CRIMINAL PROCEDURE

Third Edition

by

Leslie W. Abramson
Professor of Law
University of Louisville School of Law

QUICK REVIEW SERIES

WEST ACADEMIC PUBLISHING

Mat #41630074

Sum & Substance Quick Review Series is a Publication of West Academic Publishing.

444 Cedar Street, Suite 700
St. Paul, MN 55101
1-877-888-1330

Printed in the United States of America

ISBN: 978-1-62810-043-3

PREFACE

Besides the approaching law school exam, why do you need to know about criminal procedure? Criminal procedure is an increasingly complex matter. Lawyers who prosecute or represent criminal defendants must know not only the substantive criminal law, but also the constitutional decisions, criminal rules and pertinent statutes relating to criminal procedure.

This book consists of thirty-one chapters that review criminal procedure, through outlines of the principles traditionally covered in *both* law school courses in criminal procedure. The typical first course in criminal procedure includes extensive study of constitutional Fourth, Fifth and Sixth Amendment issues, along with the exclusionary rule. The second course is known to some as "bail to jail." That course addresses the constitutional, statutory and procedural standards relevant to criminal proceedings, from the initial appearance to collateral remedies following a conviction.

Working through these materials will teach you the basics and fine points of criminal procedure so that you will be able to both understand *and* apply the appropriate analysis of the United States Constitution, cases, statutes, rules, policies and practices. I am grateful to Elisabeth Fitzpatrick for her editing assistance.

The materials in this book are current through the end of the 2013–2014 United States Supreme Court Term.

PROFESSOR LESLIE W. ABRAMSON

July 2014

TABLE OF CONTENTS

TABLE OF CONTENTS

TABLE OF CONTENTS

TABLE OF CONTENTS

TABLE OF CONTENTS

CRIMINAL PROCEDURE

Third Edition

CHAPTER 1

INCORPORATION AND RETROACTIVITY

A. INCORPORATION

The constitutional rights included in the first ten amendments to the United States Constitution—the "Bill of Rights" apply automatically only to the federal government. *Barron v. Baltimore*, 32 U.S. (7 Pet.) 243 (1833). Prior to the adoption of the Fourteenth Amendment, the Bill of Rights was not applied to the States. Since then, the Court has been willing to apply most of the individual rights in the Bill of Rights to the States, using the Fourteenth Amendment to incorporate the various provisions of the Bill of Rights and apply them to the states.

1. Fundamental Right Approach

For the first half of the 20th century, the Supreme Court decided the applicability of the Bill of Rights on a right-by-right (not amendment-by-amendment) basis, using a standard of whether the asserted right violated in a particular case involved a "fundamental right." If the Court found that the right was fundamental, the right applied to the States through the authority of the Fourteenth Amendment Due Process Clause.

a. Fundamental Right Standard

The test used by the Court to decide whether a right was fundamental was whether the right was "implicit in the concept of ordered liberty." *Palko v. Connecticut*, 302 U.S. 319 (1937).

b. Criticism of the Test

Critics found the test overly subjective and unstructured. Two cases illustrate the problem. In *Rochin v. California*, 342 U.S. 165 (1952), the Court held that a person had a fundamental right not to have his stomach pumped forcibly, because such conduct "shocks the conscience." On the other hand, warrantless eavesdropping on bedroom conversations was permitted in *Irvine v. California*, 347 U.S. 128 (1954). The majority found that this police conduct was not as or more shocking than in *Rochin*, while the dissenters either disagreed or proposed that the whole fundamental rights approach be replaced. The dissenters' position ultimately prevailed.

2. Total Incorporation Test

Some Justices in the past advocated a simple incorporation and application of *all* parts of the Bill of Rights to the States through the Fourteenth Amendment Due Process Clause. *See, e.g., Adamson v. California*, 332 U.S. 46 (1947) (Black, J., dissenting).

a. Why Total Incorporation Failed

A majority of the Court rejected total incorporation for two reasons: it was an improper interpretation of the legislative history of the Fourteenth Amendment, and it failed to allow experimentation by the States about what and how liberties should be protected. *See, e.g., Adamson*, 332 U.S. at 67 (Frankfurter, J., concurring).

b. Total Incorporation "Plus" Also Failed

A "total incorporation plus" approach would incorporate not only all of the rights in the Bill of Rights, but also other rights deemed by the Court to be fundamental. It, too, has never been adopted by the Court.

3. Selective Incorporation Test

Selective incorporation is a hybrid between earlier analytical methods: the Fourteenth Amendment Due Process includes rights that are essential to "ordered liberty," and the protections in the Bill of Rights are the only fundamental protections. Advocates of selective incorporation believe that the fundamental right approach is too subjective and unstructured.

a. Duncan v. Louisiana

Duncan v. Louisiana, 391 U.S. 145 (1968) is the leading selective incorporation decision, applying the Sixth Amendment right to a jury trial through the Fourteenth Amendment Due Process Clause to the States.

b. Selective Incorporation Standard

To determine whether a protection from the Bill of Rights applies to the States under the selective incorporation approach, a court looks at the entirety of the right (not just as it applies to a particular set of facts, as with the fundamental right approach) and whether the provision is fundamental to Anglo-American jurisprudence. When the Supreme Court selectively incorporates a right from the Bill of Rights to the States, a majority of the Court believes that the right as well as the case law relating to that right apply to the States as though the right is being applied in a trial in a federal court.

c. Successful Application of the Selective Incorporation Test

Using the selective incorporation approach, the Supreme Court has applied almost every right in the Bill of Rights to the States through the Fourteenth Amendment. In its most recent ruling on incorporation, seven of the Justices used the selective incorporation approach to apply the Second Amendment to the States through the Fourteenth Amendment. *McDonald v. City of Chicago*, 561 U.S. 742 (2010).

d. Disagreement About the Scope of Selective Incorporation

In *Duncan*, Justice Harlan in dissent argued, as have others Justices, that even after a right was selectively incorporated, it could apply differently to the States than it does to the federal government. His view has from time to time influenced the Court's interpretation of the scope of some constitutional rights. For example, in *Apodaca v. Oregon*, 406 U.S. 404 (1972), and *Johnson v. Louisiana*, 406 U.S. 356 (1972), the Court examined whether States could constitutionally convict accused individuals with less-than-unanimous, criminal trial juries. The Court had to look at the Sixth Amendment jury-trial right that already had been selectively incorporated and applied to the States in *Duncan*. Justice Powell concluded that the Sixth Amendment criminal jury trial right required verdict unanimity in the federal courts, but not in the State courts. Because his opinion also provided the fifth and the deciding vote, the Supreme Court judgment was that federal criminal juries must be unanimous, but that State criminal juries need not be.

4. Case Law Applying Aspects of Bill of Rights to States

Bill of Right Provision	Case Applying Right to States
Second Amendment	*McDonald v. City of Chicago*, 561 U.S. 742 (2010)
Fourth Amendment	
Seizure	*Mapp v. Ohio*, 367 U.S. 643 (1961)
Search	*Ker v. California*, 374 U.S. 23 (1963)
Fifth Amendment	
Self-incrimination	*Malloy v. Hogan*, 378 U.S. 1 (1964)
Double jeopardy	*Benton v. Maryland*, 395 U.S. 784 (1969)
Grand jury indictment	NOT APPLICABLE TO STATES
Sixth Amendment	
Counsel	*Gideon v. Wainwright*, 372 U.S. 335 (1963)
Confrontation	*Pointer v. Texas*, 380 U.S. 400 (1965)
Compulsory process	*Washington v. Texas*, 388 U.S. 14 (1967)
Speedy trial	*Klopfer v. North Carolina*, 386 U.S. 213 (1967)
Jury trial	*Duncan v. Louisiana*, 391 U.S. 145 (1968)
Public trial	*Gannett Co., Inc. v. DePasquale*, 443 U.S. 368 (1979)
Notice of charge	*In re Oliver*, 333 U.S. 257 (1948)
Eighth Amendment	
Cruel punishment	*Robinson v. California*, 370 U.S. 660 (1962)
Excessive bail	*Baze v. Rees*, 553 U.S. 35 (2008)

5. Rights Inapplicable to States: Excessive Bail and Grand Jury Indictment

Although it may be regarded as fundamental, the Eighth Amendment prohibition on excessive bail does not apply to the States. As recently as the 1990s, the Court noted that the Fifth Amendment requirement for a grand jury indictment in felony cases is inapplicable to the States. *Albright v. Oliver*, 510 U.S. 266 (1994).

B. RETROACTIVITY: APPLYING A CASE THAT GENERATES A NEW RULE OF LAW

1. Traditional Application of New Constitutional Rulings

Traditionally, the prevailing litigant in a case establishing a new constitutional rule is entitled personally to the benefit of that new rule. Application of the decision to the prevailing litigant is justified as satisfying the case or controversy requirement as well as for inducing challenges to improve the law.

2. Retroactivity for Applying New Rulings to Cases Already Decided

The issue of retroactivity asks about the application of the new rule to others whose cases involve the same issue: what rule applies to them, the old or the new one?

a. What Is a New Constitutional Rule That Triggers Retroactivity?

Retroactivity becomes an issue only when a court announces a *new* constitutional rule, as opposed to a ruling or clarification driven by precedent. *Schriro v. Summerlin*, 542 U.S. 348 (2004). It is not always easy, however, to figure out whether a new Supreme Court decision has stated a new constitutional rule or, instead, whether it is simply applying an existing rule to new and different circumstances. While conceding the difficulty in making the distinction, the Supreme Court has observed that "[i]n general, . . . a case announces a new rule when it breaks new ground or imposes a new obligation on the States or the Federal Government." Conversely, a case does not "announce a new rules,[when] it '[is] merely an application of the principles that governed' " a prior decision to a different set of facts. *Teague v. Lane*, 489 U.S. 288 (1989).

b. Linkletter v. Walker

In *Linkletter v. Walker*, 381 U.S. 618 (1965), the Court held that "the Constitution neither prohibits nor requires retrospective effect." Instead, it decided to "weigh the merits and demerits in each case by looking to the prior history of the rule in question, its purpose and effect, and whether retrospective operation will further or retard its operation." Applying a case-by-case, balancing approach, *Linkletter* concluded that *Mapp v. Ohio*, 367 U.S. 643 (1961), the landmark decision applying the exclusionary rule to the States, did not apply retroactively, i.e., it did not apply to any cases that had been finally decided prior to the date when *Mapp* was decided.

c. Stovall v. Denno

In *Stovall v. Denno*, 388 U.S. 293 (1967), the Court organized the retroactivity analysis: what mattered was

"(a) the purpose to be served by the new standards,

(b) the extent of the reliance by law enforcement authorities on the old standards, and

(c) the effect on the administration of justice of a retroactive application of the new standards."

(1) No Bright Line Operative Date for Applying New Rulings

The Court did not even specify a bright-line for determining the operative date from which a new constitutional ruling applies when the Court rules that it is applies prospectively only. It is up to the Court to decide whether a prospective decision applies from the date of the decision or from the date of the police conduct in question.

(2) Difficult to Predict If New Rulings Are Applied Retroactively

The Court's decisions for the next twenty years lacked a unifying theme and produced inconsistent results, in turn making it difficult to predict how the Supreme Court would apply the *Linkletter* and *Stovall* tests to new constitutional rulings.

d. Whether a Case Is Pending or Final at the Time of New Ruling

There is clarity about whether a particular case was pending or "final" at the time that a new constitutional ruling was issued. A "final" decision is "a case in which a judgment of conviction has been rendered, the availability of appeal exhausted, and the time for a petition for certiorari elapsed or a petition for certiorari finally denied." *Griffith v. Kentucky*, 479 U.S. 314 (1987). A case is deemed to be final, even though it is theoretically possible that a State court might, as a discretionary matter, decline to enforce a procedural bar to raising an issue and choose to apply a new rule of law. *Beard v. Banks*, 542 U.S. 406 (2004).

e. Rejection of the "Clear Break" Exception

The Court soon held that a new rule for the conduct of criminal prosecutions is to be applied retroactively to *all* cases, State or federal, pending on direct review or not yet final, with no exception for cases in which the new rule constitutes a "clear break" with the past. *Griffith v. Kentucky*, 479 U.S. 314 (1987). In *Griffith*, the Court concluded that its new constitutional ruling in *Batson v. Kentucky*, 476 U.S. 79 (1986) should be applied retroactively, even though it was a "clear break" with the Court's past precedent.

3. Applying Retroactivity to Federal *Habeas Corpus* Cases

In contrast to the application of new rulings to cases still pending on direct appeal when a new constitutional ruling is handed down (i.e., not "final"), the Supreme Court concluded in 1989 that "[u]nless they fall within an exception to the general rule, new constitutional rules of criminal procedure will not be applicable to those cases which have become final before the new rules are announced." *Teague v. Lane*, 489 U.S. 288 (1989). However, *Danforth v. Minnesota*, 552 U.S. 264 (2008) held that state courts are free to give broader retroactive application than the *Teague* nonretroactivity standard which applies only in federal *habeas corpus* cases.

a. Retroactivity Inquiry Process

Federal district courts applying *Teague* in a retroactivity inquiry in *habeas corpus* proceedings, should follow three steps. "First, the court must determine when the defendant's conviction became final. Second, it must ascertain whether the rule is actually 'new.' Finally, if the rule is new, the court must consider whether it falls within either of the two exceptions to nonretroactivity." *Beard v. Banks*, 542 U.S. 406 (2004).

b. Exceptions to the *Teague* General Rule

Two exceptions exist to the general rule: (1) "a new rule should be applied retroactively if it places 'certain kinds of primary, private individual conduct beyond the power of the criminal law-making authority to proscribe' "; and (2) "watershed rules of criminal procedure: . . . those new procedures without which the likelihood of an accurate conviction is seriously diminished." *Teague*.

(1) Forbidden Punishment Exception

The first *Teague* exception "cover[s] not only rules forbidding criminal punishment of certain primary conduct but also rules prohibiting a certain category of punishment for a class of defendants because of their status or offense." *Penry v. Lynaugh*, 492 U.S. 302 (1989).

(2) Watershed Rule of Criminal Procedure Exception

A watershed rule is sweeping, and implicates the fundamental fairness and accuracy of a criminal proceeding. It changes the Supreme Court's understanding of the fundamental procedural elements essential to a proceeding's fairness. *Whorton v. Bockting*, 549 U.S. 406 (2007). The class of watershed rules is "extremely narrow." *Schriro v. Summerlin*, 542 U.S. 348 (2004). Since *Teague*, the Court has rejected every attempt to label a new holding as a watershed rule.

CHAPTER 2

EXCLUSIONARY RULE

A. SUPPRESSION OF EVIDENCE AS AN EXCLUSIONARY REMEDY

The exclusionary rule prohibits prosecutors from using evidence obtained in violation of a defendant's Fourth, *Mapp v. Ohio*, 367 U.S. 643 (1961), Fifth, *Blackburn v. Alabama*, 361 U.S. 199 (1960) or Sixth, *United States v. Wade*, 388 U.S. 218 (1967) Amendment rights. It also prohibits the use of evidence in certain circumstances in which a defendant's rights have been violated, even though the violation does not rise to the level of a constitutional infringement. See *Oregon v. Elstad*, 470 U.S. 298 (1985).

1. Purpose of Exclusionary Rule Depends on Which Right Is Violated

The purposes served by the exclusionary rule vary according to the nature of the right which has been infringed and the kind of evidence which has been obtained.

a. Fourth Amendment

In the case of an illegal arrest, search or seizure, the rule may result in the exclusion of evidence which is usually reliable, so that the integrity of the factfinding process is not at stake. In *Stone v. Powell*, 428 U.S. 465, 479 (1976), the Court held that Fourth Amendment violations are different from Fifth or Sixth Amendment violations. Exclusion of illegally seized evidence is intended to deter law enforcement officers from violating the Fourth Amendment. *Brown v. Illinois*, 422 U.S. 590 (1975).

b. Fifth Amendment

In the case of statements from police interrogation, the rule operates to ensure the voluntariness of the statement and to prevent the use of coercive techniques, and it thus serves to promote the integrity both of the factfinding process and of the judicial process.

c. **Sixth Amendment**

As the rule relates to pretrial identification, it is intended to protect against unduly suggestive procedures which might otherwise impugn the integrity of the factfinding process. *Foster v. California*, 394 U.S. 440 (1969).

2. **Exclusionary Rule Is Not a *Per Se* Rule of Exclusion**

The exclusionary rule does not establish a *per se* rule of exclusion forbidding the use of all illegally obtained evidence in all situations. For example, in *United States v. Calandra*, 414 U.S. 338 (1974), the Court found that extending the exclusionary rule to grand jury proceedings would substantially impede the grand jury's role while achieving only a speculative and minimal advance in deterring police misconduct. Instead, courts balance the interest of deterrence against the societal costs of suppressing probative evidence, concluding that in certain circumstances suppression is inappropriate. *See Massachusetts v. Sheppard*, 468 U.S. 981 (1984).

3. **Constitutional Origins of Federal Exclusionary Rule**

When the Supreme Court first adopted the exclusionary rule as a constitutional remedy, it applied to *federal* criminal trials only. *Weeks v. United States*, 232 U.S. 383 (1914).

a. **Mapp v. Ohio**

Facts: In *Mapp v. Ohio*, 367 U.S. 643 (1961), three Cleveland police officers attempted to gain entrance to Mapp's residence by claiming to have obtained information from a confidential informant. Officers forced their way into the house and searched it from top to bottom. Police found pornographic materials in her bedroom; she was charged with and convicted of possession and control of obscene material.

Law: The *Mapp* Court held that the same exclusionary rule recognized in *Weeks* applied in State court proceedings. The Court suppressed the evidence seized by the police and reversed Mapp's conviction. The Court found that the exclusionary rule was a constitutional requirement. Noting that "other remedies" for police misconduct, discussed below, "have been worthless and futile," the Court ruled that "all evidence obtained by searches and seizures in violation of the Constitution is, by that same authority, inadmissible in a state court."

b. **State Constitutional Exclusionary Rule**

State courts also may apply the exclusionary rule under their own State constitutions. Moreover, any legislative body can enact statutes which contain an exclusionary rule to serve as a remedy for police (or even private) violations of whatever criminal or civil prohibitions are set out in the legislation. A statutory exclusionary rule would apply as a matter of non-constitutional, statutory law.

4. The Costs of the Exclusionary Rule

Justice (then Judge) Cardozo criticized the exclusionary rule by noting that "under constitutional exclusionary doctrine '[t]he criminal is to go free because the constable has blundered.'" *People v. Defore*, 150 N.E. 585 (1926). What are the primary costs of the exclusionary rule?

- When a court applies the exclusionary rule, reliable evidence is unavailable to the prosecutor.
- Public respect for the criminal justice system suffers when a "technicality" results in the release of defendants.
- The exclusionary rule does not meaningfully deter police misconduct, because the exclusion of evidence often occurs long after the offending conduct and the offending officer is rarely disciplined.
- Courts might be more willing to find constitutional violations if the remedy of exclusion for the violation were not so serious.

5. Alternatives to the Exclusionary Rule

Despite criticism, the exclusionary rule survives (although without the same strong *constitutional* grounding today as when *Mapp* was decided) because a majority of the Supreme Court continues to believe that "nothing else works" to deter police misconduct. What else is there?

a. Public Opinion

Reliance on public opinion to correct and remedy police misconduct has proved problematic.

- "The public" is unaware of a significant percentage of cases when police misconduct occurs.
- Because the case law involves defendants who are "guilty," there is usually little public sympathy for constitutional claims.

b. Criminal Prosecution

Criminal prosecution of police officers who engage in constitutional misconduct as an effective remedy is generally dismissed as impractical. Prosecutors use their discretion to decide who and when (not) to prosecute. Usually, prosecutors exercise their discretion by not prosecuting police officers whose conduct might be problematic. While an occasional criminal prosecution of police officers may deter subsequent police misconduct, their infrequency dilutes the deterrence of such prosecutions.

c. Disciplinary Proceedings and Review Boards

Internal police review boards suffer from the difficulty of judging and sanctioning one's own peers. External police review boards are often composed of non-law enforcement members and suffer from the perceived lack of identity with the police officers whose conduct is under scrutiny. Those boards often lack statutory or legal power to put their recommendations of discipline into effect. Practically, disciplinary proceedings and review boards do not either prevent law enforcement officers from engaging in unconstitutional activity or remedy the consequences of such misconduct.

d. Civil Actions

Civil actions for damages against law enforcement officers for alleged constitutional rights violations are insufficient or ineffective, because as stated in *Monell v. Department of Social Services of the City of New York*, 436 U.S. 658 (1978),

- recovery is unlikely, given that a police officer's "good faith" typically is a complete defense,
- the prospect of an enforceable damage recovery is unlikely against an individual officer, and
- recovery is available against a governmental unit only to the extent that its "policy or custom, whether made by its lawmakers or by those whose edicts or acts may fairly be said to represent official policy, inflicts the injury. . . ."

B. LIMITS ON THE EXCLUSIONARY RULE'S APPLICATION

1. Official Misconduct v. Private Actors

Because one purpose for the exclusionary rule is to discourage *official* misconduct, it is necessary to show that the person searching or seizing was the government or an agent of the government. The rule applies to conduct by any state actor, and is not confined to law enforcement. *New Jersey v. T.L.O.*, 469 U.S. 325 (1985) (a school principal must follow the Fourth Amendment).

a. Private Actors

By contrast, evidence illegally obtained by private persons not acting in concert with the police is admissible. *Burdeau v. McDowell*, 256 U.S. 465 (1921). For example, in *United States v. Jacobsen*, 466 U.S. 109 (1984), the Court found no Fourth Amendment violation where employees of a private freight carrier opened a damaged package, made an examination of its contents, discovered plastic bags filled with white powder, and then called a federal agent who took a trace sample of the powder and tested it.

b. Cooperation Between Police and Private Persons

Evidence obtained as a result of cooperative or coercive action between police officers and private citizens *is* subject to the exclusionary rule. *See Abel v. United States*, 362 U.S. 217 (1960).

2. Non-Criminal Proceedings: Incremental Deterrence

Since the 1970s, the Supreme Court has stated that the Fourth Amendment exclusionary rule is not a constitutional requirement *per se* as was suggested in *Mapp*. Instead, the Court has said that the exclusionary rule is a required remedy to deter the future misconduct of law enforcement officials. *United States v. Calandra.* The exclusionary rule's deterrence aim is furthered when it is applied to suppress unconstitutionally-seized evidence sought to be introduced by the government in the prosecution's case-in-chief at trial. However, if police misconduct is not deterred by applying the exclusionary rule in a particular setting, the Court has stated that the rule should not be used because the social costs of the rule's application (i.e., some criminals will go free) are so great.

3. Forfeiture Proceedings

Many American jurisdictions have enacted statutes that permit the government to seek the forfeiture to the government of instrumentalities used in the commission of specified criminal activity (e.g., cars, boats, or airplanes used to smuggle narcotics). Such "forfeiture proceedings" are civil rather than criminal in nature. However, in a decision handed down before the Supreme Court began limiting the application of the exclusionary rule to situations where incremental deterrence of police misconduct is achieved, the Court ruled that the exclusionary rule applies with full force to suppress unconstitutionally-seized evidence sought to be introduced in such forfeiture proceedings because of the "quasi-criminal nature" of these proceedings. *One 1958 Plymouth Sedan v. Commonwealth of Pennsylvania*, 380 U.S. 693 (1965).

4. Grand Juries

United States v. Calandra noted the concern about permitting the exclusionary rule to prevent grand juries from hearing about illegally obtained evidence. "Any incremental deterrent effect which might be achieved by extending the [exclusionary] rule to grand jury proceedings is uncertain at best." As a result, the exclusionary rule was held inapplicable by the Court to the use of unconstitutionally-seized evidence presented to a grand jury.

5. Civil Proceedings

For similar reasons, the exclusionary rule does not usually apply in civil cases. In *United States v. Janis*, 428 U.S. 433 (1976), the Supreme Court permitted evidence seized illegally by Los Angeles police officers to be introduced in the prosecution's case-in-chief in a federal, civil tax proceeding for back taxes brought by the Internal Revenue Service. The exclusionary rule also does not apply in (civil) deportation proceedings. *Immigration & Naturalization Service v. Lopez-Mendoza*, 468 U.S. 1032 (1984).

6. "Silver Platter" Doctrine

Because the constitutional limitation on obtaining evidence is intended to deter all public officers, unlawful evidence obtained by an agent of one governmental unit does not lose its taint merely because the evidence is handed to another governmental unit on a "silver platter." For example, in *Elkins v. United States*, 364 U.S. 206 (1960), State officers, without involvement of federal officers, conducted an unreasonable search and seizure. The Court held that the evidence obtained as result of that illegal State search is also inadmissible in defendant's federal criminal trial.

7. Federal Habeas Corpus

The exclusionary rule does not apply to Fourth Amendment claims raised in federal *habeas corpus* proceedings where the petitioner had a full and fair opportunity to litigate these issues in her prior State court proceedings. *Stone v. Powell*, 428 U.S. 465 (1976).

There is no reason to believe, however, that the overall educative effect of the exclusionary rule would be appreciably diminished if search-and-seizure claims could not be raised in federal *habeas corpus* review of state convictions. . . . Even if one rationally could assume that some additional incremental deterrent effect would be presented in isolated cases, the resulting advance of the legitimate goal of furthering Fourth Amendment rights would be outweighed by the acknowledged costs to other values vital to a rational system of criminal justice.

8. "Ker-Frisbie Doctrine"

The "body" or identity of a defendant or respondent in a criminal or civil proceeding is never itself suppressible as a fruit of an unlawful or unconstitutional arrest. *Ker v. Illinois*, 119 U.S. 436 (1886); *Frisbie v. Collins*, 342 U.S. 519 (1952).

9. Violation of Internal Agency Standards

If evidence is obtained in violation of the rules or standards of a governmental agency rather than in violation of federal constitutional or statutory law, the exclusionary rule does not prevent admission of that evidence. *United States v. Caceres*, 440 U.S. 741 (1979).

10. Revocation Proceedings

The exclusionary rule is inapplicable to parole revocation proceedings. *Pennsylvania Board of Probation and Parole v. Scott*, 524 U.S. 357 (1998). Applying a cost-benefit analysis from earlier cases, the Court noted the governmental interest in returning parolees to prison if they violate their release conditions because parolees commit more offenses than other persons.

C. GOOD-FAITH EXCEPTION TO EXCLUSIONARY RULE

In 1984, the Supreme Court adopted a significant exception to the exclusionary rule, holding that it does not apply where a law enforcement officer has acted in reasonable "good faith" on the basis of an unconstitutional search warrant. *United States v. Leon*, 468 U.S. 897 (1984). The Court adopted this exception, because police officers acting in good faith on the basis of what reasonably appears to them (even erroneously) to be a valid and lawful search warrant would not ordinarily be deterred by application of the rule.

1. Exception Is Based on Objective Test

The "good-faith exception" to the exclusionary rule is an objective test, i.e., the police officer's reliance on the otherwise invalid search warrant must be reasonable: "whether a reasonably well trained officer would have known that the search was illegal despite the magistrate's authorization."

2. Good-Faith Exception Initially Applied Only to Warrants

The good-faith exception adopted in *Leon* applies only to searches pursuant to defective *search warrants*; not *warrantless* searches by law enforcement officers.

3. Extending the Good-Faith Exception Beyond Warrants

The Supreme Court has extended the good-faith exception to the exclusionary rule to otherwise unconstitutional actions by law enforcement officers' based upon:

- a computerized police record erroneously indicating the existence of an outstanding arrest warrant, *Arizona v. Evans*, 514 U.S. 1 (1995),
- reasonable reliance upon a statute subsequently found to be unconstitutional. *Illinois v. Krull*, 480 U.S. 340 (1987),
- an officer's reliance on negligent recordkeeping by other officers leading to an illegal search. *Herring v. United States*, 555 U.S. 135 (2009), and
- an officer's reasonable reliance on precedent that was binding at the time but subsequently overruled. *Davis v. United States*, 131 S.Ct. 2419 (2011). "The extent to which the exclusionary rule is justified by . . . deterrence principles varies with the probability of the law enforcement conduct."

4. When the Good-Faith Exception Does Not Apply, Per *Leon*

Leon states that the good-faith exception is always inapplicable in any of four situations, where:

- the magistrate or judge in issuing a warrant was misled by information in an affidavit that the affiant knew was false or would have known was false except for his reckless disregard of the truth,
- where the issuing magistrate wholly abandoned his judicial role, *Lo-Ji Sales, Inc. v. New York*, 442 U.S. 319 (1979),
- an officer . . . rel[ied] on a warrant based on an affidavit "so lacking in indicia of probable cause as to render official belief in its existence entirely unreasonable." *Nathanson v. United States*, 290 U.S. 41 (1933), and
- depending on the circumstances of the particular case, a warrant was so facially deficient, i.e., in failing to particularize the place to be searched or the things to be seized, that the executing officers cannot reasonably presume it to be valid.

5. States Can Reject the Exception Under State Constitutional Law

The good-faith exception to the exclusionary rule was adopted as a matter of *federal* constitutional law. A number of State courts, disagreeing with the Supreme Court's deterrence analysis, have concluded that the good-faith exception does not exist under their own State constitutions. The dichotomy thereby created is that, in some States, the unconstitutional actions of a federal law enforcement agent would be subject to application of the good-faith exception to the exclusionary rule, but the unconstitutional actions of a State or city police officer would not be.

6. Good-Faith Exception in Civil Cases

In *Groh v. Ramirez*, 540 U.S. 551 (2004), the Court distinguished *Leon* and limited the Court's application of the good faith exception in the context of a civil rights lawsuit. A government agent who executed a search warrant that failed to identify the property sought was not entitled to qualified immunity, because no reasonable officer could have believed that the warrant was valid on its face.

7. Good Faith Exception Inapplicable for "Knock and Announce" Violations

In *Hudson v. Michigan*, 547 U.S. 586 (2006), the Court refused to apply the exclusionary evidence rule in the context of a violation of the "knock and announce" rule. Although the police searched Hudson's house pursuant to a warrant, they had waited only three to five seconds after knocking before entering. The Court held that the wait was insufficient and the question was whether the fruits of the search should be suppressed because of the premature entry. The Court answered that question in the negative, applying the cost-benefit test and noting that the exclusionary rule should not be indiscriminately applied, but rather should be reserved for situations "where its remedial objectives are thought most efficaciously served," i.e., "where its deterrence benefits outweigh its substantial social costs." Justice Scalia wrote that the knock-and-announce rule was meant to prevent violence, property damage, and impositions on privacy, *not* to prevent police from conducting a search for which they have a valid warrant.

D. USING ILLEGALLY OBTAINED EVIDENCE FOR IMPEACHMENT

The exclusionary rule applies only to the use of unconstitutionally-seized evidence offered at a criminal trial during the prosecution's case-in-chief. It does not apply to the same evidence introduced by the prosecution at trial to "impeach" the defendant's credibility on cross-examination. *Harris v. New York*, 401 U.S. 222 (1971); *Kansas v. Ventris*, 556 U.S. 586 (2009). Impeachment also is necessary to prevent the *Miranda* doctrine from being used as a "shield" for the commission of perjury by defendants who could contradict their incriminating statements to police without those statements being used to impeach them.

1. Impeaching Defendant's Statements

A defendant's direct or cross-examination testimony can be impeached with illegally obtained evidence bearing *directly* on the current charge, e.g., a confession admitting to the charged offense. Courts permit the prosecution to use most illegally obtained evidence to impeach a defendant's direct testimony, *Oregon v. Hass*, 420 U.S. 714 (1975), or to impeach statements elicited on cross-examination when it is "reasonably suggested" by the defendant's direct testimony. *United States v. Havens*, 446 U.S. 620 (1980). In *Havens*, the defendant testified at trial that he did not own an incriminating item of clothing, a T-shirt. The Supreme Court ruled that this testimony by the defendant was impeached constitutionally by the prosecution when, in response to this statement, it introduced into evidence the T-shirt to which the statements pertained, even though the T-shirt had been seized unconstitutionally by the government.

a. Illegally Obtained Confession Must Be Voluntary

Before a defendant can be impeached with an illegally obtained confession, the prosecution must show that the confession was given voluntarily, i.e., not in violation of Due Process. *Mincey v. Arizona*, 437 U.S. 385 (1978). See Chapter 13. The impeachment rules apply to confessions regardless of whether the police acted negligently or intentionally in eliciting the statement from the defendant.

2. Witness Cannot Be Impeached with Illegally Obtained Evidence

The impeachment exception to the exclusionary rule applies only to impeachment of the *defendant*'s testimony by the government, not to the attempted impeachment of other defense witnesses with unconstitutionally-seized evidence. *James v. Illinois*, 493 U.S. 307 (1990). Extension of the impeachment exception to all defense witnesses would compromise the deterrent effect of the exclusionary rule.

3. Impeachment with Defendant's Silence Is Limited

A defendant's post-arrest silence, after receiving her *Miranda* warnings, cannot be used as substantive evidence, *Wainwright v. Greenfield*, 474 U.S. 284 (1986) (the silence cannot be used to rebut an insanity defense), or for impeachment at trial, *Doyle v. Ohio*, 426 U.S. 610 (1976).

a. Post-Arrest Silence to Impeach Is Not Permitted

When the defense successfully objects to a prosecutor's question as to why the defendant failed to reveal an exculpatory story earlier and the judge instructs the jury to ignore the question, no *Doyle* violation occurs. *Greer v. Miller*, 483 U.S. 756 (1987). However, a reference to post-arrest silence for impeachment purposes is reversible error when it is deliberately used to impeach an explanation subsequently offered at trial or where there is a similar reason to believe that a defendant has been prejudiced by reference to the exercise of her constitutional right to remain silent, e.g., where the prosecutor focuses on defendant's silence in a way that is linked to the defendant's testimony.

b. Exceptions When Defendant's Silence May Be Used to Impeach

This prohibition on the use of defendant's prior silence does not apply to:

- cross-examination that merely inquires into prior inconsistent statements, *Anderson v. Charles*, 447 U.S. 404 (1980);
- pre-arrest silence, *Jenkins v. Anderson*, 447 U.S. 231 (1980); and
- post-arrest silence without *Miranda* warnings, *Fletcher v. Weir*, 455 U.S. 603 (1982).

E. STANDING

1. Constitutional Limitation

A criminal defendant must have "standing" to raise the issue of unconstitutional law enforcement conduct. Standing exists only where the defendant seeks to remedy a violation of her own personal constitutional rights, not the rights of another person. *Alderman v. United States*, 394 U.S. 165 (1969).

a. Standing Example

If the police arrest *A* illegally and then interrogate *A* without giving her *Miranda* warnings, any statement that *A* makes as a result of that unconstitutional conduct (arrest and custodial interrogation) could be suppressed by *A* in a criminal proceeding brought against her. But the same statement could *not* be challenged by *B*, even if the statement directly implicates him in the same (or different) criminal conduct (e.g., *A* said "*B* and I killed *C*."). *B* lacks standing because the unconstitutional conduct (illegal arrest; failure to give *Miranda* warnings) violated only *A's* constitutional rights, not *B's* constitutional rights.

b. Obvious Applications of Standing Rules

Some applications of the standing rules are self-evident. For example, only the person identified can challenge her identification. Only the person who made an incriminating statement can challenge the admissibility of her statement. Only the person seized can challenge her arrest or stop, and only the person searched can challenge the search of her person.

2. Standing = Violation of Defendant's Reasonable Expectation of Privacy

Personal constitutional rights are violated where the constitutional harm is done to that individual personally, at a place (e.g., her home), or to some thing (e.g., her car or backpack) where and when she possessed a "reasonable expectation of privacy" (sometimes referred to as a "legitimate expectation of privacy"). *Rakas v. Illinois*, 439 U.S. 128 (1978).

a. Standing Concerns Which Police Conduct Is Objectionable

Rakas concerned whether a passenger in a motor vehicle has standing to challenge a search of the vehicle in which she is riding. In standing cases, it is important to isolate which police act is objectionable. If the passengers in *Rakas* had challenged the *stop* of the car in which they were riding or had challenged the *seizure* of their persons, they would probably have had standing to challenge the evidence seized as a fruit of the violation of their personal rights.

b. No Standing to Challenge Violation of Another's Rights

A defendant does not have standing to object simply because evidence has been seized unconstitutionally from her co-defendant or co-conspirator. Similarly, a defendant does not have standing to complain about the constitutionality of the search of another person's container (containing the defendant's drugs). *Rawlings v. Kentucky*, 448 U.S. 98 (1980).

c. Person Engaged in "Commerce" v. Social Guest

An individual also lacks standing, when a police officer illegally peeped through a gap in a closed window blind and the individual's presence in that apartment was strictly as part of a commercial transaction, not as a social guest or invitee. *Minnesota v. Carter*, 525 U.S. 83 (1998). An individual does have standing to challenge the constitutionality of a search of an apartment where he was present as an "overnight guest." *Minnesota v. Olson*, 495 U.S. 91, 98 (1990).

d. Standing Does Not Yield to Exercise of Supervisory Powers

Standing doctrine (which is a part of substantive constitutional law) cannot be ignored, on the basis of the court's inherent, non-constitutional "supervisory powers" over law enforcement. *United States v. Payner*, 447 U.S. 727 (1980).

3. Standing REOP v. Fourth Amendment REOP

An individual's "reasonable expectation of privacy" (REOP) is the same concept used to define when police conduct is subject to Fourth Amendment requirements. See Chapter 3. However, unlike Fourth Amendment standing which is about whether there is *a* REOP, standing is about whether *this specific defendant* complaining about police conduct has a REOP to challenge the evidence obtained by the police conduct.

4. The Standing Spectrum: Hitchhiker v. Absent Owner

At one extreme of the standing spectrum, a hitchhiker just picked up by the driver would not have standing to challenge a later search of the car, although she would argue that her recent arrival in the vehicle negates her guilt on the substantive charge. At the other end of the standing spectrum, the owner of the vehicle would have standing to challenge a search of her vehicle, even if she was a passenger in the vehicle or absent from the vehicle at the time of the search. For any vehicle passenger, the reasonableness of her expectation of privacy would depend on such factors as the regularity of her presence in the vehicle, her ownership of the vehicle, and her relationship to the vehicle owner.

5. Burden of Proof for Standing

How does a defendant sustain the burden of proving that her Fourth Amendment rights have been violated? Factors to be considered include:

- property ownership,
- whether the defendant has a possessory interest in the thing seized,
- whether the defendant has a possessory interest in the place searched,
- whether the defendant has the right to exclude others from that place,

- whether the defendant has exhibited a subjective expectation that the place would remain free from governmental invasion, and
- whether the defendant took normal precautions to maintain her privacy.

6. History of Fourth Amendment Standing Since 1960

Pre-*Jones*	*Jones*	*Rakas*
Possessory interest in property seized or premises searched———>	**Adds:** automatic standing if: either charged with possessory offense OR legitimately on premises at time of search————>	**Substitutes**: Reasonable expectation of privacy in the area searched

7. Automatic Standing in State Cases

Some States have retained an automatic standing rule under their own State constitutions. Prior to *Rakas*, *Jones v. United States*, 362 U.S. 257 (1960) adopted an "automatic standing" rule for defendants charged with possessory crimes (e.g. possession of narcotics). However, the automatic standing rule was overruled by the Supreme Court in *Rakas* as a matter of federal constitutional law.

8. Defendant's Testimony to Obtain Standing Is Inadmissible at Trial

The suppression hearing testimony of a defendant about her relationship to evidence sought to be suppressed cannot be used against her at trial on the issue of her substantive guilt. *Simmons v. United States*, 390 U.S. 377 (1968).

F. DERIVATIVE EVIDENCE: "FRUIT OF THE POISONOUS TREE" DOCTRINE

Evidence derived from law enforcement's unconstitutional activity is inadmissible in criminal proceedings not only when it is obtained as a direct result of that activity, but also when it has been derived only as an *indirect* result of such a constitutional breach. This rule is formally referred to as the "derivative evidence rule," but more commonly it is called "the fruit of the poisonous tree" doctrine [FOPT]. *Nardone v. United States*, 308 U.S. 338 (1939).

1. Wong Sun v. United States

In *Wong Sun v. United States*, 371 U.S. 471 (1963), where police illegally entered the defendant's home, a statement made by the defendant immediately following the illegal entry and drugs discovered based on the information in the defendant's statement were inadmissible against defendant. The statement was inadmissible, not because it was illegally obtained but because the statement was derived from the illegal entry.

2. FOPT Provides an Alternative Method for Challenging Evidence

FOPT is an alternative method for challenging the admissibility of evidence. Assume that the defendant was arrested and the police subsequently seized contraband from the defendant's briefcase. Typically, the defendant would move directly to suppress the admissibility of the contraband from her briefcase. FOPT doctrine enables the defendant also to challenge the admissibility of the contraband by attacking the legality of the arrest, even if the search of the briefcase was legal.

3. FOPT Step-by-Step Analysis

In order for a defendant to invoke the FOPT doctrine, the issues are:

- Does she have standing to challenge the original violation, i.e., the tree?
- Did the original police activity violate her rights?
- Was the evidence sought to be admitted against her, i.e., the fruit, obtained as a result of the original violation?

FOPT analysis specifically addresses the last issue. If the answer for any of these posed questions is in the negative, the FOPT analysis fails, and the defendant would have to rely on the direct challenge to the conduct yielding the evidence in order to suppress it. The burden of proving that the evidence is not the FOPT is on the prosecution.

4. Why FOPT Is Useful

The doctrine may be especially useful for defendants who lack standing to challenge the alleged fruit of the original violation. For example, if a confession was obtained from codefendant *A* in reaction to the illegal arrest of codefendant *B*, codefendant *B* cannot directly attack the admissibility of *A*'s confession because *B* lacks standing. However, under the FOPT doctrine, *B* can prevent the admission of *A*'s confession because *B* has standing to challenge *B*'s own illegal arrest, which violated *B*'s rights, and if *B* can show a direct link between *B*'s illegal arrest and *A*'s confession.

5. FOPT Analysis Applies to Physical and Testimonial Evidence

Traditionally, the FOPT doctrine applies both to physical and testimonial evidence. *Wong Sun v. United States*. However, in *United States v. Patane*, 542 U.S. 630 (2004), the Court dealt with the question of whether a failure to give a suspect *Miranda* warnings necessitated suppression of physical evidence (e.g., a gun) located as a result of the suspect's unwarned but voluntary statements. A plurality of the Court refused to suppress the gun noting that the *Miranda* rule protects against violations of the Self-Incrimination Clause, and that clause is not implicated by the introduction at trial of physical evidence resulting from voluntary statements. Justice Kennedy, joined by Justice O'Connor, concurred, arguing that the admission of "nontestimonial physical fruits (the gun in this case) [does] not run the risk of admitting into trial an accused's coerced incriminating statements against himself." In other words, the *Patane* Court questioned the application of the FOPT analysis when the fruit is physical evidence that was located as a result of a voluntary statement.

6. FOPT Is Not a "But For" Test

The *Wong Sun* Court made clear that the FOPT doctrine is *not* applied by using a mechanistic and broad "but for" type of causation test (e.g., "but for" the police officer's unconstitutional activity, the government would never have discovered the hidden marijuana). Some evidence that would satisfy a "but for" test will nonetheless be deemed admissible where it was either not acquired "by exploitation" of the officers' unconstitutional activity, and/or because it was obtained "by means sufficiently distinguishable" from that unconstitutional activity to warrant such admission.

7. Exceptions to FOPT Analysis

A court will, however, admit the fruit of the poisonous tree if the prosecutor establishes that:

- the evidence was obtained from a source independent of the primary illegality,
- the evidence inevitably would have been discovered in the course of the investigation, or
- the connection between the challenged evidence and the illegal conduct is so attenuated that it dissipates the taint of the illegal action.

a. Independent Source

The essence of the exclusionary rule is that the prosecution should not be permitted to use illegally obtained evidence at all. However, when the police obtain knowledge of the same facts through an independent source, the prosecution is not barred from attempting to prove such facts. *Silverthorne Lumber Co. v. United States*, 251 U.S. 385 (1920). In other words, the fruit of the illegality was in fact located by means unrelated to the illegal source.

(1) Rationale for Independent Source Rule

In *Murray v. United States*, 487 U.S. 533 (1988), the Court offered the rationale for the independent source exception to the FOPT analysis. When challenged evidence has an independent source, application of the exclusionary rule would place the police in a worse position than they would have been in the absence of any violation. If no violation had occurred, the evidence would have been admitted due to the operation of the independent legal source.

(2) Identification Evidence as Independent Source Exception

Identification evidence is a recognized context for the operation of the independent source exception. For example, if a trial judge has ruled that the police conducted an unconstitutional out-of-court identification procedure, the prosecutor still has the opportunity to show that the victim or witness can make an in-court identification that is based on what he saw at the time of the crime rather than what he saw at the improper out-of-court identification procedure. In other words, the in-court identification has a source independent of the improper out-of-court identification. *United States v. Crews*, 445 U.S. 463 (1980). See Chapter 14.

b. Inevitable Discovery

The inevitable discovery exception is a "hypothesized independent source" exception to the FOPT rule, i.e., evidence seized by unconstitutional law enforcement activity is nonetheless admissible into evidence (again, as another exception to the FOPT doctrine) where the government can prove that it would have discovered this same evidence anyway or "inevitably," absent the constitutional violation. In other words, the fruit of the illegality would have been located by means unrelated to the illegality.

(1) Inevitable Discovery Endorsed by Supreme Court

The Supreme Court has formally endorsed the inevitable discovery exception to the fruit of the poisonous tree doctrine. In *Nix v. Williams*, 467 U.S. 431 (1984), the defendant's illegally obtained confession led to expedited discovery of the murder victim. Because the prosecution proved that a search party was approaching the actual location of body and would have found it even if defendant had not confessed, evidence pertaining to the discovery and condition of the victim was properly admitted. If "the prosecution can establish by a preponderance of the evidence that the information ultimately or inevitably would have been discovered by lawful means . . . then the deterrence rationale has so little basis that the evidence should be received."

c. Attenuation

Evidence that would not have been discovered except for police misconduct may be admissible if it is sufficiently attenuated from the illegal action. In *Wong Sun v. United States*, where the defendant had been released for several days after his illegal arrest and then returned to the police station voluntarily to make a statement, the statement was admissible despite the initial illegal arrest because "the connection between the arrest and the statement had become so attenuated as to dissipate the taint."

(1) Rationale for Attenuation

The rationale for the exception is that an attenuated connection between the illegal activity and other evidence reduces the deterrent value of the exclusionary rule. Thus, the cost of excluding the evidence outweighs the benefit of deterrence. Yes, the illegality has in some manner resulted in procurement of the evidence, but the improper police activity played a *de minimis* role. The facts of each case must be examined.

(2) Attenuation Criteria

The Court has noted that relevant attenuation criteria include the temporal proximity of "tree" and the "fruit," the presence of intervening circumstances, and the purpose and flagrancy of the police misconduct. *Brown v. Illinois*, 422 U.S. 590 (1975). The defendant in *Brown* made a statement less than two hours after his illegal arrest. On the other hand, a statement obtained at the station house following an unlawful home entry to arrest was admissible because the statement was obtained later and thus was not an exploitation of the illegal entry. *New York v. Harris*, 495 U.S. 14 (1990).

(3) Attenuation Between Illegal Search and Testimony

In *United States v. Ceccolini*, 435 U.S. 268 (1978), the Supreme Court held that the connection between an illegal search and live witness testimony that was the fruit of that search was sufficiently attenuated to allow admission of the testimony. The witness had freely decided to testify and a long time had elapsed between the illegal search and the witness's testimony. Excluding live witness testimony is so costly to the prosecution that only a close connection between the testimony and the illegal conduct justifies exclusion.

(4) Attenuation Between Illegal Arrest and Confession

In *Dunaway v. New York*, 442 U.S. 200 (1979), the police seized, detained, and interrogated defendant without probable cause. During the interrogation, the defendant made incriminating statements; the Court held that the connection between the unconstitutional police conduct and the incriminating statements was not sufficiently attenuated to permit use of the statements against the defendant at trial.

(5) (No) Attenuation in Consecutive Confessions

When the Court examined a case involving consecutive confessions, the first unwarned and the second warned, it held that a technical *Miranda* violation of failing to warn a suspect does not poison the second statement. *Oregon v. Elstad*, 470 U.S. 298 (1985). In *Missouri v. Seibert*, 542 U.S. 600 (2004), known as the "question first, warn later" case, the Court excluded a statement when the police deliberately failed to administer *Miranda* warnings in hopes that they could obtain a later, "Mirandized" confession. The Court criticized the police approach of rendering the "warnings ineffective by waiting for a particularly opportune time to give them, after the suspect has already confessed." See Chapter 13.

(6) No Attenuation Between Illegal Confession and Evidence

On the other hand, the Court has held that "[a]ttenuation also occurs when, even given a direct causal connection, the interest protected by the constitutional guarantee that has been violated would not be served by suppression of the evidence obtained." *Hudson v. Michigan*, 547 U.S. 586 (2006). In *United States v. Patane*, 542 U.S. 630 (2004), the police deliberately violated *Miranda* in the hope of obtaining statements that would lead them to physical evidence. Although there was substantial evidence that the *Miranda* violation was designed to facilitate discovery of the evidence, the Court applied *Elstad* and held that the physical evidence acquired from the *Miranda* violation was admissible.

Chapter 3

Search and Seizure: Fourth Amendment Activity

A. INTRODUCTION

The Fourth Amendment states:

> The right of the people to be secure in their persons, houses, papers, and effects, against unreasonable searches and seizures, shall not be violated; and no Warrants shall issue but upon probable cause, supported by Oath or affirmation, and particularly describing the place to be searched, and the persons or things to be seized.

If police conduct is classified as Fourth Amendment activity, the police must follow the legal standards governing their behavior. If the conduct is not Fourth Amendment activity, law enforcement officials are free to disregard the legal structures of the Fourth Amendment. The amendment applies only to conduct that can be classified as a search or seizure, and seeks to protect conduct that an individual legitimately seeks to preserve as private. A court determines the reasonableness of a search by evaluating the degree of intrusion on a person's privacy and the extent to which the search is necessary to promote legitimate governmental interests. *Wyoming v. Houghton*, 526 U.S. 295 (1999).

1. Defining a Search

A search involves a visual observation or physical intrusion that infringes upon a person's reasonable expectation of privacy. *Kyllo v. United States*, 533 U.S. 27 (2001). For example, although passengers on a commercial bus expect fellow passengers to handle or move carry-on baggage, a police officer's "probing tactile examination" of soft-sided luggage constitutes a search. *Bond v. United States*, 529 U.S. 334 (2000).

2. Defining a Seizure

A seizure in the Fourth Amendment context requires some meaningful interference with an individual's liberty (an arrest) or possessory interests (a seizure of property). *Michigan v. Chesternut*, 486 U.S. 567 (1988). A seizure such as an arrest is subject to Fourth Amendment scrutiny even though no Fourth Amendment search has occurred.

a. Seizure of an Individual

Seizure of an individual occurs by taking a person physically or constructively into custody and detaining that person, thus causing a deprivation of the person's freedom of movement in a significant way. A law enforcement officer's use of physical force is a seizure regardless of whether the suspect submits to detention. *California v. Hodari D.*, 499 U.S. 621 (1991). However, if an officer engages in a nonphysical show of authority, a seizure occurs only if a reasonable person would not feel free to leave and actually submits to authority. *See Florida v. Bostick*, 501 U.S. 429 (1991); Chapter 12 for further discussion of investigative seizures of people and property.

b. *California v. Hodari D.*: Has a Seizure Occurred?

Facts: In *California v. Hodari D.*, 499 U.S. 621 (1991), police officers on patrol in a high crime area saw youths who panicked and ran. As they chased the youths, they came close to Hodari D., who tossed away what turned out to be cocaine. The officer tackled Hodari and handcuffed him.

Law: The Court concluded that Hodari had not been seized when he abandoned the cocaine. An arrest requires either "physical force" or "submission to the assertion of authority." *Hodari*. To constitute an arrest, "the mere grasping or application of physical force with lawful authority, whether or not it succeeded in subduing the arrestee, was sufficient." At the time he threw away the cocaine, Hodari had not been grasped or subjected to any physical force, but had simply been subjected to a "show of authority." There was no seizure when Hodari refused to yield to that show of authority.

Extending *Hodari*: If Hodari D. had been seized when he abandoned the cocaine, the Court would have been forced to determine whether the seizure was legal or illegal. If the seizure was illegal, and discovery of the contraband was directly attributable to the seizure, the evidence might be deemed "fruit of the poisonous tree" of the illegal seizure. As a result, the evidence might be subject to exclusion. See Chapter 2.

c. Michigan v. Chesternut

Facts: *Hodari D.'s* logic was applied in other cases. In *Michigan v. Chesternut*, when Chesternut saw a patrol car, he began to run. The officers drove alongside him for a short distance, when Chesternut discarded a number of packets that were found to contain illegal narcotics.

Law: The Court concluded that Chesternut had not been seized when he threw away the narcotics: a reasonable person in Chesternut's position would not have believed that there was an attempt to capture or otherwise intrude upon his freedom of movement.

> The record does not reflect that the police activated a siren or flashers; or that they commanded respondent to halt, or displayed any weapons; or that they operated the car in an aggressive manner to block respondent's course or otherwise control the direction or speed of his movement.

B. *KATZ* AND THE REASONABLE EXPECTATION OF PRIVACY

The modern Fourth Amendment privacy definition was articulated in *Katz v. United States*, 389 U.S. 347, 360 (1967) (Harlan, J., concurring): "[T]here is a twofold requirement, first that a person have exhibited an actual (subjective) expectation of privacy and, second, that the expectation be one that society is prepared to recognize as 'reasonable.' " When the Court determines that a defendant's expectation of privacy is unreasonable, the police do not have to comply with the Fourth Amendment, e.g., there is no probable cause requirement for police to satisfy in order to search. When the Court rules that the expectation of privacy is reasonable, police conduct must satisfy the Fourth Amendment's requirements.

1. Katz v. United States

Katz held that a person inside a closed public phone booth had a reasonable expectation of privacy in his conversations. Therefore, agents' use of an electronic listening and recording device attached to the outside of the booth required compliance with the Fourth Amendment. *Katz* declared that

The Fourth Amendment protects people, not places. . . . What a person knowingly exposes to the public, even in his own home or office, is not a subject of Fourth Amendment protection. But what he seeks to preserve as private, even in an area accessible to the public, may be constitutionally protected.

a. Rationale for *Katz*

The rationales for the *Katz* holding focus on the context of Katz's reliance on his expectation of privacy from police surveillance.

> One who occupies [a public phone booth], shuts the door behind him, and pays the toll that permits him to place a call is surely entitled to assume that the words he utters into the mouthpiece will not be broadcast to the world.

The defendant's privacy expectation also reflected concern about the government's power to gain access to the contents of that communication anywhere, anytime.

b. Nature of Privacy as a Constitutional Right

The privacy interest is a constitutional right that depends in part on the person's behavior (e.g., talking loudly in a public place) and in part on the social context (e.g., using a telephone booth to conduct a phone conversation). Talking loudly in a booth does not make the person's expectation reasonable. If the speaker's expectation is unreasonable, an officer eavesdropping on the conversation from outside the booth does not have to satisfy the Fourth Amendment in order to listen and testify later about what she heard.

c. When *Katz* Does Not Apply

Katz does not apply when a government agent is one of the parties to the conversation or listens to it. *United States v. White*, 401 U.S. 745 (1971). Defendants cannot reasonably expect that the person to whom they are talking is not a government agent recording the conversation or is not reporting the conversation to the police. (When neither party to the conversation is aware that the government is listening, the legality of the seizure of the conversation through electronic surveillance is governed by the same Fourth Amendment standards as any other police investigative practices.) The Court has similarly ruled that *Katz* is inapplicable when defendants (actually or constructively) convey other information to third parties, who then provide that information to law enforcement personnel. *See, e.g.*, *United States v. Miller*, 425 U.S. 435 (1976) (bank received custody of suspect's checks and financial records); *Smith v. Maryland*, 442 U.S. 735 (1979) (by making a phone call, the suspect conveyed information to the telephone company about the numbers he was calling).

2. Curtilage v. Open Fields

Fourth Amendment activity may include police conduct on the "curtilage" (the land "immediately surrounding and associated with the home"), which generally is a protected area. The difficulty relates to defining its boundaries. The status of a potential "curtilage" area is evaluated with reference to four factors: its proximity to the home, whether it is enclosed, the nature of its uses, and the steps taken to protect it from observation. *United States v. Dunn*, 480 U.S. 294 (1987) (defining scope of curtilage). Police can observe activity on the curtilage from a public street, but police presence *on* the curtilage itself is Fourth Amendment activity.

a. Police Conduct in Open Fields Is Not Fourth Amendment Activity

"Open fields" are the area beyond the curtilage, and are exempt from Fourth Amendment requirements and can be entered and searched without a warrant. The "open fields" exception is consistent with the *Katz* privacy analysis. *Oliver v. United States*, 466 U.S. 170 (1984). Thus, police presence on a person's property that is an open field (i.e., beyond the curtilage) does not require compliance with the Fourth Amendment (even though it constitutes a trespass). The police can stand in an open field and observe what is occurring on the curtilage or in a house.

C. *JONES* AND THE PHYSICAL TRESPASS OF A PROTECTED AREA

"Fourth Amendment rights do not rise or fall with the *Katz* formulation." The Supreme Court historically interpreted the Fourth Amendment to represent a specific concern for government trespass in the areas enumerated in its text. Neither the *Katz* test nor the trespass test is the exclusive test for measuring Fourth Amendment activity. *United States v. Jones*, 132 S.Ct. 945 (2012).

1. United States v. Jones

United States v. Jones, 132 S.Ct. 945 (2012) held that police installation of a GPS tracking device on a vehicle and warrantless use of the device to monitor the vehicle's movements constitute a "search" and violate a defendant's Fourth Amendment rights. An essential component of the Fourth Amendment claim requires that 1) one's own personal "effects" have been trespassed (e.g., Scalia's majority view that emphasized the trespassory nature of the secret installation of a GPS device on one's automobile), or 2) one's own expectation of privacy was impinged (e.g., the focus of the *Jones*'s concurrences and dissent upon the continuous monitoring and tracking of one's movements for a material period of time).

a. The *Jones* majority

The Court disagreed about why this was a Fourth Amendment violation. Writing for the majority, Justice Scalia found that the *Katz* reasonable expectation of privacy standard had not changed the historical principle that the Government cannot engage in a physical intrusion of a constitutionally protected area in order to obtain information. In other words, *Katz's* reasonable expectation of privacy standard was *an addition, not a substitute for*, the common-law trespass test.

b. The *Jones* Concurrences

Five other members of the Court concluded that Justice Scalia's trespass theory does *not* form a sufficiently comprehensive analysis of the Fourth Amendment implications of GPS monitoring. They instead argued that GPS monitoring should be analyzed to determine whether it has invaded a reasonable expectation of privacy. Even Justice Scalia noted that cases "involving merely the transmission of electronic signals without trespass would *remain* subject to *Katz* analysis."

2. Florida v. Jardines

Police use of a trained drug-sniffing dog on a homeowner's porch to investigate the possibility of drugs in the home is a Fourth Amendment search, thereby requiring probable cause. Relying upon the *Jones* trespass analysis (instead of the *Katz* privacy approach). The police obtained information about drugs inside the house by the dog sniffing (and thereby physically intruding) at the base of the front door of the defendant's home. Without probable cause, the dog-sniff violated the Fourth Amendment. *Florida v. Jardines*, 133 S.Ct. 1409 (2013).

3. When *Katz* Applies and When *Jones* Applies

Jones held that a trespass test applies when state actors physically trespass on a person's legally recognized property interest, while the *Katz* reasonable expectation of privacy test applies in cases when no physical trespass has occurred. In either situation, law enforcement must obtain a warrant, unless the government identifies an exception to the warrant requirement. *See* Chapters 5–12.

D. HUMAN SURVEILLANCE AND ENHANCED SURVEILLANCE

The Court's cases also address issues of "human" surveillance and issues of "enhanced" surveillance, using technologies that are as varied as canine sniffs, tracking beepers, helicopter "flyovers," aerial mapping cameras, and thermal-imaging devices.

1. Protected Vantage Points

Case law suggests that certain questions are relevant to whether vantage points are protected:

- whether the public at large has access to the vantage point,
- whether the public has access to technology being used by the government, and
- whether the surveillance reveals intimate activities.

An example of the first question occurs when the police walk by a vehicle and look through a vehicle windshield to obtain a vehicle identification number. The owner of the vehicle has no privacy interest in that number because anyone can walk by the vehicle and see that information. *New York v. Class*, 475 U.S. 106 (1986). Police use of a device like a flashlight merely to artificially enhance sensory perceptions is an example of the second issue; there is no Fourth Amendment activity if the device aids the police in obtaining information that they could have obtained through their own senses. *Texas v. Brown*, 460 U.S. 730 (1983). If the person had no privacy interest to begin with, the use of enhancement devices likewise is not Fourth Amendment activity.

2. *California v. Greenwood*: Garbage on the Curb

In a controversial decision emphasizing public access, the Court held that a defendant had no reasonable expectation of privacy in garbage that was placed in opaque trash bags, left on the curb, and searched by police who procured the bags from the garbage collector. *California v. Greenwood*, 486 U.S. 35 (1988). The *Greenwood* defendants were in the unprotected *Katz* category of those who knowingly expose private information to the public, e.g., garbage collectors, scavengers. A different conclusion would follow if police went into the garage, i.e., on the curtilage, to take the garbage bags.

3. *Bond v. United States*: Squeezing Luggage

Greenwood's logic did not prevail for carry-on luggage placed in an overhead bin by a bus passenger and squeezed by a police officer in *Bond v. United States*, 529 U.S. 334 (2000). While "public access" and "conveyance to a third party" were present in *Bond*, given that other passengers and bus employees could handle or touch the luggage, the Court recognized that public customs do not extend beyond mere "handling" to encompass the "exploratory" feeling of a bag. The Court also emphasized that "tactile" observation is "more intrusive than purely visual inspection." *Bond*, however, did not hold that luggage in a public area is protected *per se* from all intrusions.

4. United States v. Place: Dog Sniff of Luggage

In a pre-*Bond* decision, the Court approved canine sniffs by narcotics detection dogs of the exterior of luggage in a public place; such an intrusion does not violate a reasonable expectation of privacy. *United States v. Place*, 462 U.S. 696 (1983). The Court relied on the sniff as:

- minimally intrusive (contrasted with opening the luggage), and
- disclosing "only the presence or absence of narcotics," thereby protecting innocent citizens from general police "rummaging" in their possessions.

The Court later recognized in *City of Indianapolis v. Edmond*, 531 U.S. 32 (2000) that a canine sniff of the exterior of a car at a roadblock is not a "search" or a "seizure" under *Place*. Likewise, a dog sniff of a vehicle's exterior during a traffic stop of one vehicle is not a "search." *Illinois v. Caballes*, 543 U.S. 405 (2005). When a drug-detection dog alerts, a court's determination of probable cause arising from that alert is determined by considering the totality of circumstances about the dog's reliability. A bona fide organization's certification of the drug dog's reliability raises a rebuttable presumption that the dog's reaction is reliable to satisfy probable cause. *Florida v. Harris*, 133 S.Ct. 1050 (2013).

5. Tracking Beepers

The Court approved of beepers as a substitute for visual surveillance in *United States v. Knotts*, 460 U.S. 276 (1983), when the police attached a tracking beeper inside a container, and then followed the defendant's car in which the container was located. After the police lost visual surveillance of the car, the beeper allowed them to track the car to the area of the defendant's cabin. *Knotts* limited its approval of "tracking beepers" to a situation where "there is no indication that the beeper was used in any way to reveal information as to the movement of the [container] inside the [defendant's premises]." By contrast, *United States v. Karo*, 468 U.S. 705 (1984) held that police cannot use "tracking beepers" to obtain information that could not have been obtained through visual surveillance. *Karo* found that a violation of a reasonable expectation of privacy occurred when police used a beeper in a container to discover "a critical fact about the interior of the premises," i.e., the container with the beeper was moved inside the home.

6. Aerial Surveillance

The Court's aerial surveillance cases indicate that there is no reasonable expectation of privacy from some police "fly overs" of property, aerial surveillance of a home's curtilage from a helicopter flying as low as 400 feet, and the use of an aerial mapping camera during "fly overs" of commercial property. *Florida v. Riley*, 488 U.S. 445 (1989); *Dow Chemical v. United States*, 476 U.S. 227 (1986). These cases rely on the "public access" rationale of *Greenwood*, because members of the "flying public" could make "naked eye" observations of the curtilage like the police in *Riley*, and could use a "conventional" mapping camera like the one in *Dow Chemical*. *Riley* noted, though, that the police observed marijuana growing in a greenhouse, but not "intimate details connected with the use of the home or the curtilage," e.g., observing private activity in a home through a skylight.

7. *Kyllo v. United States*: Thermal Imaging Devices

Facts: In *Kyllo v. United States*, 533 U.S. 27 (2001), a "thermal imaging device" was aimed at a private home from across the street, and the heat scan showed that the garage was hotter than the rest of the house and "substantially warmer than neighboring homes." That evidence established the probable cause required for the issuance of a warrant to search the home for an "indoor growing operation" using halide lights to grow marijuana.

Law: The *Kyllo* majority determined that the homeowner had a reasonable expectation of privacy from the use of the thermal imaging device: obtaining information about the interior of home by sense-enhancing technology by physical "intrusion into a constitutionally protected area" constitutes a search (requiring a finding of probable cause *prior* to using the imager), at least where the technology used is not available to the general public.

a. *Kyllo*'s Rationales

Kyllo's rationales relied on *Katz*, *Karo*, and *Dow Chemical*. The Court rejected the argument that the device detected heat only from the external surface of the home, reasoning that such a "mechanical interpretation" of privacy was rejected in *Katz*. *Karo* implies that a homeowner should not without prior probable cause be subject to police use of technology that may discern human activity inside the home. The majority also rejected the government's alternate argument that the heat device did not "detect private activities occurring in private areas," reasoning that "[i]n the home, all details are intimate details, because the entire area is held safe from prying government eyes."

8. United States v. Jacobsen: Reopening Packages

Facts: A common carrier employee opened a package, sealed it, and then notified the police about suspicions about its contents. A government agent reopened the package while it was still in the custody of the common carrier.

Law: No Fourth Amendment search by the police occurred, because the package at the time had already been legally opened by the private employee and the contents did not change after the original opening. *United States v. Jacobsen*, 466 U.S. 109 (1984).

9. City of Ontario v. Quon: Text Messages

Facts: The city of Ontario claimed that it had the right to read text messages being sent and received by SWAT team members on pagers owned and issued by the city to its employees. The team members previously read and signed a statement that they understood the city's Computer policy that stated text message transcripts could be reviewed by their supervisors.

Law: The Court in *City of Ontario v. Quon*, 560 U.S. 746 (2010) characterized Quon's privacy expectation as "limited." He already knew that his messages were subject to audits. Because "Quon had received no assurances of privacy, he could have anticipated that it might be necessary for the city to audit pager messages to assess the SWAT team's performance in particular emergency situations." The Court found that the audit of the messages on the "employer-provided pager was not nearly as intrusive as a search of his personal e-mail account or pager, or a wiretap on his home phone line would have been." A supervisor's review of pager messages while the officers are on duty "might be justified for other reasons, including performance evaluations, litigation concerning the lawfulness of police actions, and perhaps compliance with state open records laws."

CHAPTER 4

SEARCH AND SEIZURE: SEARCH AND ARREST WARRANTS

A. THE SIGNIFICANCE OF USING A WARRANT

The Warrant Clause of the Fourth Amendment requires that "no Warrants shall issue, but upon probable cause, supported by Oath or affirmation, and particularly describing the place to be searched, and the persons or things to be seized." There is a strong preference for search warrants. The Court generally determines whether to exempt a given type of search from the warrant requirement "by assessing, on the one hand, the degree to which it intrudes upon an individual's privacy and, on the other, the degree to which it is needed for the promotion of legitimate governmental interests." *Wyoming v. Houghton*, 626 U.S. 295 (1999). For example, given the pervasive types and amounts of cell phone information, "[o]fficers must generally secure a warrant before conducting . . . a search" for digital inforamtion. *Riley v. California*, 134 S.Ct. 2473 (2014). In cases where it is a close question about whether probable cause exists, courts lean toward upholding searches based upon warrants.

1. The "Warrant Requirement"

Searches conducted without prior approval by a judge are *per se* unreasonable under the Fourth Amendment, subject to a few well-delineated exceptions. *Thompson v. Louisiana*, 469 U.S. 17 (1984).

> A warrant assures the citizen that the intrusion is authorized by law, and that it is narrowly limited in its objectives and scope. . . . A warrant also provides the detached and neutral scrutiny of a neutral judge, and thus ensures an objective determination whether an intrusion is justified in any given case.

Skinner v. Railway Labor Executives' Ass'n, 489 U.S. 602 (1989).

2. Reasons for Using an Arrest Warrant.

Absent exigent circumstances (see Chapter 11), an arrest warrant is required in order to arrest a person in her own home. *Payton v. New York*, 445 U.S. 573 (1980). Entry into the defendant's home without a lawful arrest warrant makes any seized evidence inadmissible. "Entry into the home is the chief evil against which the wording of the Fourth Amendment is directed." *United States v. United States District Court*, 407 U.S. 297 (1972).

B. PROBABLE CAUSE

The Warrant Clause requires probable cause for issuance of a search warrant or an arrest warrant. Probable cause requires a showing of "a fair probability" on each of the points that the prosecution must establish in order for a warrant to issue. For an arrest warrant, the government must prove a fair probability that a crime has been committed and that the person to be arrested committed the crime. To demonstrate probable cause sufficient to obtain a search warrant, the government must establish a fair probability that the specified items sought are evidence of criminal activity and that those items are presently located at the specified place described in the search warrant application.

1. Scope and Sources of Probable Cause

As discussed in this and the following chapters, the Supreme Court has applied the probable cause requirement both to the Warrant Clause *and* to the Amendment's first clause that prohibits "unreasonable searches and seizures." Probable cause is measured by the information available to law enforcement *prior* to an arrest or search. What is learned afterwards is irrelevant to *that* arrest or search. Probable cause is evaluated on the basis of information from other police, private citizens, informants, and anonymous tipsters.

2. A Common Sense Approach to Probable Cause

For probable cause, the issuing judge makes a "common sense decision" whether under the circumstances articulated in the affidavit there is a fair probability that evidence of a crime will be found in a particular place. *Illinois v. Gates*, 462 U.S. 213 (1983). Using a "common sense" test, the Supreme Court has concluded that probable cause existed to arrest a driver and both of his two passengers in a car where baggies of cocaine and large amounts of cash had been discovered during a routine traffic stop: "We think it an entirely reasonable inference from these facts that any or all three of the occupants had knowledge of, and exercised dominion and control over, the cocaine." *Maryland v. Pringle*, 540 U.S. 366 (2003).

3. Informant Information and Probable Cause

Prior to 1983, the Supreme Court used the so-called *Aguilar-Spinelli* test to evaluate the existence of probable cause based upon information obtained from an informant. Under *Aguilar v. Texas*, 378 U.S. 108 (1964) and *Spinelli v. United States*, 393 U.S. 410 (1969), the government needed to provide the judge with information that sufficiently explained:

- how the informant obtained her information (the "underlying circumstances" prong); and
- why the informant is reliable (the "credibility" prong).

a. Totality of Circumstances Test

In 1983, in *Illinois v. Gates*, 462 U.S. 213 (1983), while finding the *Aguilar-Spinelli* test "highly relevant" to the probable cause determination, the Court rejected the rigid categories of proof as necessary to show probable cause. In its place, the Court adopted a "totality-of-the-circumstances" test to evaluate probable cause based upon informant information. As the *Gates* Court pointed out, "a deficiency in one category", e.g., basis of knowledge, may be offset by a strong showing as to the other category, e.g., why the informant is reliable, or by some other indicia of reliability. Other "indicia of reliability" may include corroboration by police of some of the informant's factual details (even if the specific corroborated facts show only otherwise innocent activity, e.g., the wearing of clothing of a particular color or style, the same color or style as a criminal suspect), and the informant's status as a "citizen" (as opposed to an informant with a criminal past).

(1) Proving Probably Cause from a Drug-Sniffing Dog's Alert

The totality of circumstances determines probable cause based upon a dog's alert. "[E]vidence of a dog's satisfactory performance in a certification or training program can itself provide sufficient reason to trust his alert. " Thereafter, a defendant is entitled to challenge the dog's reliability, by cross-examining the testifying officer or by introducing fact or expert witnesses. In *Florida v. Harris*, 133 S.Ct. 1050 (2013), the record supported the trial court's conclusion that the dog's alert gave the officer probable cause to search the defendant's truck.

b. Informer's Privilege

The government may try to keep informants' identities confidential, out of fear for their safety and/or a desire for their continued effectiveness as informants. As a result, the Court recognizes an "informer's privilege" when defense counsel seeks an informant's actual identity at a suppression hearing. *McCray v. Illinois*, 386 U.S. 300 (1967). Judges have discretion to order disclosure of an informant's identity when there is some reason to believe that her information is not believable (or that the informant does not even exist). Disclosure of an informant's identity may occur out of the presence of the defendant and defense counsel.

4. Staleness of Probable Cause

Probable cause information for a search warrant may be stale depending on the relationship between the length of time between discovery of the information and the time that a search warrant is sought. (Because *arrest* warrants may be served anytime, the staleness issue is inapplicable.) Some evidence may: disappear quickly (a marijuana cigarette), or persist for a long time (e.g., a corpse buried in a basement). Additional factors relevant to the staleness inquiry are:

- the nature of the criminal evidence sought (e.g., large or small, moveable or fixed),
- the location of the evidence (e.g., in plain view or buried),
- the condition in which the evidence was observed (e.g., solid or liquid, easily disposable or permanent), and
- the nature of the place to be searched (e.g., readily moveable vehicle or a residential home).

5. Prospective Probable Cause and Anticipatory Warrants

In *United States v. Grubbs*, 547 U.S. 90 (2006), the Supreme Court upheld the constitutionality of an "anticipatory warrant," which is a search warrant issued based only upon a showing of *prospective* probable cause. In other words, there is a showing that evidence of crime will be or is likely to be present on the premises sought to be searched at some specified time in the future subsequent to the occurrence of some specified triggering condition.

a. Prerequisites for an Anticipatory Warrant

"The supporting affidavit must provide sufficient information to evaluate both aspects of the probable cause determination." The triggering condition does not have to be set forth in the warrant itself. Two prerequisites of probability must be satisfied:

- if the triggering condition occurs, a fair probability exists "that contraband or evidence of a crime will be found in a particular place," and

- "probable cause exists to believe the triggering condition will occur."

b. When the Triggering Event Does Not Occur

Many anticipatory warrants involve information that narcotics will be delivered to a certain place at a certain time in the future (the "triggering condition"). Often, law enforcement agents know for a virtual certainty that such a delivery will be made (and when it will be made), because their own agents are making or monitoring the delivery. Such anticipatory warrants become invalid and cannot be executed when and if the contingent event (e.g., the delivery of narcotics) that established prospective probable cause does not in fact occur (e.g., no delivery appears to have been made).

C. OBTAINING WARRANTS

Information supporting the issuance of a search warrant or arrest warrant must be disclosed to the issuing judge *ex parte* at the time she is considering the application for a warrant. Ordinarily, the information is presented in the form of written affidavits, sworn to by the affiant under oath. However, some jurisdictions have rules which authorize warrants to be obtained upon oral testimony communicated by telephone or other means "if the circumstances make it reasonable to dispense with an affidavit." Fed.R.Crim.P. 41(c).

1. "Four Corners" of the Affidavit

Most jurisdictions require that the issuing judge may consider only the information that is contained within "the four corners" of the affidavits in evaluating whether probable cause exists. In some jurisdictions, however, the issuing judge may also consider sworn oral statements made by affiants or other witnesses as supplements to information contained in the affidavits themselves.

2. Challenging Affidavits

Affidavits offered as support for probable cause may be challenged by defense counsel in two different ways:

- "on their face," i.e., counsel argues that the facts in the affidavit are insufficient to establish probable cause, or
- because some or all of the statements in the affidavit were false.

a. *Franks* Hearing to Challenge the Affidavit

The mere falsity of affidavit information is not enough to make the warrant defective and unconstitutional, because search warrant affidavits are presumptively valid. *Franks v.*

Delaware, 438 U.S. 154 (1978). A *Franks* hearing is a pretrial hearing at which defense counsel attempts to show that the affiant deliberately lied or made a statement in reckless disregard of the truth. Because an affidavit is presumed to be valid, the first step requires the defendant to make a preliminary showing that there are specific false statements in the affidavit for the warrant, making the warrant defective. If the defendant cannot do that, there is no right to a *Franks* hearing. If the defendant does make that showing, the defendant next must show that the false statements were deliberately or recklessly made. If the mistakes were negligent or innocent, there is no *Franks* hearing. If the mistakes were deliberate or reckless, the court holds a *Franks* hearing to determine whether *without* those false statements, the affidavit still contains probable cause. If probable cause would still exist, the exclusionary rule is inapplicable. If probable cause would not exist, the exclusionary rule applies *but* the warrant still is subject to the good faith of officers in executing it, unless *those* officers knew or should have known that the affiant was deliberately or recklessly lying.

3. Review of Probable Cause Determinations

Probable cause determinations where a search warrant has been issued are reviewed for whether the issuing judge had a substantial basis for concluding that a search would uncover evidence of wrongdoing. *Illinois v. Gates*, 462 U.S. 213 (1983). *Gates* noted that a reviewing court must pay "great deference" to the trial judge's conclusion that probable cause existed.

4. Issuing Judges

A judge authorized by a jurisdiction to issue a warrant is generically referred to as an "issuing judge." She ordinarily may issue search warrants only for the search of places located within the issuing court's jurisdiction. Likewise, she may issue arrest warrants only for the arrest of persons in the issuing court's jurisdiction.

a. The Issuing Judge Must Be Neutral, Detached, and Impartial

An issuing judge must be neutral, detached, and capable of determining whether probable cause exists for a requested arrest or search warrant. *Shadwick v. City of Tampa*, 407 U.S. 345 (1972) (a statutorily authorized person to issue warrants does not have to be a lawyer). A State Attorney General is not sufficiently neutral and detached to be empowered to issue warrants. *Coolidge v. New Hampshire*, 403 U.S. 443 (1971). An "officer engaged in the often competitive enterprise of ferreting out crime" cannot make probable cause determinations. *Johnson v. United States*, 333 U.S. 10 (1948).

b. The Judge Cannot Have a Pecuniary Interest in Issuing Warrants

A defendant may also attack the validity of a warrant by pointing to specific examples of partiality to show that the issuing judge was not acting in a neutral and detached manner in the particular case. For example, Georgia judges who received $5.00 each time they issued a search warrant (and received nothing each time that they declined to issue a warrant) had a pecuniary interest in the issuance of the warrants. *Connally v. Georgia*, 429 U.S. 245 (1977).

5. The Particularity Requirement

The Fourth Amendment prescribes that Warrants must particularly describe "the place to be searched, and the persons or things to be seized."

a. Rationale for Particularity Requirement

The requirement ensures that the search will not become an exploratory, wide-ranging rummaging. *Maryland v. Garrison*, 480 U.S. 79 (1987). In another words, the requirement "prevents the seizure of one thing under a warrant describing another. As to what is to be taken, nothing is left to the discretion of the officer executing the warrant." *Marron v. United States*, 275 U.S. 192 (1927). The Supreme Court has noted that the "Fourth Amendment specifies only two matters that must be 'particularly describ[ed]' in the warrant: 'the place to be searched' and 'the persons or things to be seized.' " *United States v. Grubbs*, 547 U.S. 90 (2006).

b. Particularity of Person to be Seized

An arrest warrant must specify the name of the defendant or otherwise describe the defendant with information by which she may be identified with reasonable certainty. A photograph of the person would assist law enforcement, as would a general description that includes distinctive physical characteristics, e.g., white male, age 25, who walks with a limp and has a cardinal bird tattoo on his face.

c. Particularity of the Search Premises

When describing search premises, the important question is whether the description is so specific that it identifies only the premises intended to be searched, and no other place. If the description fails this test, the warrant is constitutionally deficient. Typical forms of descriptive information of the search premises are:

- street numbers, geographic indicators, or apartment numbers,
- city, county, and State locations,
- legal property descriptions or plat map references,
- directions on a map (sometimes attached to the affidavit or warrant),
- descriptions of the house or building by color, style, composition, or size,
- description of the neighborhood character (e.g., urban, suburban, rural), and
- the name of the owner and/or residents.

(1) Catch-All Descriptive Clauses Are Acceptable

Property descriptions in an affidavit or a warrant often conclude with language such as "any other evidence of the crime" or "together with other fruits instrumentalities and evidence of crime." As long as this language is preceded by reference to specifically described property, evidence seized pursuant to the catch-all clause of the warrant is admissible. *Andresen v. Maryland*, 427 U.S. 463 (1976).

(2) Warrant for Part of a Building

When the warrant authorizes a search of only part of a building, e.g., a single apartment in a multi-unit, residential building, that limitation must be expressed in the search warrant description to meet the constitutional test. Most courts are willing to evaluate the particularity of a warrant description (the place to be searched or things to be seized) on the basis of the description contained in the search warrant itself and in any physically attached affidavits or lists, assuming that appropriate words of reference to those documents are included in the warrant itself.

d. Particularity of Things to Be Seized

The description in the warrant must be only as particular as the circumstances require, e.g., a description of contraband like "narcotics" or "drugs" is sufficiently specific, but a reference to "stolen property" is too general and unconstitutionally deficient. A reference to stolen "jewelry," on the other hand, described by detailed reference to characteristics as to nature, appearance, dimensions and initialing is constitutional. A less-detailed description may be constitutional when that is the most that can be said under the circumstances, e.g., a "brown puppy."

e. Minor or Partial Errors Irrelevant

A minor error in the search warrant about the place to be searched does not automatically render the warrant constitutionally defective, e.g., "2620 McCoy Way" instead of "2620A McCoy Way." As long as the place where the search is to take place is clear to the executing officers, e.g., from an otherwise accurate description aside from the error in the address number, the warrant is constitutional despite the descriptive error. The same is true of minor errors in the description of the things to be seized contained in a search warrant, e.g., a serial number on an appliance when only one appliance of the type described is on the premises. Even if some items seized must be suppressed for violating the particularity requirement, any remaining items seized pursuant to the warrant and described particularly are admissible.

f. "All Persons" Warrants

Some search warrants list as search targets "all persons on the premises." Normally, if a person is a search target of a search warrant, she must be described particularly (although not necessarily by name), just as with any non-human search target like a residence, business, or vehicle. The rationale justifying "all persons" warrants is that they are proper when the search premises are being used for such clearly criminal purposes, e.g., a "crack house," that all persons present are necessarily involved with criminal activity. The Supreme Court has expressly reserved judgment on the constitutionality of such "all persons on the premises" warrants, *Ybarra v. Illinois*, 444 U.S. 85 (1979), and the lower courts are split on the question.

D. EXECUTION OF SEARCH OR ARREST WARRANTS

While the particularity requirement limits the officer's discretion in executing a warrant, a search or arrest warrant for a specific place includes both the buildings and other areas within the curtilage.

1. Persons Who May Execute

A search or arrest warrant may be executed by the specific law enforcement officers directed in the warrant itself or by any other law enforcement officers authorized by applicable statutes in that jurisdiction. The executing officers must be acting within their own jurisdiction but they may use the services of officers from other law enforcement agencies or, where necessary, private citizens.

2. Time Limits

Search warrants must be executed both within the jurisdiction's maximum time limit for execution (usually established by court rule or by statute) and prior to the time the probable cause information supporting the warrant becomes stale. Prescribed maximum time limits vary widely, from two to sixty days. After the time limit passes, unless it is renewed with a fresh showing of probable cause prior to its execution, evidence seized will be suppressed. *Sgro v. United States*, 287 U.S. 206 (1933). A delay in the execution of an arrest warrant does not render the warrant invalid.

3. Nighttime Searches

Most jurisdictions (including the federal courts) require, by statute or court rule, a special showing if a search warrant is to be executed at night. Searches at night are more intrusive of individuals' privacy, and raise a greater risk of a violent response from the occupants who may not realize who is forcing their way on the premises. Officers seeking a nighttime warrant must specify why they need to search at night, e.g., evidence of easily destructible or mobile evidence on the search premises.

4. Knock-and-Announce Doctrine

The common-law "knock-and-announce" doctrine for warrants is part of the Fourth Amendment and applicable to all federal and State executing officers. *Wilson v. Arkansas*, 514 U.S. 927 (1995). The doctrine requires executing officers to do four things:

- audibly "knock" or otherwise make their presence known at the outer door, thereby giving notice to the occupants about the law enforcement presence,
- "announce" the identity of the executing officers (e.g., "It's the Police!"),
- "announce" the purpose of the executing officers (e.g., "We have a warrant!"), and
- "delay" for a period of time sufficient to permit the occupants to reach and to open the door.

a. When Police May Enter Premises

After a sufficient delay when no one answers the door, officers may then enter the premises forcibly, including breaking down doors and engaging in the destruction of other property, if it is necessary and reasonable to enter. *United States v. Ramirez*,

523 U.S. 65 (1998); 18 U.S.C. § 3109. In *Alderman v. United States*, 394 U.S. 165 (1969), the court stated in *dicta* that there is no need to wait for someone to be at the premises before police may make a forcible entry. Nor do executing officers need to look for or obtain the cooperation of search premises' occupants before beginning their search of the premises named in the warrant or for the person designated in the arrest warrant.

(1) Delay before Police May Enter

In general, a delay of thirty seconds is sufficient in most jurisdictions to meet the Fourth Amendment delay requirement. The Supreme Court has upheld a delay of only 15 to 20 seconds, however, where the premises occupant was suspected of selling cocaine which can be quickly destroyed. *United States v. Banks*, 540 U.S. 31 (2003). By contrast, "[p]olice seeking a stolen piano [i.e., evidence that cannot be quickly destroyed] may be able to spend more time to make sure they really need the battering ram."

(2) Effect of Violating Knock-and-Announce

Violation of the knock-and-announce doctrine by executing officers renders the search warrant defective as a constitutional matter, but the federal exclusionary rule does *not* apply to law enforcement officers' knock-and-announce violations. *Hudson v. Michigan*, 547 U.S. 586 (2006). "[T]he social costs of applying the exclusionary rule to knock-and-announce violations are considerable; the incentive to such violations is minimal to begin with, and the extant deterrences against them are substantial—incomparably greater than the factors deterring warrantless entries when *Mapp* was decided." See Chapter 2.

b. Exceptions to Knock-and-Announce

There are a number of permissible exceptions to the knock-and-announce requirement:

- nonviolent "entry by trick," e.g., law enforcement officer pretending to be a hotel desk clerk,
- the exigency exception, which must be specific to the particular circumstances, *see Richards v. Wisconsin*, 520 U.S. 385 (1997), and
- when adherence to the knock-and-announce doctrine would be futile.

For the last two exceptions, police must have a reasonable suspicion that knocking and announcing their presence would be dangerous or futile, or that it would inhibit an effective investigation by, for example, allowing the destruction of evidence. Requiring executing officers who have already been spotted by search premises' occupants to follow all of the requirements of the knock-and-announce doctrine may be a futile gesture and is not required.

c. Justifying Knock-and-Announce Provision in Advance

When individuals obtaining a search warrant can show in advance that the conditions that would excuse compliance with the knock-and-announce doctrine at the scene will be present at the search premises (e.g., danger to the officers or the destructibility of evidence), the Court has stated in *dicta* that executing officers may obtain a no-knock warrant.

5. Post-Execution Requirements

By rule or statute, most jurisdictions require executing officers to leave a copy of the search warrant and a receipt for items seized at the search premises. They also must promptly file a "return" with the court, noting when the warrant was executed and specifying precisely what was seized. Most jurisdictions do not treat these requirements as requiring application of the exclusionary rule. As for the return of property seized, governments are not constitutionally required to give detailed instructions to individuals seeking to obtain their lawfully-seized property after the property is no longer needed for investigative or prosecutorial purposes. *City of West Covina v. Perkins*, 525 U.S. 234 (1999).

6. Seizures Pursuant to Search Warrant

a. What Can Be Seized?

Items specified and particularly described in a search warrant as evidence of crime may be seized under the authority of the warrant. In addition, executing officers may seize non-described items that they see in "plain view" while they are lawfully present at a place to execute a search warrant, provided that the items are "incriminating on their face," i.e., connected with some criminal activity. *Horton v. California*, 496 U.S. 128 (1990). See Chapter 5.

b. Where Can Seizures Be Made?

Executing officers may search anywhere on the search premises that the items particularly described in the search warrant may be hidden. As long as the officers are searching in such a place, they may lawfully seize items particularly described in the warrant and/or plain view items.

(1) Permitted Scope of Search Area

A search warrant description for a particular home, building or place usually includes permission to search the land immediately surrounding and associated with the search target, any and all buildings located thereon (e.g., a garage), and any vehicles found there. However, a search pursuant to a search warrant cannot extend to neighboring areas outside of or beyond the search premises.

(2) Exception: When Police Must Discontinue Search

The exception is where a neighboring area reasonably appears to the executing officers to be part of the search premises covered by a warrant. For example, the Supreme Court upheld a search of a third-floor apartment in a building where the executing officers reasonably did not realize that the third floor was divided into two separate apartments, and that they were searching the wrong one. *Maryland v. Garrison*, 480 U.S. 79 (1987). However, the Court warned that

> the officers . . . were required to discontinue the search of [the wrong] apartment as soon as they discovered that there were two separate units on the third floor and therefore were put on notice of the risk that they might be in a unit erroneously included within the terms of the warrant.

c. Intensity of Search

The permissible intensity of a search is dictated and limited by the nature of the items being sought under the warrant.

> A warrant that authorizes an officer to search a home for illegal weapons also provides authority to open closets, chests, drawers, and containers in which the weapon might be found. A warrant to open a footlocker to search for marijuana would also authorize the opening of packages found inside. A warrant to search a vehicle would support a search of every part of the vehicle that might contain the object of the search.

United States v. Ross, 456 U.S. 798 (1982).

d. Property Damage or Destruction

Executing officers may damage or destroy property in conducting a search where such damage is reasonably necessary to effect the search. *Dalia v. United States*, 441 U.S. 238 (1979). Nonetheless, there are limits to the permissible extent of property destruction in the execution of a warrant. "Excessive or unnecessary destruction of property in the course of a search may violate the Fourth Amendment, even though the entry itself is lawful and the fruits of the search not subject to suppression." *United States v. Ramirez*. An excessive search may lead to a civil action for damages.

e. Duration of Search

Searches are limited in duration by a similar rule of reasonable necessity. Searches of a home that last for several hours are not uncommon, but once all of the objects particularly described and sought under a warrant have been found or the police leave, no further searches are permissible under the authority of *that* warrant.

f. Detaining Occupants on the Premises During Warrant Execution

Officers executing a search warrant may "detain the occupant of the premises while a proper search is conducted," even without any suspicion that the person is involved in a crime. *Muehler v. Mena*, 544 U.S. 93 (2005); *Michigan v. Summers*, 452 U.S. 692 (1981). Three law enforcement interests justify the detention: officer safety, facilitation of the warrant's execution, and preventing flight. *Summers*. If there is reasonable suspicion that any person is armed, police may frisk the outer clothing of that person for weapons. In *Los Angeles County v. Rettele*, 550 U.S. 609 (2007), the Court held that the police acted reasonably when, during the execution of a search warrant, they found two unclothed people in bed and required them to stand naked briefly before permitting them to dress.

(1) Detaining Occupant Outside Immediate Vicinity of Premises

In *Bailey v. United States*, 133 S.Ct. 1031 (2013), police did not detain the occupant of the premises until he was almost a mile away. The Court held that the foregoing rationales for a detention outside the immediate vicinity of the premises were inapplicable, and remanded the case to determine if the detention was justified on other grounds.

(2) Searching Property Belonging to Non-Suspect Third Party

When executing officers either know or reasonably should know that property found on search premises belongs to a non-suspect third-party, e.g. a purse belonging to a social guest, that property cannot be searched pursuant to the search warrant. However, this rule is inapplicable to the search of property belonging to a non-suspect, third-party vehicle passenger subject to a lawful search of the car for contraband. "Police officers with probable cause to search a car may inspect passengers' belongings found in the car that are capable of concealing the object of the search." *Wyoming v. Houghton*, 526 U.S. 295 (1999).

CHAPTER 5

WARRANTLESS SEARCHES: PLAIN VIEW

A. INTRODUCTION

Although the Fourth Amendment prohibits "unreasonable" searches and seizures, it does not require that all searches or seizures be conducted pursuant to a warrant. Although the Court has articulated a "preference" for warrants, it has frequently found that warrantless searches are "reasonable." Even though warrantless arrests are generally permissible, warrantless searches are disfavored and are "*per se* unreasonable subject only to a few specifically established and well-delineated exceptions." *Katz v. United States*, 389 U.S. 347 (1967). The next few chapters discuss those exceptions.

B. PLAIN VIEW EXCEPTION

"Plain view" is a frequently used exception to the warrant requirement. When the police are in a place where they have the right to be (as when they are conducting a lawful search), either pursuant to a warrant or pursuant to an exception to the warrant requirement, the exception allows them to seize items that they find in "plain view." While a seizure of property is an invasion of the owner's possessory interest, the search is justified by the fact that the officer found it in "plain view."

1. Plain View Criteria

For the plain view exception to apply, the contraband's incriminating character must be "immediately apparent." If the police see a defendant carrying what looks like a cigarette, it must be "immediately apparent" that the cigarette contains marijuana rather than ordinary tobacco, i.e., the police must be able to ascertain the cigarette's incriminating character based on their training and experience.

a. "Immediately Apparent" Requirement

- In *Coolidge v. New Hampshire*, 403 U.S. 443 (1971), the police seized defendant's car from his driveway because they thought that it might contain microscopic fibers that would implicate him in a crime. The Court held that the seizure of the car was invalid, because the incriminating character of the car (containing the fibers) was not immediately apparent.
- In *Arizona v. Hicks*, 480 U.S. 321 (1987), although the police validly entered an apartment to search for evidence relating to a shooting, they observed expensive stereo components which they moved in order to observe the serial numbers. The Court invalidated the search, because the serial numbers were not "immediately apparent" before the police moved (i.e., seized) the components to observe the numbers.
- In *Minnesota v. Dickerson,* 508 U.S. 366 (1993), a police officer stopped Dickerson and forced him to submit to a frisk for weapons. The frisk revealed no weapons, but the officer felt a small "lump" in his nylon jacket. The officer examined the lump by sliding it back and forth until he was able to determine that it was crack cocaine. The officer then seized the cocaine. The Court held that the contraband was not in plain view and that the seizure therefore was invalid, because the officer was unaware that the "lump" was contraband until he manipulated it.

b. Police Have a Right to Be Where They Are

The plain view exception also requires that the police have a right to be where they are when they make their observation. For example, suppose that a police officer on a public sidewalk looks through a window and sees marijuana on a table inside a house. If the officer does not possess a warrant to enter the house, and cannot enter under one of the recognized exceptions to the warrant requirement, the officer cannot justify entry under the plain view exception. However, the officer's observation of the marijuana in plain view may provide probable cause to obtain a warrant to search the house for the marijuana.

c. Plain View Discovery Does Not Have to Be "Inadvertent"

The plain view exception applies even if the discovery of contraband was accidental or "inadvertent." *Horton v. California,* 496 U.S. 128 (1990). "The fact that an officer is interested in an item of evidence and fully expects to find it in the course of a search should not invalidate its seizure if the search is confined in area and duration by the terms of a warrant or a valid exception to the warrant requirement."

CHAPTER 6

WARRANTLESS SEARCHES: SEARCH INCIDENT TO ARREST

A. SEARCH INCIDENT TO LEGAL ARREST

Search incident to legal arrest is a well-established exception to the warrant requirement. When the police make a legal arrest, they have the implicit right to conduct a search incident to that arrest. The scope of that search is a search of the person and the area within her immediate control.

1. A Legal Arrest as a Prerequisite

An arrest is a prerequisite to being able to search incident to that arrest. When the applicable statute requires a citation or summons instead of an arrest, the search incident to arrest theory is inapplicable. *Knowles v. Iowa*, 525 U.S. 113 (1998). A "legal" arrest occurs when the police take a suspect into custody in order to bring charges.

a. Arrest in Public Place

United States v. Watson, 423 U.S. 411 (1976) held that the police may arrest a person in a public place without a warrant, provided that they have probable cause to believe that the arrestee committed a felony. Essentially, the Court reaffirmed the common law rule which allowed peace officers to arrest without a warrant "for a misdemeanor or felony committed in his presence as well as for a felony not committed in his presence if there [are] reasonable ground[s] for making the arrest."

b. Arresting a Suspect at Home

The Court qualified *Watson* for an arrest at a person's home in *Payton v. New York,* 445 U.S. 573 (1980). The Court held that, absent exigent circumstances, police cannot arrest a person at his home without a warrant. In *Steagald v. United States*, 451 U.S. 204 (1981), the Court extended *Payton* by holding that a law enforcement officer may not search for the subject of an arrest warrant in the home of a third party without first obtaining a *search* warrant for that place.

c. Arrest as Pretext to Search

Even if the arrest is a "sham" or "pretext" to allow the police to search, the police may still arrest the suspect and conduct the search. In *Arkansas v. Sullivan*, 532 U.S. 769 (2001), the Court noted that individual officers' "[s]ubjective intentions play no role in ordinary, probable cause Fourth Amendment analysis."

d. When a Search May Precede the Arrest

Except in rare circumstances, the arrest must precede the search in order to fit within this exception. However, in *Rawlings v. Kentucky*, 448 U.S. 98 (1980), after petitioner admitted ownership of a sizeable quantity of drugs, the police searched his person (the search revealed money and a knife) and then placed him under arrest. The Court viewed the search of Rawlings' person as "incident to arrest" even though it preceded the arrest. After Rawlings admitted ownership of the drugs found in Cox's purse, the police clearly already had probable cause to arrest him. "Where the formal arrest followed quickly on the heels of the challenged search of petitioner's person, we do not believe it particularly important that the search preceded the arrest rather than vice versa."

2. The Rationale and Scope of a Search Incident to Arrest

Once a legal arrest occurs, the police are allowed to make a search incident to arrest. A search incident to legal arrest is "reasonable" because the arrestee might have:

- a weapon on her person or within her reach that she can use to endanger the police or to effect an escape, or
- incriminating evidence in her possession that she might try to destroy.

a. Scope of Search of a Person Is Limited

In *Chimel v. California*, 395 U.S. 752 (1969), Chimel was legally arrested at his home for burglary, and the police searched the entire house and seized various stolen coins and other objects. Although the Court held that the police may conduct searches incident to arrest, it held that the police had exceeded the permissible scope of the search incident to the arrest. The scope of a search incident to arrest is limited to the arrestee's person and the areas within her immediate control. By searching Chimel's entire house, the police went beyond the area of her "immediate control," i.e., the area within which she could reach for a weapon or to destroy evidence.

(1) Seizure of Evidence, Regardless of Reason for Arrest

The search incident to legal arrest exception applies, regardless of the type of crime for which the arrest is made and regardless of whether the police can prove that the arrestee is carrying a weapon or contraband. *United States v. Robinson*, 414 U.S. 218 (1973).

(2) Opening Containers on the Person

If police conduct a search incident to arrest and find a container in the arrestee's pocket, the police may open the container and search it at that time or later.

(3) Containers Immediately Associated with the Arrestee

Police may seize a container like a purse or bag that the person is holding, and may search that container at the time of seizure or later.

(4) Containers within the Arrestee's Immediate Control

Police may seize a container that an arrestee can reach and may search it contemporaneous with the arrest. However, if police do not search the container immediately, they must obtain a warrant to open and search it later.

(5) The Limitations of an Arrestee's Immediate Control

In *Vale v. Louisiana*, 399 U.S. 30 (1970), the Court held that police who arrested a suspect outside his home for drug trafficking could not enter and search his home as incident to the arrest.

(6) The Area of Immediate Control May Change

Facts: In *Washington v. Chrisman*, 455 U.S. 1 (1982), a police officer approached a student who was carrying liquor and appeared too young to possess it. Because the student was not carrying any identification, the officer went with him to his dormitory room to obtain his student identification card. After entering the room, the officer found marijuana in plain view.

Law: The Court upheld that authority of an officer to maintain custody and to accompany an arrested person to a different location than the site of the arrest without having to prove a risk of danger. Because the student's area of immediate control had changed, the officer was able to seize the drugs as a search incident to an arrest.

(7) A Search Incident to an Arrest for Digital Information Generally Is Prohibited

Riley v. California, 134 S.Ct. 2473 (2014) found that a search of digital information on a cell phone does not further the government interests (police protection, preventing the arrestee's escape, and evidence destruction), and implicates much greater privacy interests than a brief physical search. "Officers must generally secure a warrant before conducting . . . a search" of a cell phone incident to an arrest.

b. Protective Sweep to Expand Area Where Police Can Search

Facts: Sometimes, especially when the police execute a warrant, they find other persons present on the scene, or they fear the presence of others. In *Maryland v. Buie*, 494 U.S. 325 (1990), the police arrested Buie as he emerged from the basement of his home, and an officer went to the basement to make sure that no one else was there. In the basement, the officer found a red running suit in plain view that implicated Buie.

Law: The Court held that the officer acted properly in entering the basement. The police are entitled "in such circumstances to take reasonable steps to ensure their safety after, and while making, the arrest," and that this "interest is sufficient to outweigh the intrusion such procedures may entail." Incident to the arrest, the police can automatically, i.e., without probable cause, "look in closets and other spaces immediately adjoining the place of arrest from which an attack could be immediately launched." To search further beyond those spaces, there must "be articulable facts which, taken together with the rational inferences from those facts, would warrant a reasonably prudent officer in believing that the area to be swept harbors an individual posing a danger to those on the arrest scene." The protective sweep is a cursory inspection for persons, and should last "no longer than is necessary to dispel the reasonable suspicion of danger and in any event no longer than it takes to complete the arrest and depart the premises."

During the protective sweep, the police may seize evidence in plain view, even if they find no other persons.

c. Scope of a Search Incident When the Arrest Is in or Near a Vehicle

For purposes of safety or evidentiary concerns, "[p]olice may search a [passenger compartment of a] vehicle incident to a recent occupant's arrest only if the arrestee is within reaching distance of the passenger compartment at the time of the search *or* it is reasonable to believe the vehicle contains evidence of the offense of arrest." *Arizona v. Gant*, 556 U.S. 332 (2009).

(1) Automatic Search of Passenger Compartment Is Prohibited

An automatic search incident to an arrest of the passenger compartment after the defendant is arrested, handcuffed and secured in a patrol car is unreasonable. A proper search incident may extend to items found in containers within the passenger compartment, e.g., the glove compartment.

(2) *Gant* Is Inapplicable to Cell Phone Cases

Riley v. California, 134 S.Ct. 2473 (2014) prohibited warrantless cell phone searches incident to arrest. Given the pervasive types and amounts of cell phone information, the Court refused to apply *Gant* to cell phone cases because "[t]he sources of potential pertinent information are virtually unlimited.". If the police need to look at the cell phone to prevent harm to themselves or others, they can rely on the "emergency" exception to the general rule that a warrant is always required. If they are concerned about destruction of evidence, they can turn off the phone or remove the battery.

d. Spatial Limitations

Chimel and *Gant* are subject to temporal and spatial limitations. The police can search only the area within the arrestee's "immediate control." In *Coolidge v. New Hampshire*, 403 U.S. 443 (1971), the defendant was arrested inside his home and the police searched his car that was sitting outside in the driveway. The Court held that the car search did not fit within the scope of a permissible search incident to arrest.

e. Time Limitations

The "temporal limitation" requires that the search incident to legal arrest be conducted relatively contemporaneously with the arrest.

(1) Search of the Arrestee

Although a search incident of the person incident to the arrest usually occurs immediately, it may occur hours later at the police station. *United States v. Edwards*, 415 U.S. 800 (1974).

(2) Searching Area Within the Arrestee's Immediate Control

The search of the area within the arrestee's immediate control must occur contemporaneously with the arrest. In *Preston v. United States*, 376 U.S. 364 (1964), Preston and his companions were arrested while riding in an automobile and taken to the police station for booking. A police officer towed their car to a garage. After the men were booked, police officers searched the passenger compartment of the car and found two loaded revolvers. The Court invalidated the search as "too remote in time or place to have been made as incidental to the arrest."

CHAPTER 7

WARRANTLESS SEARCHES: VEHICLE SEARCHES

A. VEHICLE EXCEPTION

When the police have probable cause to believe that a vehicle contains the fruits, instrumentalities or evidence of crime, the vehicle exception provides that they may search the vehicle without a warrant.

1. Vehicle Search Rationales: Mobility and Reduced Privacy Expectations

In *Carroll v. United States*, 267 U.S. 132 (1925), the Court noted that, although owners or drivers have constitutionally protected privacy interests in their cars, the owners are given less protection than when they are at home because of the "ready mobility" of automobiles. This mobility creates exigent circumstances to justify a warrantless search. Recent cases have recognized that a vehicle is subject to less rigorous warrant requirements "because the expectation of privacy with respect to one's automobile is significantly less than that relating to one's home or office" due to the "pervasive regulation" of vehicles on the highway. *California v. Carney*, 471 U.S. 386 (1985). "Pervasive regulation" includes the possibility of periodic inspections as well as licensing requirements, e.g., police stop and examine vehicles when license plates or inspection stickers have expired.

2. Probable Cause Is the Threshold Standard

In light of the mobility and diminished expectation of privacy, the existence of probable cause alone justifies an immediate warrantless search "before the vehicle and its occupants become unavailable." It does not matter whether the vehicle is being driven at the time of the stop and the subsequent search so long as it is capable of moving and therefore has "ready mobility."

3. What Is a Vehicle?

In *California v. Carney*, the Court treated a mobile home like an automobile, concluding that its mobility is similar to an automobile, and therefore is subject to the diminished expectation of privacy associated with automobiles. The Court emphasized that this particular mobile home was "readily mobile." In addition, it was subject to the pervasive regulation associated with vehicles, and the vehicle was so situated that an objective observer would conclude that it was being used not as a residence, but as a vehicle.

4. Scope of a Vehicle Search

a. No Time Limitation to Search

Most decisions have loosely applied the contemporaneous requirement to the vehicle exception. For example, in *Chambers v. Maroney*, 399 U.S. 42 (1970), although petitioner was riding in a vehicle at the time of his arrest, it was searched at the police station rather than at the scene. The court upheld the search even though it had been immobilized and it would have been relatively easy to obtain a warrant. Given the existence of probable cause to search, the police may choose to search later at the police station or elsewhere.

b. Searching the Entire Vehicle

In *United States v. Ross*, 456 U.S. 798 (1982), the police searched Ross's car after receiving information that he had completed a drug transaction with drugs from the trunk of his car. In the trunk, police found a brown paper bag containing illegal drugs. In upholding the search, the Court gave guidance regarding the scope of the automobile exception. "If probable cause justifies the search of a lawfully stopped vehicle, it justifies the search of every part of the vehicle and its contents that may conceal the object of the search."

(1) Police Happen to See Container During Search

Police may seize a container found during the search of the vehicle and open it to examine its contents. Any incriminating items found in the container are admissible under the plain view doctrine.

c. Seizures When Probable Cause Is Limited

If the police have probable cause to search for a container only, once they find the particular container they can open it but that is the end of the search unless its contents suggest probable cause for a broader search. If the police come across criminal evidence in plain view on the way to finding the specific container for which there is probable cause, they can seize it as well. They also may open larger containers in which the smaller container for which probable cause exists could be located.

d. To Search or Seize a Container in the Vehicle

In *California v. Acevedo*, 500 U.S. 565 (1991), the Court appeared to offer the police the choice of securing the container or opening it: "a container found after a general search of the automobile and a container found in a car after a limited search for the container are equally easy for the police to store and for the suspect to hide or destroy." In *Acevedo*, the police had probable cause to seize and search only a paper bag that happened to be in a vehicle.

e. Searching a Container Belonging to a Passenger

In *Wyoming v. Houghton*, 526 U.S. 295 (1999), the Court upheld a vehicle search that produced incriminating evidence from a container clearly belonging to a passenger. The Court noted that passengers and drivers alike have a reduced expectation of privacy in property carried in vehicles; passengers "will often be engaged in a common enterprise with the driver, and have the same interest in concealing the fruits or the evidence of their wrongdoing."

CHAPTER 8

WARRANTLESS SEARCHES: BOOKING & INVENTORY SEARCHES

A. BOOKING SEARCHES

Closely related to the search incident to legal arrest exception is the so-called "booking" exception. After the police arrest and "book" a suspect at police headquarters, and before they place the suspect in jail, the police usually conduct a "booking" search. In *Illinois v. Lafayette*, 462 U.S. 640 (1983), the Court upheld this type of search, noting that it "is reasonable for police to search the personal effects of a person under lawful arrest as part of the routine administrative procedure at a police station house incident to booking and jailing the suspect." Under the booking exception, jail officials can remove both contraband and valuables without a warrant. For example, in the case of a person with a backpack, the officials have the right not only to take the backpack but to search its interior as well.

1. Rationales for Booking Searches

A number of governmental interests justify booking searches. Jail officials:

- prevent personal items from being stolen while the arrestee is in the jail population,
- help protect themselves against false claims of theft,
- prevent the arrestee from introducing contraband, weapons, etc. into the jail that could be used by inmates, and
- are better able to ascertain a suspect's identity.

2. DNA Collection

Warrantless, routine collection by police of DNA samples from individuals arrested and taken into custody for specified serious crimes is a legitimate booking procedure that is reasonable under the Fourth Amendment. *Maryland v. King*, 133 S.Ct. 1958 (2013). A statute required officials to collect a DNA sample when the arrest is for a crime of violence or burglary, or an attempt to commit a crime of violence or burglary. As in prior cases, the Court balanced legitimate governmental interests against the intrusion upon an individual's privacy.

3. Strip Searches

Striking "a reasonable balance between inmate privacy and the security needs of the institutions," the Court has upheld routine, suspicionless strip searches of all arrestees who end up in the general population, regardless of the seriousness of the crimes charged. *Florence v. Board of Chosen Freeholders of the County of Burlington*, 132 S.Ct. 1510 (2012).

4. Temporal Limitations

Courts loosely apply temporal limitations in this context. For example, in *United States v. Edwards*, 415 U.S. 800 (1974), the Court upheld a booking search which took place nearly ten hours after a defendant's arrest: "searches and seizures that could be made on the spot at the time of arrest may legally be conducted later when the accused arrives at the place of detention."

B. INVENTORY EXCEPTION

Inventory searches may be conducted without probable cause or a warrant. Prior to an inventory search, the vehicle must have been legally impounded, according to local standards. Once a vehicle is lawfully impounded, the scope of an inventory search is broad; police may search the passenger compartment, the trunk, and any closed containers.

1. Colorado v. Bertine

The leading decision is *Colorado v. Bertine*, 479 U.S. 367 (1987), a case that involved an inventory search of a vehicle following its operator's arrest for drunk driving. Upholding the search, the Court emphasized that the inventory exception developed in response to three distinct needs: "(i) the protection of the owner's property while it remains in police custody; (ii) the protection of the police against claims or disputes over lost or stolen property; and (iii) the protection of the police from potential danger."

2. Scope of Inventory Search

Pursuant to the rationales for the inventory search offered by the Court in *Bertine*, the police are not required merely to lock the vehicle at the impoundment lot. Instead, they may search containers and unlock areas like the trunk or glove compartment in order to list the vehicle's contents. Whatever the police recover during the inventory search may be used as evidence in a later criminal prosecution.

3. The Police Motive Cannot Solely Be Investigatory

An inventory search may be important to determine the identities of the vehicle's owner or passengers, or for the many reasons police have for taking a vehicle into police custody. An inventory search cannot be conducted solely for criminal investigative motives. Thus, before conducting an inventory search, the police are not required to show that the particular vehicle contains dangerous items.

4. *Florida v. Wells*: Inventory Searches Pursuant to Regulations

Facts: Courts sometimes require that inventory searches be conducted pursuant to departmental regulation so that the discretion of individual police officers is minimized. For example, in *Florida v. Wells*, 495 U.S. 1 (1990), Wells was arrested and his car was impounded. An inventory search at the impoundment facility revealed two marijuana cigarettes, and a locked suitcase that was found to contain a considerable quantity of marijuana.

Law: Because the Florida Highway Patrol "had no policy whatever with respect to the opening of closed containers encountered during an inventory search," the Court held that the search was "not sufficiently regulated to satisfy the Fourth Amendment." The Court did not preclude individual police officers from exercising all discretion, provided that "discretion is exercised according to standard criteria and on the basis of something other than suspicion or evidence of criminal activity."

CHAPTER 9

WARRANTLESS SEARCHES: CONSENT SEARCHES

A. CONSENT SEARCHES

The consent exception is not really an "exception" to the warrant requirement. Any constitutional right can be waived voluntarily, including the Fourth Amendment right to be free from unreasonable searches and seizures.

1. *Schneckloth v. Bustamonte*: Totality of Circumstances

Facts: Six men were traveling in an automobile. When the vehicle was stopped (because one headlight and a license plate light were burned out), and the driver could not produce a driver's license, the officer asked the driver and passengers to step out of the vehicle. The officer then asked Alcala, a passenger who claimed that his brother owned the car, if he could search the vehicle. Alcala replied, "Sure, go ahead." The officer testified that it "was all very congenial at this time." The driver testified that Alcala actually helped in the search of the car by opening the trunk and glove compartment. In the car, the officer found three stolen checks which were introduced at Bustamonte's subsequent trial.

Law: The *Schneckloth* Court held that consent searches are permissible, but that the State bears the burden of showing "that the consent was, in fact, freely and voluntarily given." Consent does not exist when the suspect was "coerced." In determining whether consent was voluntary or coerced, a "totality of the circumstances" test is applied, using a variety of factors peculiar to the suspect (e.g., if the suspect is particularly vulnerable because of lack of schooling), and factors that suggest coercion (e.g., police guns were drawn, police demanded the right to search). *Schneckloth v. Bustamonte*, 412 U.S. 218 (1973).

a. Assertions of Police Authority May Negate Consent

Facts: In *Bumper v. State of North Carolina,* 391 U.S. 543 (1968), the police went to an elderly widow and asked for permission to search her house (the police believed that her grandson had committed a crime). One officer lied when he stated "I have a search warrant to search your house." The grandmother responded, "Go ahead," and opened the door.

Law: The Court held that the consent was invalid because it was obtained involuntarily, noting that the State bears the burden of showing that consent did not exist simply because the woman acquiesced to a "claim of lawful authority."

b. No Requirement to Inform Person of Right to Refuse Consent

One potential factor in the "totality of circumstances" is whether the suspect knows that she has the right to refuse consent. However, the *Schneckloth* Court refused to require the police to inform a suspect of her right to refuse. The Court regarded Fourth Amendment rights as different because they are designed to protect the "security of one's privacy against arbitrary intrusion by the [police]," rather than to guarantee a fair trial. In addition, the community has an interest in encouraging consent, because "the resulting search may yield necessary evidence for the solution and prosecution of crime, evidence that may insure that a wholly innocent person is not wrongly charged with a criminal offense."

c. Needn't Say Person Is "Free to Leave" Before Seeking Consent

Facts: In *Ohio v. Robinette*, 519 U.S. 33 (1996), where the defendant was lawfully stopped for speeding and given a verbal warning, the officer asked whether Robinette was carrying contraband. When Robinette answered in the negative, the officer asked for and obtained permission to search Robinette's car. The search revealed a small amount of marijuana.

Law: The Court held that the officer was *not* required to tell Robinette that he was "free to go" before asking for consent to search the vehicle. "The Fourth Amendment test for a valid consent to search is that the consent be voluntary, and 'voluntariness is a question of fact to be determined from all the circumstances.' "

d. Scope of Consent May Extend to Closed Containers

The scope of consent can extend to closed containers. In *Florida v. Jimeno*, 500 U.S. 248 (1991), believing that respondent was carrying narcotics, a police officer asked for permission to search his car. Respondent consented stating that he had nothing to hide. When the search revealed cocaine in a paper bag on the floorboard, the Court held that the consent extended to the paper bag because Jimeno "did not place any explicit limitation on the scope of the search. [I]t was objectively reasonable for the police to conclude that the general consent to search respondent's car included consent to search containers within that car which might bear drugs."

B. THIRD PARTY CONSENT

When a third party consents to a search of property, a court must decide about not only whether the consent was voluntarily given and the scope of the search, but also whether the third party could consent to the search. In *United States v. Matlock*, 415 U.S. 164 (1974), a woman consented to the search of a house that she shared with Matlock, including their bedroom where police found evidence that they used against Matlock. The Court held that the woman could consent to a search of the room because she had "common authority" over the area. "Common authority" rests on

> mutual use of the property by persons generally having joint access or control for most purposes, so that it is reasonable to recognize that any of the co-inhabitants has the right to permit the inspection in his own right and that the others have assumed the risk that one of their number might permit the common area to be searched.

1. *Illinois v. Rodriguez*: Reasonable Reliance on Apparent Authority

Facts: In *Illinois v. Rodriguez*, 497 U.S. 177 (1990), police made a warrantless entry into Rodriguez's apartment with the consent of his girlfriend who had lived there for several months and who possessed a key. She referred to the apartment as "our apartment" and she claimed to have clothing and furniture there. In fact, although she had lived in the apartment with Rodriguez, she had moved out more than a month before, her name was not on the lease, she did not pay rent, and she had taken the key without Rodriguez's knowledge or consent (although she had not yet moved all of her furniture). Inside the apartment, the police found cocaine and seized the drugs and related paraphernalia.

Law: Although the Court stated that the girlfriend did not possess "common authority" over the apartment, the Court upheld the search, focusing on the reasonableness of the police in believing that she had "apparent authority" to consent. Someone who lacks "common authority" still may consent to a search if police reasonably believe that she appears to have authority to consent.

The Court required only that the officers make a "reasonable" judgment regarding the facts before them. The Court noted that this approach would sanction a "reasonable mistake." In the Court's view, the police act "reasonably" when they enter a dwelling based on a reasonable but erroneous belief "that the person who has consented to their entry is a resident of the premises." An objective standard applies: "would the facts available to the officer at the [moment] 'warrant a man of reasonable caution in the belief' that the consenting party had authority over the premises?" In *Rodriguez*, the Court concluded that the officers reasonably believed that the girlfriend had authority over the apartment to provide her consent to search.

2. Consenting and Nonconsenting Parties

Georgia v. Randolph, 547 U.S. 103 (2006) held that a wife's consent to search was not valid because her husband objected. *Fernandez v. California*, 134 S.Ct. 1126 (2014) characterized *Randolph* as a "narrow exception" to *Matlock*'s normal rule that "police officers may search jointly occupied premises" without a warrant "if one of the occupants consents." *Fernandez* made clear that *Randolph* "was limited to situations in which the objecting occupant is present." In *Fernandez*, consent was provided by an abused victim well after her male partner was removed from the apartment they shared. After the objecting person was removed by police for "objectively reasonable" reasons, the consenting victim then provided sufficient authority to search. As for children, *Randolph* suggested that the authority to consent depends on the circumstances. "[A] child of eight might well be considered to have the power to consent to the police crossing the threshold into that part of the house where any caller, such as a pollster or salesman, might well be admitted," but no one could "reasonably expect such a child to be in a position to authorize anyone to rummage through his parents' bedroom."

CHAPTER 10

WARRANTLESS SEARCHES: ADMINISTRATIVE SEARCHES

A. ADMINISTRATIVE SEARCHES

Administrative agencies regularly conduct various types of inspections, e.g., health inspectors enter restaurants to determine whether food preparation and service areas are clean, as well as to make sure that food is being properly maintained. Government inspectors examine industrial sites for safe and healthy conditions. *See, e.g., United States v. Biswell*, 406 U.S. 311 (1972) (search of a locked storeroom of a firearms warehouse during reasonable hours permitted); *North American Cold Storage v. City of Chicago*, 211 U.S. 306 (1908) (warrantless search for contaminated food allowed). Recall, however, that no Fourth Amendment search occurs when a public official enters and investigates an area that is open to the public because there is no expectation of privacy. For example, in *Donovan v. Lone Steer, Inc.*, 464 U.S. 408 (1984), the Court held that the Fourth Amendment did not apply to a fire inspector's entrance to a hotel lobby to check for fire exits.

1. Camara v. Municipal Court

Facts: In *Camara v. Municipal Court*, 387 U.S. 523 (1967), a San Francisco city ordinance authorized city inspectors to enter buildings "to perform any duty imposed upon them by the Municipal Code." When Camara refused to allow inspectors to enter his apartment without a warrant, he was ultimately convicted of refusing to permit a lawful inspection.

Law: Overturning the conviction, the Court emphasized that the Fourth Amendment was designed to prevent "arbitrary invasions by governmental officials," and reiterated its long-standing preference for warrants. An important aspect of *Camara* was the balancing of competing interests which shows up in many future cases defying categorization. In determining whether the search was "reasonable," the Court balanced the governmental interest against the private interest. The governmental interest in administrative inspections ensures "city-wide compliance with minimum physical standards for private property" and prevents "the unintentional development of conditions which are hazardous to public health and safety." The Court also recognized that administrative searches involve "significant intrusions" on individual privacy, but held that warrants help protect individual security.

2. Administrative Warrants

After balancing these interests, *Camara* noted that the Fourth Amendment warrant requirement could effectively function in the administrative context, because it both notifies the homeowner about the purpose of the inspection and about the limits of the inspector's power. It also checks administrative discretion by requiring a neutral judge to determine whether the inspection is justified.

a. Administrative Probable Cause Is Not as Specific as Traditional Probable Cause

The Court held that the Fourth Amendment imposes a warrant requirement on administrative inspections based on "administrative" probable cause. The Court did not describe historically-required, building-specific probable cause for building inspections. Instead, the Court held that one warrant can be sought to inspect all buildings in a particular area based on an assessment of "conditions in the area as a whole, not on its knowledge of conditions in each particular building."

b. Criteria for Issuing Administrative Warrants

Camara held that "area inspections" required reasonable legislative or administrative standards that could focus on general criteria such as "the passage of time, the nature of the building (e.g., a multifamily apartment house), or the condition of the entire area." Many conditions (e.g., faulty wiring) "are not observable from outside the building and indeed may not be apparent to the inexpert occupant himself," and administrative inspections "involve a relatively limited invasion of the urban citizen's [privacy]."

3. Administrative Warrants Are Unnecessary for Emergencies

The Court also recognized that there are situations when warrantless inspections are constitutionally permissible. For example, a warrant is not required in "emergency situations" involving the seizure of unwholesome food, smallpox vaccinations, health quarantines, or the inspection of a fire scene. *Michigan v. Tyler*, 436 U.S. 499 (1978); *See v. Seattle*, 387 U.S. 541 (1967).

4. Warrants Are Also Not Needed for "Closely Regulated" Businesses

The Court also established an exception to the warrant requirement for certain "closely regulated" businesses that have "such a history of government oversight that no reasonable expectation of privacy could exist for a proprietor over the stock of such an enterprise." *Marshall v. Barlow's, Inc.*, 436 U.S. 307 (1978).

- In *Donovan v. Dewey*, 452 U.S. 594 (1981), the Court held that underground and surface mines qualified as closely regulated businesses.
- In *United States v. Biswell*, 406 U.S. 311 (1972), the Court upheld a warrantless inspection of a pawnshop operator who was federally licensed to sell sporting weapons: a businessperson who engages in a pervasively regulated business under a license knows that her business records, firearms, and ammunition are subject to effective inspection.

a. *New York v. Burger*: Establishing the "Closely Regulated" Exception

Facts: The outer limits of the "closely regulated" exception were established in *New York v. Burger*, 482 U.S. 691 (1987), in which a junkyard was in the business of dismantling cars and selling car parts. Police officers sought to inspect under a New York law authorizing warrantless inspections of junkyards. During the inspection, officers recorded vehicle identification numbers on a number of vehicles that were later determined to be stolen. Burger was charged with possession of stolen property and operation of a junkyard in non-compliance with State law.

Law: Upholding the search, the Court held that junkyards qualified as "closely regulated" businesses. Junkyards had to maintain a book showing the acquisition and disposition of motor vehicles and vehicle parts, and these records must be available for inspection by governmental agents. The Court analogized the industry to secondhand shops and general junkyards which "long have been subject to regulation." As a result, junkyard owners engaged in vehicle dismantling had a reduced expectation of privacy.

5. Criteria for "Closely Regulated" Designation

Not all businesses can be regarded as "closely regulated." Warrantless searches are upheld if:

- there is a "substantial government interest that informs the regulatory scheme pursuant to which the inspection is made", and
- the warrantless inspections are "necessary to further [the] regulatory scheme."

a. Nature of the Regulatory Statute

In *Marshall v. Barlow's*, the court invalidated an OSHA warrantless inspection provision because its scope applied to a wide variety of industries instead of a limited regulated business. The regulatory statute must perform the two basic functions of a warrant:

- advising the owner of the commercial premises that the search is being made with a properly defined scope; and
- limiting the discretion of the inspecting officers. Inspectors' discretion is limited by time, place, and scope.

b. Upholding the Regulatory Scheme in *Burger*

The New York statute met the criteria for warrantless inspections of closely regulated businesses. First, the interest in regulating the industry was substantial, "because motor vehicle theft has increased in the State and because the problem of theft is associated with this industry." Second, the statute provided a "constitutionally adequate substitute for a warrant," because it informed the operator of a vehicle dismantling business about regular inspections and the scope of the inspections. Finally, the administrative scheme is an adequate substitute for a warrant by limiting the discretion of inspectors regarding the "time, place, and scope" of the inspection.

c. *Burger* Search Upheld Despite Police Participation

The *Burger* search did not involve ordinary administrative inspections by administrative officials, but instead involved a police search for evidence of criminal activity. Still, the Court upheld the police search as an administrative inspection: "a State can address a major social problem both by way of an administrative scheme and through penal sanctions."

CHAPTER 11

WARRANTLESS SEARCHES: EXIGENT CIRCUMSTANCES & SPECIAL NEEDS

A. EXIGENT CIRCUMSTANCES

The police can conduct a warrantless search when "exigent circumstances" exist. Many of the already discussed Fourth Amendment warrantless search exceptions involve exigent situations when there is insufficient time to obtain a warrant, e.g., search incident to arrest, vehicle searches. Courts have devised a separate category for exigent circumstances in fact patterns which occur less frequently.

1. Rationale for Exigent Circumstances Searches

The exigent circumstances exception applies to cases where there is a concern about imminent destruction of evidence, risk of danger to police or others, or hot pursuit of fleeing suspects.

2. Entering the Premises Without Exigent Circumstances

When the police lack a search warrant or an arrest warrant upon entering a suspect's home to conduct a search, the ensuing search is illegal absent pre-existing exigent circumstances, regardless of whether they subsequently obtain a warrant or believed that probable cause for the search already existed. *Kirk v. Louisiana*, 536 U.S. 635 (2002).

3. Requirements for an Exigent Circumstances Search

Probable cause that an emergency situation exists will justify entry into private premises, and an ensuing search may last only as long as the exigency exists. *Flippo v. West Virginia*, 528 U.S. 11 (1999). For example, in a hot pursuit case of the police seeking a person for a crime of violence, the police may search for weapons as they are seeking the suspect, and the exigency ends when the suspect is captured, i.e., without another justification such as search incident to arrest the police may not continue to search the premises after the suspect is taken to the police station. *Warden v. Hayden*, 387 U.S. 294 (1967). Several case examples of the scope of the exigent circumstances exception follow.

a. Brigham City v. Stuart

Facts: In *Brigham City v. Stuart*, 547 U.S. 398 (2006), police officers responded to a call regarding a loud party at a residence at 3:00 a.m. On arriving, they heard shouting from inside, proceeded to investigate, and saw an altercation through a screen door in the kitchen. At this point, an officer opened the screen door and announced his presence. Nobody noticed. When the officer entered, the argument ceased as the occupants became aware that the police were on the scene. The officers arrested respondents and charged them with contributing to the delinquency of a minor, disorderly conduct, and intoxication.

Law: The Court upheld the entry into the house, holding that the exigent circumstances exception includes a need to enter "to assist persons who are seriously injured or threatened with such injury." The officers "had an objectively reasonable basis for believing both that the injured adult might need help and that the violence in the kitchen was just beginning." The Fourth Amendment did not require the police to delay until someone was unconscious, semi-conscious, or in an even worse condition before entering.

b. Michigan v. Fisher

Facts: In *Michigan v. Fisher*, 558 U.S. 45 (2009), after receiving a tip to go to the defendant's home because someone there was "going crazy," police saw the defendant inside the house with a cut on his hand. After he refused their offer of assistance, the police pushed the front door open and went inside the house, where the defendant was pointing a long gun at them.

Law: On appeal from his conviction for assault, the Court held that the police "do not need ironclad proof 'of a likely serious, life-threatening' injury to invoke the emergency aid exception." Here, it "was reasonable to believe that Fisher had hurt himself (albeit nonfatally) and needed treatment that in his rage he was unable to provide, or that Fisher was about to hurt, or had already hurt, someone else."

c. **Warden v. Hayden**

Facts: In *Warden v. Hayden,* 387 U.S. 294 (1967), following an armed robbery, police received a description of the robbers and followed them to a nearby house. A search revealed Hayden in a bedroom. In other parts of the house, officers found weapons and clothing used in the robbery.

Law: The Court held that the warrantless search of the entire house was valid. "Speed here was essential, and only a thorough search of the house for persons and weapons could have insured that Hayden was the only man present and that the police had control of all weapons which could be used against them or to effect an escape."

d. **United States v. Santana**

Facts: In *United States v. Santana,* 427 U.S. 38 (1976), after an undercover drug buy, the police went to Santana's home to arrest her (Santana provided the drugs to the seller). They found her standing in the doorway with a brown paper bag in her hand. When Santana retreated into the vestibule of her house, the officers followed through the open door and caught her.

Law: The Court upheld the entry into the house, applying the "hot pursuit" exception. "Once Santana saw the police, there was [a] realistic expectation that any delay would result in destruction of evidence."

e. **Minnesota v. Olson**

Facts: In some cases, the Court has held that the circumstances were not sufficiently exigent to justify a warrantless entry. For example, in *Minnesota v. Olson,* 495 U.S. 91 (1990), the morning after an armed robbery that resulted in the death of a gas station attendant, a woman called the police and said that Olson admitted his participation in the robbery to two other women. When the police learned that Olson had gone to the home of the two women, police surrounded the home. Without seeking permission and with weapons drawn, the police entered and found Olson hiding in a closet.

Law: The Court found insufficient exigent circumstances to justify the warrantless entry into the home: 1) Olson was the driver of the getaway car, not the one who pulled the trigger; 2) the murder weapon already was recovered; and 3) no showing existed that either of the women was in danger or that Olson could escape.

f. Welsh v. Wisconsin

Welsh v. Wisconsin, 466 U.S. 740 (1984) is another example when the exception did not apply. Police received eyewitness reports that Welsh had been driving under the influence of alcohol, and went to Welsh's home. When Welsh's stepdaughter answered the door, the police entered and proceeded to Welsh's bedroom where they found him lying in bed. The Court concluded that the police acted improperly since they were unable to show that exigent circumstances existed. The Court found that there was no hot pursuit or continuing threat to "public safety," because Welsh had abandoned his car and returned home, unaware that that the police were looking for him. The only need for immediate action was that the police wanted to test Welsh's blood-alcohol level before the level dissipated. The State's interest in the evidence was minimal given that the State had chosen to classify the offense as "noncriminal," i.e., a conviction carried no jail time.

g. Kentucky v. King

Facts: In *Kentucky v. King*, 131 S.Ct. 1849 (2011), after smelling marijuana outside an apartment door, law enforcement officers repeatedly knocked and banged loudly on the door while identifying themselves as police. They heard noises inside that were consistent with the destruction of evidence. After announcing their intent to enter, they kicked in the door and saw drugs in plain view.

Law: The Court held that the officers did not engage in, or threaten to engage in, conduct that would have violated the Fourth Amendment. Law enforcement officers may rely on the exigent circumstances exception even when they had a role in creating the exigency, as long as they did not engage in, or threaten to engage in, conduct that violates the Fourth Amendment.

4. Assessing the Imminent Risk of Destruction of Evidence

The destruction or loss of evidence often justifies invoking exigent circumstances in order to avoid the necessity of a search warrant. Courts in the aforementioned and other cases have noted the importance of the following factors in assessing the imminent risk of the destruction or loss of physical evidence:

- degree of urgency v. the amount of time to obtain a warrant,
- reasonable belief that evidence is about to be removed or that the suspect has a firearm,
- possible danger to police and others,

- whether the suspect is aware that the police are looking for her and the likelihood of an escape, and
- whether the evidence can be easily destroyed.

5. Exigencies to Search the Suspect's Body

Other exigent circumstances cases have dealt with police attempts to gather evidence from the body of a suspect that is likely to disappear absent prompt or immediate action.

a. Cupp v. Murphy

Facts: In *Cupp v. Murphy*, 412 U.S. 291 (1973), Murphy's wife died by strangulation at her home. During questioning, the police noticed a dark spot on Murphy's finger. Suspecting that the spot might be dried blood, the police took a sample without a warrant. Tests revealed that the samples included traces from the victim's skin and blood.

Law: The Court upheld the search, "considering the existence of probable cause, the very limited intrusion undertaken incident to the station house detention, and the ready destructibility of the evidence."

b. Rochin v. California

Facts: In *Rochin v. California*, 342 U.S. 165 (1952), the police believed that Rochin was selling narcotics, and went to his home where they found two capsules which might have been narcotics. When the officers inquired about the capsules, Rochin immediately swallowed them. Rochin was handcuffed and taken to a hospital where the police instructed doctors "pump" his stomach. The procedure caused Rochin to vomit and the police recovered the capsules which were found to contain morphine.

Law: Concluding that the police had violated Rochin's rights, the Court relied upon the Due Process Clause in ruling that the officer's conduct had shocked the conscience of the Court.

c. Schmerber v. California

Facts: In *Schmerber v. California*, 384 U.S. 757 (1966), Schmerber was arrested at a hospital while receiving treatment for injuries suffered in an automobile accident. A police officer, who believed that Schmerber's intoxication caused the accident, directed a physician to take a blood sample from him.

Law: The Court upheld the blood sample extraction even though it involved an intrusion into Schmerber's body. The Court noted that the officer had probable cause to arrest

Schmerber, and upheld the search on the basis that there was an "emergency" which would have led to the destruction of evidence. The test used was:

- highly effective in determining whether an individual is intoxicated,
- commonly used in routine physical examinations,
- extracted a minimum amount of blood,
- one involving virtually no risk, trauma, or pain, and
- performed in a reasonable manner "by a physician in a hospital environment according to accepted medical practices."

d. Missouri v. McNeely

Facts: McNeely was stopped for speeding and crossing the centerline. After he declined to take a breath test to measure his blood alcohol concentration [BAC], the officer arrested him and took him to a hospital for a blood test that showed that McNeely's BAC exceeded the legal limit. The trial judge granted McNeely's motion to suppress the test results.

Law: *Missouri v. McNeely*, 133 S.Ct. 1552 (2013) held that the natural dissipation of alcohol in DUI investigations does not automatically qualify as an exigency to justify a nonconsensual, warrantless blood test to measure BAC. "Whether a warrantless blood test of a drunk-driving suspect is reasonable must be determined case by case based on the totality of the circumstances."

B. SPECIAL NEEDS

Traditional warrant/probable cause analysis is unnecessary for a category of searches based on "special needs." Courts evaluate whether the public interest in support of the warrantless search is a special need that is beyond the normal need for law enforcement. Using the test articulated in *Camara v. Municipal Court*, 387 U.S. 523 (1967), courts balance the state's interest justifying the search against the intrusion upon privacy caused by the search. Special needs searches have been upheld in distinct contexts such as drug testing for employees and for public school students.

1. Drug Testing of Employees: *Skinner v. Railway Labor Executives' Association*

Facts: *Skinner v. Railway Labor Executives' Association*, 489 U.S. 602 (1989) involved a challenge to federal regulations mandating blood and urine tests of railroad employees involved in "major" train accidents, and authorizing breath and urine tests of employees who violate certain safety rules.

Law: The Court upheld the regulations, emphasizing: 1) the governmental interest "in ensuring the safety of the traveling public and of the employees themselves"; 2) the need to make sure that restrictions on drug and alcohol use are being observed; and 3) the need to act quickly to take samples after an accident. The intrusion on privacy was limited, because the employees worked "in an industry that is regulated pervasively to ensure safety, a goal dependent, in substantial part, on the health and fitness of covered employees." The Court found that the tests were not intrusive, could be conducted safely outside a hospital environment "with a minimum of inconvenience or embarrassment," and "reveal the level of alcohol in the employee's bloodstream and nothing more." The Court held that drug testing could be required even in the absence of a reasonable suspicion, because the employees' jobs involved them in "duties fraught with such risks of injury to others that even a momentary lapse of attention can have disastrous consequences." In addition, the testing provided "invaluable information about the causes of major accidents."

a. City of Ontario v. Quon

Facts: The city of Ontario claimed that it had the right to read text messages being sent and received by government employees on pagers owned and issued by the city to its employees. To reduce the intrusiveness of the search, the city had redacted all messages sent while each employee was off-duty. The employees read and signed a statement that they understood the city's computer policy that stated text message transcripts could be reviewed by his supervisors.

Law: Applying standards from the plurality in *O'Connor v. Ortega*, 480 U.S. 709 (1987), *City of Ontario v. Quon*, 560 U.S. 746 (2010) stated that a government employer's warrantless search is reasonable if it is "justified at its inception" and if "the measures adopted are reasonably related to the objectives of the search and not excessively intrusive in light of" the circumstances giving rise to the search. Reading the transcripts was a justifiable search because there were reasonable grounds for suspecting that the search was necessary to learn whether city employees' use of pagers was work-related or for personal use. The Court found that the search was not excessive in scope, noting the fact that a search could have been conducted in a less intrusive manner does not render the actual search unreasonable.

2. Drug Testing Pregnant Mothers: *Ferguson v. City of Charleston*

The Court struck down a hospital's policy of drug testing pregnant mothers suspected of cocaine use in *Ferguson v. City of Charleston*, 532 U.S. 67 (2001). Unlike the earlier cases, the Court held that these tests were not "special needs" searches because their "central and indispensable feature" was to promote law enforcement goals. The results of this drug testing were turned over to the police without the knowledge or consent of the tested women so that they could be prosecuted for child neglect and/or drug offenses. The Court distinguished the earlier drug-testing cases because those policies protected against dissemination of the test results to third parties like the police, and the special need in those cases was "divorced from the State's general interest in law enforcement."

3. Drug Testing Candidates for Public Office: *Chandler v. Miller*

The Court in *Chandler v. Miller*, 520 U.S. 305 (1997) held that drug testing of candidates was invalid, because there was no demonstrated drug problem. Without a showing that a problem exists, the government must prove that a suspicionless plan is necessary to protect against a public hazard. While *Skinner* involved a risk that railroad employees could create serious harm if they were under the influence of drugs, there was no comparable risk that candidates would use drugs.

4. Special Rules for School-Age Children: *New Jersey v. T.L.O*

Facts: The Court has applied special rules to searches of school-age children. In *New Jersey v. T.L.O.*, 469 U.S. 325 (1985), the Court upheld a limited search of a high school student. A teacher found two girls smoking in a lavatory, and took both girls to the assistant principal, who demanded to see their purses where he found cigarettes as well as rolling papers, marijuana and a large number of one-dollar bills. At that point, T.L.O. confessed to the crime of selling marijuana.

Law: The Court upheld the search, balancing the child's interest in privacy against "the substantial interest of teachers and administrators in maintaining discipline in the classroom and on school grounds." Noting that public schools had been the scene of drug use and violent crimes, the Court held that the "school setting requires some easing of the restrictions to which searches by public authorities are ordinarily subject." Searches should be evaluated under a two-part test which ultimately focused on the "reasonableness" of the school's action: 1) the search must be "justified at its inception" i.e., a school official must have "reasonable grounds" to think that a search would yield evidence of legal or school rule violations; and 2) the search must be "reasonably related to the objectives of the search and not excessively intrusive in light of the age and sex of the student and the nature of the infraction." Applying these criteria, the Court upheld the assistant principal's action. Since a teacher had reported that he saw T.L.O. smoking in a lavatory, he had reason to believe that she was carrying cigarettes in her purse. Although the search extended to a zippered compartment in the purse, the Court held that he acted reasonably because he had already found rolling papers and marijuana.

a. Safford Unified School District #1 v. Redding

In *Safford Unified School District #1 v. Redding*, 557 U.S. 364 (2009), the Court found that school officials had reasonable suspicion to search the student's backpack and outer clothing for drugs, but it held that they did not have sufficient suspicion to conduct a strip search of her underwear.

b. Vernonia School District v. Acton

Vernonia School District v. Acton, 515 U.S. 646 (1995) upheld suspicionless drug-testing of high school athletes, because of their reduced expectation of privacy when they participate in a school activity and a documented drug problem among athletes in the district. The Court emphasized that the testing occurred in a "public school environment where the State is responsible for maintaining discipline, health and safety."

c. Board of Education of Independent School District No. 92 of Pottawatomie County v. Earls

Facts*:* *Board of Education of Independent School District No. 92 of Pottawatomie County v. Earls*, 536 U.S. 822 (2002) extended *Acton* in two ways to drug testing for all middle and high school students involved in competitive extracurricular activities. The policy of drug-testing applied to students participating in *all* extracurricular activities, rather than athletes only. There was *no* documented problem of drug abuse among the students in the school district.

Law: The Court stated that drug testing for all students was preferable to a standard of "individualized reasonable suspicion of wrongdoing," which would place various burdens on schools and might subject them to lawsuits, thereby making the overall program of drug detection less effective. Again applying a balancing test examining the governmental interest and the intrusion on privacy, the Court upheld the constitutionality of the policy, which was aimed at promoting health and safety of all students by detecting and preventing drug use. The students had a diminished expectation of privacy and the urine samples were not collected in an intrusive manner; the faculty monitor waited outside the room to collect the sample and the collection method constituted a "negligible" intrusion. The test results were:

- maintained in a file separate from students other educational records,
- released to school personnel only on a "need to know" basis, and
- never the basis for school discipline and never turned over to the police.

C. SPECIAL SEARCH SITUATIONS

1. Probationers and Parolees

Even after their release from prison, inmates who become probationers and parolees are subject to special rules. In *Griffin v. Wisconsin,* 483 U.S. 868 (1987), the Court held that a State's operation of its probation system presented a "special need" for the "exercise of supervision to assure that [probation] restrictions are in fact observed." As a result, warrantless searches of probationers were deemed to be reasonable.

a. United States v. Knights

Facts: In *United States v. Knights*, 534 U.S. 112 (2001), the Court held that warrantless searches might be permissible of one who was on probation. Knights' condition required him to submit to a "search at anytime, with or without a search warrant, warrant of arrest or reasonable cause by any probation officer or law enforcement officer." An arson investigation revealed that Knights was involved. A police officer, who was aware of the condition of Knights' probation, then made a warrantless search of Knights' apartment that produced evidence incriminating Knights in the fire.

Law: The Court upheld the search. The Court emphasized that the probation order clearly stated the condition, and "Knights was unambiguously informed of it." As a result, the condition diminished Knights' reasonable expectation of privacy. In assessing the governmental interest, the Court emphasized that "the very assumption" of probation is that the probationer "is more likely than the ordinary citizen to violate the law." As a result, the Court held "that the balance of these considerations requires no more than reasonable suspicion to conduct a search of this probationer's house." The Court concluded that the police had the necessary reasonable suspicion to make a warrantless search of Knights' home.

b. Samson v. California

In *Samson v. California*, 547 U.S. 843 (2006), the Court upheld a California statute providing that parolees, as a condition of their release, could be searched "at any time of the day or night, with or without a search warrant and with or without cause." Relying on *Knights*, the Court noted that "parolees have fewer expectations of privacy than probationers," and that "parole is more akin to imprisonment than probation is to imprisonment." The parole conditions were clearly expressed to Samson, who did not have an expectation of privacy that society would recognize as legitimate. In addition, the Court concluded that the State has an "overwhelming interest" in supervising parolees because "parolees . . . are more likely to commit future criminal offenses."

2. Border Searches

Special rules have always applied to searches conducted at or near the United States border, because of the interest in protecting those borders. *United States v. Montoya de Hernandez*, 473 U.S. 531 (1985). Routine border searches are "reasonable simply by virtue of the fact that they occur at the border." *United States v. Ramsey*, 431 U.S. 606 (1977). At the border, customs and immigration officials have the right to "stop" those who seek to enter the United States, and to force them to prove their right to enter (by presenting their passport and relevant immigration documents).

a. Customs Officials

Customs officials have usually enjoyed the right to conduct limited searches of those who enter the United States. These searches are designed to make sure that entrants 1) are not carrying contraband, 2) do not have dutiable items that they have failed to declare, and 3) are not carrying harmful or dangerous items (e.g., agricultural products with dangerous parasites).

(1) United States v. Flores-Montano

Facts: In *United States v. Flores-Montano*, 541 U.S. 149 (2004), customs officials dismantled a gasoline tank at the United States border in a successful search for marijuana hidden in the tank. The dismantlement required a 20 to 30 minute delay to obtain a mechanic, and an additional 15 to 25 minutes to dismantle the tank.

Law: The Court upheld the search, refusing to make fine distinctions between "routine" searches and more "intrusive" searches at international borders. The Court noted the "Government's interest in preventing the entry of unwanted persons and effects is at its zenith at the international border."

b. Vehicle Stops of Illegal Aliens

Inside the United States, the rules regarding searches and seizures are somewhat more complicated and tend to parallel the ordinary search and seizure rules. Sometimes, for example, the police seek to stop a vehicle in an area near the border because they believe that it contains illegal aliens. In *United States v. Brignoni-Ponce*, 422 U.S. 873 (1975), the Court held that such stops could be justified by a "reasonable suspicion."

(1) Reasonable Suspicion

Facts: *United States v. Arvizu*, 534 U.S. 266 (2002) illustrates the reasonable suspicion standard. A border patrol agent was conducting a checkpoint near the Mexican border when a magnetic sensor indicated the presence of traffic that might be consistent with smuggling on a nearby road. An officer found a vehicle that slowed dramatically when it saw the officer. The vehicle then turned at the last place that it could turn before it reached an immigration checkpoint. Radio communication revealed that the vehicle was registered to a place near the Mexican border that was "notorious for alien and narcotics smuggling." At that point, the officer stopped the vehicle and the driver consented to a search that revealed the existence of marijuana.

Law: Based on these facts, the Court concluded that a reasonable suspicion of illegal activity existed to stop the vehicle.

c. Near-Border Roadblocks or Checkpoints

Despite the general rules regarding automobile stops (requiring reasonable suspicion), the Court has established special rules for near-border roadblocks or checkpoints.

(1) United States v. Martinez-Fuerte

Facts: *United States v. Martinez-Fuerte*, 428 U.S. 543 (1976) involved near-border fixed checkpoints at which agents slowed all traffic "to a virtual, if not a complete, halt" at a highway roadblock, and referr[ed] vehicles chosen at the discretion of Border Patrol agents to an area for "secondary inspection."

Law: Although the stops were not justifiable as border searches because of their distance from the border, they still were upheld because the state interest in investigating and deterring illegal aliens outweighed the drivers' interests in being free from such seizures. The Court noted that the "objective intrusion—the stop itself, the questioning, and the visual inspection—also existed in roving-patrol stops. But we view checkpoint stops in a different light because the subjective intrusion—the generating of concern or even fright on the part of lawful travelers—is appreciably less in the case of a checkpoint stop."

CHAPTER 12

WARRANTLESS SEARCHES: STOP AND FRISK

A. STOP AND FRISK

The "stop and frisk" exception to the warrant requirement has reshaped Fourth Amendment law in important respects. A stop is a temporary seizure of a person short of an arrest; its purpose is to clarify ambiguous situations that a police officer observes. *Terry v. Ohio*, 392 U.S. 1 (1968) establishes that a stop is proper when an officer reasonably concludes in light of his experience and observation that criminal activity may be afoot *and* that the person is armed and presently dangerous. (Since *Terry*, the case law has de-emphasized the armed and dangerous requirement for a stop.) The test for a stop has both objective and subjective aspects: the test is objective because it focuses on whether the officer reached a reasonable conclusion, but the test is also subjective because the officer is relying on his experiences and observations. A mere hunch that someone is involved in illegal activity is not enough to justify a stop. *Sibron v. New York*, 392 U.S. 40 (1968).

1. Terry v. Ohio

Facts: In *Terry v. Ohio*, a police officer observed suspicious behavior (three men walked back and forth in front of a business) and became concerned that a robbery was about to take place. Because robbers carry guns, the officer believed that the men were armed. He approached them and asked for their names. When they "mumbled" a response, he grabbed Terry, spun him around, and patted down the outside of his clothing, revealing a revolver. The officer then "patted down" the other two men and found a second weapon. The officer arrested the men and charged them with carrying concealed weapons.

Law: Upholding the officer's actions, the Court provided detailed guidance for police-citizen street encounters. Because Terry was protected by the Fourth Amendment on public streets, the "stop" involved a "seizure" and the "frisk" involved a "search." A seizure occurs when the police "accost an individual and restrain his freedom to walk away," and a search occurs even when the police simply explore a person's outer clothing in an effort to discover weapons. The Court then focused on whether the officer had acted "reasonably" as that term is defined in the Fourth Amendment. The Court concluded that a stop and frisk constituted a "serious intrusion . . . upon the sanctity of the person, which may inflict great indignity and arouse strong resentment." In reaching its conclusion, the Court applied the "need" versus "intrusion" balancing test which it had announced a year earlier in *Camara v. Municipal Court*. See Chapter 10.

a. The *Terry* Stop Was Proper

The Court found a governmental interest in "effective crime prevention and detection." Because the officer believed that a "stick-up" might be in progress and that the suspects might be armed and dangerous, he was justified in believing that immediate action was needed. Because he did not have "probable cause" to arrest the suspects, he began with a limited intrusion as he approached the men and asked them to identify themselves. When he received an unsatisfactory response, he seized Terry to pat him down. His actions were justified by the circumstances.

b. The *Terry* Frisk Was Permissible

Because the stop and frisk exception was designed to allow the police to protect themselves and others from a suspect who might be armed and dangerous, the search must be designed to discover hidden weapons. The frisk of Terry was permissible because the officer patted down only the outer clothing until he found a weapon, therefore confining "his search strictly to what was minimally necessary to learn whether the men were armed and to disarm them once he discovered the weapons." Police must be able to point to "specific and articulable facts which, taken together with rational inferences from those facts, reasonably warrant that intrusion." Courts apply an objective standard: "would the facts available to the officer at the moment of the seizure or the search warrant a man of reasonable caution in the belief that the action taken was appropriate?" In *Terry*, this standard was met because the officer observed the suspects' activity which suggested that they might be "casing" a store in preparation for an armed robbery.

2. Evaluating Whether a Stop/Seizure Occurred: Would a Reasonable Person Believe She Was Free to Leave?

No seizure occurs when the individual "remains free to disregard the questions and walk away." *United States v. Mendenhall*, 446 U.S. 544 (1980). The question of whether a reasonable person would have believed that she was not free to leave is made under a "totality of the circumstances" test with the government bearing the burden of proof. Without evidence of coercion, there is no seizure. *United States v. Drayton*, 536 U.S. 194 (2002). Relevant factors include:

- "the threatening presence of several officers,
- the display of a weapon by an officer,
- some physical touching of the person of the citizen,
- the use of language or tone of voice indicating that compliance with the officer's request might be compelled,"
- leaving an available departure route,
- brevity,
- retaining identification, or tickets for transportation, or
- informing the citizen of the right to terminate the encounter or to refuse consent.

3. Encounter v. Stop of Person

In measuring whether a stop has occurred, so that the requisite proof can be assessed, the Court has posed the issue as whether a reasonable person would have felt free to leave the scene. If the answer is yes, the situation constitutes an encounter and not even a stop, and the police do not have to satisfy any proof standard.

a. Florida v. Bostick

Facts: The "free to leave" concept does not apply if the citizen's choice to stay is extraneous to the police presence, such as being on a common carrier. For example, in *Florida v. Bostick*, 501 U.S. 429 (1991), two armed police officers boarded a bus bound from Miami to Atlanta during a stopover in Ft. Lauderdale. The officers randomly picked out Bostick (a passenger), asking for permission to inspect his ticket and identification. The ticket matched Bostick's identification and both were returned to him. The officers then explained that they were narcotics agents looking for illegal drugs, and requested permission to search Bostick's luggage. The police specifically advised Bostick that he had the right to refuse consent, and did not threaten him with a weapon.

Law: The Court concluded that he had not been "stopped" under the Fourth Amendment. Instead of applying the "free to leave," standard, the Court stated that the applicable question was whether a reasonable person would feel free to decline the officer's request or otherwise terminate the situation.

4. The Reasonable Suspicion Standard

The reasonable suspicion standard requires less proof than either probable cause or even a preponderance of evidence. *United States v. Sokolow*, 490 U.S. 1 (1989). The legal standard to stop expresses a concern for danger that flows from the nature of the crime for which reasonable suspicion exists. Measuring reasonable suspicion is based on an assessment of the totality of the circumstances for suspecting the person of criminal activity. For example, in *Sokolow*, the Court found a "reasonable suspicion of criminal activity" when a suspect:

- paid $2,100 for two airplane tickets from a roll of $20 bills,
- traveled under a name that did not match the name under which his telephone number was listed,
- went to Miami as his original destination, a source city for illicit drugs,
- stayed in Miami for only 48 hours, even though a round-trip flight from Honolulu to Miami takes 20 hours,
- appeared nervous during his trip, and
- checked none of his luggage.

a. Proof to Satisfy Reasonable Suspicion Standard

Efforts to avoid the police or avoid being seen may contribute to the grounds for a stop. Other facts that may support reasonable suspicion are the nature of the suspected crime, what conduct caused the suspicion, whether the area is a high crime area or a luxury home area, whether the suspect is engaged in conduct for which he already has a criminal record, and the suspect's age, race, dress, demeanor, as well as the police officer's experience.

(1) Illinois v. Wardlow

In *Illinois v. Wardlow*, 528 U.S. 119 (2000), the suspect ran from police in a heavy drug trafficking area as soon as he saw them. After catching Wardlow, they subjected him to a patdown search for weapons, during which they squeezed a bag he was carrying and felt a heavy hard object similar to the shape of a gun. The officer opened the bag and found a handgun with ammunition. The Court upheld the stop and frisk. "Headlong flight . . . is the consummate act of evasion: it is not necessarily indicative of wrongdoing, but it is certainly suggestive of such."

b. Informant's Information May Be Used for Reasonable Suspicion

Reasonable suspicion may be based on a tip from an informant, even an anonymous tipster, to develop reasonable suspicion. "If a tip has a relatively low degree of reliability, more information will be required to establish the requisite quantum of suspicion than would be required if the tip was more reliable." *Alabama v. White*, 496 U.S. 325 (1990).

(1) Navarette v. California

In *Navarette v. California*, 134 S.Ct. 1683 (2014), a motorist's anonymous 911 call, reporting that a pickup truck had run her off the road, was legally sufficient for the police to stop the truck, *without* having to independently corroborate the tip. Reasonable suspicion derives from the totality of the circumstances showing that the tip was reliable. Here, the phone caller was credible because (1) the tipster claimed eyewitness knowledge of an incident, and (2) the call was made almost immediately after the incident.

(2) Florida v. J.L.

Facts: In *Florida v. J.L.*, 529 U.S. 266 (2000), an anonymous tipster called the Miami police to say that a young black male was wearing a plaid shirt while carrying a concealed weapon and standing with others at a bus stop. Apart from the tip, the officers had no reason to believe that any of the persons was engaged in illegal conduct. The officers immediately frisked the defendant and found a gun in his pocket.

Law: The Court reversed the conviction, because of the nature of the information in the tip. "The reasonable suspicion . . . requires that a tip be reliable in its assertion of illegality, not just in its tendency to identify a determinate person." In other words, police action must be based on objective criteria rather than simply a "hunch."

c. Profiling Does Not Support Reasonable Suspicion

As with probable cause, reasonable suspicion is based on an *individualized* assessment of the circumstances. Drug courier profiles have been used at least since the 1970s to support stopping persons based upon certain characteristics and behavioral traits. However, such profiles do not necessarily amount to reasonable suspicion to justify a stop, which must be based on actual facts. *United States v. Cortez*, 449 U.S. 411 (1981) notes that reasonable suspicion is based upon the totality of circumstances, which involves the cumulative effect of facts rather than the presence of a fact that happens to match a profile fact.

d. Scope of Reasonable Suspicion: A Completed or an Imminent Crime

The police are not restricted to stopping people for crimes that have not yet been committed. They also may stop a suspect who is found near the scene of a recent or completed crime. *United States v. Hensley*, 469 U.S. 221 (1985). In these situations, reasonable suspicion may be based upon the specificity of the description of a person or vehicle, the elapsed time since the crime, the number of persons in the area, the known or probable direction of the offender's flight, and other suspicion that the person or vehicle stopped has been involved in other criminality of the type under investigation.

5. Duration of Stop

A stop must be temporary and last no longer than is necessary to effectuate the stop's purpose. *Florida v. Royer*, 460 U.S. 491 (1983). In *Royer*, the officer's decision to remove the suspect from the initial location of the stop to the detective office rendered the seizure unreasonable. However, a stop does not become unreasonable simply because the police could have used a less intrusive means of investigation. "Such a rule would unduly hamper the police's ability to make swift, on-the-spot decisions." *United States v. Sokolow*. Police may justify a longer time period for a stop as long as they are diligently pursuing their investigation during the detention.

a. Police Must Pursue Investigation to Confirm Reasonable Suspicion

Although the Court has not fixed any outer time limit for the duration of a stop, the police must pursue a means of investigation that is likely to confirm or dispel their suspicion quickly. In each case, courts must consider the length and intrusiveness of the stop and "the enforcement purposes to be served by the stop as well as the time reasonably needed to effectuate those purposes." *United States v. Sharpe*, 470 U.S. 675 (1985). When the actions by the police exceed what is permitted for a stop, the seizure becomes an arrest, which must be supported by probable cause.

6. Frisk Procedures

After a stop, if police still suspect that the person seized is about to or has committed a crime, *Terry* permits them to frisk him if they also have reasonable grounds to believe that the person is armed and dangerous. Even if the officer is not certain, a protective search is permitted if "a reasonably prudent man in the circumstances would be warranted in the belief that his safety or that of others was in danger," considering "the specific reasonable inferences which he is entitled to draw from the facts in light of his experience." That standard of proof may be satisfied by the nature of the investigation, a bulge in the suspect's clothing, a sudden movement by the suspect toward a pocket or other place where a weapon may be hidden, and police awareness that the suspect was armed on a prior occasion.

a. Frisk Begins with a Patdown

A frisk typically must begin with a patdown. (An exception occurred in *Adams v. Williams*, 407 U.S. 143 (1972), when the officer was allowed to bypass the patdown and reach beneath the suspect's clothing immediately because an informant told him the exact location of a weapon and the suspect failed to exit the vehicle when requested.) In a patdown, the officer is seeking a weapon which the suspect could use to harm the officer.

b. When Police Legally Can Reach Beneath the Surface of Clothing

During the patdown, if the officer feels a weapon, he may reach beneath the surface and retrieve it. If the hard object turns out to be a container, the officer may open it if he still believes that a weapon is inside the container. If he finds a weapon in the container, he may have probable cause to arrest the suspect for carrying a concealed weapon.

c. Problem for Police Who Feel a Soft Object

During the patdown, if the officer feels something soft, he may not continue a tactile examination in an effort to determine whether the object is incriminating. *Minnesota v. Dickerson*, 508 U.S. 366 (1993). If the office retrieves the soft item from beneath the surface and tries to admit it into evidence, the prosecutor may be forced to argue that there already had been an arrest and that the soft item was found as part of a search incident to arrest. In that situation, the prosecutor would have to prove that there was probable cause to have already made an arrest of the suspect.

7. Vehicle Stops and Frisks

As with any stop, a traffic stop requires reasonable grounds to suspect that a crime is or has been committed. It is a seizure of the passengers as well as the driver. *Brendlin v. California*, 551 U.S. 249 (2007). For a passenger, the pertinent inquiry is whether a reasonable passenger would have perceived that the police show of authority was at least partly directed at him. In a vehicle stop, without any showing that the suspect may be armed, police have the authority to order both the driver and any passengers from the vehicle to protect themselves. *Pennsylvania v. Mimms*, 434 U.S. 106 (1977); *Maryland v. Wilson*, 519 U.S. 408 (1997). The intrusion on passengers is minimal, and that the motivation of a passenger to use violence to prevent detection and apprehension for a crime is great. During a vehicle stop, the driver and passengers are not free to end the encounter with the police or to move about at will. *Arizona v. Johnson*, 555 U.S. 323 (2009).

a. Pretext Vehicle Stops

Suppose the police are determined to find some reason to stop a suspect. Are they allowed to follow the suspect's car, waiting for him to do something illegal like running a stop sign? In *Whren v. United States*, 517 U.S. 806 (1996), although the defendants conceded that grounds existed to stop their vehicle for traffic violations, they argued that it was a pretextual stop designed to search for drugs. The Court held that the actual motivations of the police are irrelevant, as long as reasonable suspicion for a stop or probable cause for an arrest exists.

b. *Michigan v. Long*: Frisking a Vehicle

Facts: In *Michigan v. Long*, 463 U.S. 1032 (1983), when police saw Long's car swerve into a ditch, they stopped to investigate. Long appeared to be "under the influence of something" and both officers observed a large hunting knife on the floorboard of the driver's side of the car. A *Terry* frisk of Long revealed no weapons, and a vehicle frisk for weapons yielded marijuana.

Law: A frisk may extend beyond the suspect's person, especially during a vehicle stop. The Court upheld the "frisk" of the passenger compartment as reasonable, because it was limited to areas where a weapon may be placed or hidden. The frisk was permissible because the police had reasonable grounds to believe that Long was dangerous and could gain immediate control of weapons upon reentering his vehicle.

c. *Delaware v. Prouse*: Vehicle Safety Checkpoints

Police have attempted to justify vehicle checkpoints to check licenses and vehicle registration, and to determine whether a vehicle is in proper mechanical condition. Using the intrusion v. need formula to determine the reasonableness of Fourth Amendment seizures and searches, the Court held in *Delaware v. Prouse*, 440 U.S. 648 (1979) that discretionary spot checks do not significantly advance the interest of ensuring that only qualified, licensed drivers are driving on American roads, Police can just as easily make a visual check of license plates on vehicles to monitor whether they are properly registered. Finally, random safety inspections do not advance safety goals, because many safety violations can be seen without stopping the vehicle.

d. *Michigan Dept. of State Police v. Sitz*: Sobriety Checkpoints

Courts have treated sobriety checkpoints with more deference. In *Michigan Dept. of State Police v. Sitz*, 496 U.S. 444 (1990), the Court upheld the use of these checkpoints if supervisory personnel rather than officers in the field select when and where to conduct the checkpoints, the checkpoint's location is publicized in advance, police stop every approaching vehicle or stop those selected by neutral criteria, e.g., every fourth car, and the standard for detaining drivers suspected of driving while intoxicated is based on the *Terry* test of reasonable grounds.

e. *City of Indianapolis v. Edmond*: Checkpoints to Solve Crimes

By comparison, the Court has invalidated a vehicle checkpoint where the goal was to intercept persons using illegal drugs. *City of Indianapolis v. Edmond*, 531 U.S. 32 (2000). Part of the Court's concern was that there was a low likelihood of apprehension compared to a sobriety checkpoint or a check for license and registration. Because law enforcement as a goal was too general, the intrusion outweighed the need for the brief stop. The Court, however, did recognize an exception for police to use a roadblock for ordinary crime control in an emergency or for an imminent terrorist attack.

(1) Informational Checkpoints for Past Crime

In *Illinois v. Lidster*, 540 U.S. 419 (2004), a person challenged his DUI conviction because his arrest occurred while police were conducting an informational checkpoint.

The Court upheld a roadblock for the purpose of gathering information about a recent hit-and-run crime. The Court distinguished its holding in *Edmond* on the basis that "special law enforcement" concerns will sometimes justify highway stops without individualized suspicion. The *Lidster* Court found that:

- the public interest was served by the seizure to assist in finding the perpetrator of a specific and known crime,
- the checkpoint fit the specific investigative needs of police because it was set up at about the same location and time of night as the crime being investigated to increase the likelihood of getting useful information from stopped drivers, and
- the intrusion was minimal, involving a brief wait in line, a request for information and distribution of a flyer about the past crime.

8. (Prolonged) Investigatory Seizures of Property

Terry's analysis extends to investigative seizures of property. An intrusion on possessory interests can vary "both in its nature and extent," ranging from an "on the spot" inquiry (as with the use of a dog to sniff the luggage) to the relinquishment of custody and control. The seizure of the property requires reasonable suspicion of criminal activity. Some brief seizures are so minimally intrusive that they can be justified based "only on specific articulable facts that the property contains contraband or evidence of a crime." *United States v. Place*, 462 U.S. 696 (1983). As with detentions of persons, however, a seizure of property at some point requires probable cause to continue. The relevant factors for deciding whether probable cause has replaced reasonable suspicion for a seizure are:

- the diligence of the investigation,
- the length of the seizure, and
- information given to the suspect about the seizure.

a. United States v. Place

Facts: In *United States v. Place*, Place's behavior aroused the suspicions of police at the Miami airport. After he was allowed to depart for New York, Miami agents contacted DEA authorities in New York to relay their suspicions. In New York, two agents approached him and suggested that he was carrying narcotics. When Place refused to consent to a search of his luggage, the agents decided to seize it while they sought a warrant from a judge. The agents then subjected the bags to a "sniff test" by a trained narcotics detection dog. The dog reacted positively to one bag. Although the sniff was conducted within a 90-minute period, the agents kept the bags over a weekend, when they obtained a search warrant from a judge. In the subsequent search, they found cocaine in the bag.

Law: Although the Court invalidated this luggage search, the Court noted that containers can be seized while the police seek a warrant, because "the risk of the item's disappearance or use for its intended purpose before a warrant may be obtained outweighs the interest in possession." Based on a reasonable conclusion that a traveler's luggage contains narcotics, the police can briefly detain the luggage for investigative purposes provided that the detention is limited in scope. A luggage "seizure can effectively restrain the person," because he may disrupt his travel plans to remain with the luggage or to arrange for its return. Applying these rules, the Court concluded that the seizure of Place's luggage went too far. The 90-minute detention of Place's luggage was too long, especially given that the agents had advance notice of Place's arrival and could have prepared for the additional investigation. The additional step of holding the bags over the weekend was also unreasonable. They failed to inform Place about where they were taking the luggage and what arrangements would be made for returning the luggage if the investigation dispelled their suspicion.

b. Inherently Coercive Nature of Station House Questioning

In deciding custody issues, a trial court should examine "whether the relevant environment presents the same inherently coercive pressures as the type of station house questioning in *Miranda*." *Howes v. Fields*, 132 S.Ct. 1181 (2012). In *Howes*, a prison inmate was not entitled to *Miranda* warnings, because he was not in custody while being questioned by sheriff's deputies in a prison conference room. The Court distinguished between the inherently coercive situation where a citizen is taken from familiar surroundings and interrogated in a police station and one involving prisoners being taken from controlled environment to another.

c. United States v. Van Leeuwen

Facts: The Court upheld the seizure of mailed packages in *United States v. Van Leeuwen*, 397 U.S. 249 (1970). Respondent mailed two 12-pound packages at a post office near the Canadian border. One package was addressed to a post office box in California, and the other to a post office box in Tennessee. Respondent stated that the boxes contained coins. Each package was sent by registered mail and insured for $10,000, a type of mailing that did not subject them to discretionary inspection. The postal clerk relayed his suspicions to a policeman who alerted the appropriate officials. Customs officials learned that both of the addressees were under investigation for trafficking in illegal coins. A customs official then obtained a search warrant, and the packages were opened and inspected.

Law: The Court upheld the seizure. On the facts, a 29-hour delay between the mailings and the service of the warrant was reasonable.

> No interest protected by the Fourth Amendment was invaded by forwarding the packages the following day rather than the day when they were deposited. The significant Fourth Amendment interest was in the privacy of this first-class mail; and that privacy was not disturbed or invaded until the approval of the judge was obtained.

B. OTHER INVESTIGATIVE SEIZURES

While seizures range from an investigatory stop to an arrest, most seizures are investigative in nature and can be relatively brief. Roadside stops usually fit this description. But police also "seize" individuals for fingerprinting, lineups and interrogation purposes. These seizures are subject to differing constitutional requirements.

1. United States v. Mendenhall

Facts: In *United States v. Mendenhall*, 446 U.S. 544 (1980), two Drug Enforcement Agency (DEA) agents believed that Mendenhall's conduct was characteristic of persons illegally carrying narcotics as she disembarked from an airplane. After the agents approached her, identified themselves, and asked to see her identification and airline ticket, she produced her driver's license. Because her airline ticket was issued in a different name, the agent inquired about the discrepancy. When one agent stated that he was a federal narcotics agent, Mendenhall became very nervous. At that point, she went with the agent to the DEA office at the agent's request. The issue was whether Mendenhall had been seized or whether she went to the office voluntarily.

Law: The Court concluded that Mendenhall had not been seized. The encounter occurred in a public area; the agents were not wearing uniforms, did not display weapons, and did not "summon" Mendenhall. Instead, they approached her, identified themselves, and "requested" rather than demanded to see her identification and ticket. As a result, she had no reason to believe "that she was not free to end the conversation in the concourse and proceed on her way." The fact that Mendenhall was not explicitly told that she was free to leave was not determinative. The movement from the public area to the DEA office did not change the encounter to a seizure. The "totality of the evidence" suggested that Mendenhall had voluntarily agreed to accompany the DEA officers to their office.

a. The Significance of the Seizure Issue

Whether a seizure has occurred is important for a variety of reasons. In cases like *Mendenhall,* when a suspect has consented to a subsequent search, the existence of a "seizure" is relevant to the question of whether the consent was voluntary or coerced. If the seizure is illegal, that factor suggests coercion.

2. *Immigration and Naturalization Service v. Delgado*: Immigration Sweeps

The Court has applied similar rules to immigration "sweeps" of factories. In *Immigration and Naturalization Service v. Delgado*, 466 U.S. 210 (1984), the INS surveyed the work force at a factory in search of illegal aliens. The agents approached employees, identified themselves, and asked questions relating to the employees' citizenship. If the employee gave an uncredible response or admitted that he was an alien, the employee was asked to produce his immigration papers. During the survey, employees continued with their work and were free to walk around within the factory. The Court rejected the employees' claim that they had been "seized" at the time of the questioning. Because they were at work, their freedom of movement was restricted "by the workers' voluntary obligations to their employers." No employees were detained unless they tried to flee or evade the agents.

3. *Dunaway* and *Davis*: Seizure for Questioning and Fingerprinting

Between an arrest and an investigative stop, there are other types of seizures. For example, in *Dunaway v. New York*, 442 U.S. 200 (1979), the Court held that, if the police want to pick up a suspect and take him to the station for questioning, they must have probable cause. The Court regarded this type of seizure as tantamount to an arrest. In *Davis v. Mississippi*, 394 U.S. 721 (1969), the Court held that probable cause is also required when the police want to pick up a suspect and take him to the station for fingerprinting. However, in *Hayes v. Florida*, 470 U.S. 811 (1985), in *dicta*, the Court suggested that when fingerprinting is done in the field, reasonable suspicion of criminal activity might justify that brief detention.

4. ***Hiibel v. Sixth Judicial District Court*: Requests for Identification**

In *Hiibel v. Sixth Judicial District Court*, 542 U.S. 177 (2004), the Court held that the police could demand identification from a suspect, and upheld an officer's decision to arrest for a statutory refusal to comply with the demand. The Court relied on the *Terry* balancing test, concluding that an "officer's reasonable suspicion that a person may be involved in criminal activity permits the officer to stop the person for a brief time and take additional steps to investigate further." Questioning a suspect "may help clear a suspect and allow the police to concentrate their efforts elsewhere."

5. ***Illinois v. McArthur*: Temporary Detentions While Seeking a Warrant**

Facts: In *Illinois v. McArthur*, 531 U.S. 326 (2001), a woman told police that her husband had drugs in their home hidden under the couch. After the husband refused to consent to a search, an officer remained at the home and prevented the man from re-entering his home without a police officer. McArthur moved to suppress the pipe, box, and marijuana found during the later search.

Law: The Court held that the police could temporarily detain a man while seeking a warrant to search his home. The Court balanced the "privacy-related and law-enforcement-related concerns" and held that the police acted properly in temporarily seizing McArthur. The Court emphasized that the contraband would be destroyed before they could obtain a warrant, and that the police imposed only a limited restraint by preventing McArthur from re-entering his home while a search warrant was sought. The search did not occur until after the warrant was obtained. *McArthur* extended the Court's holding in *Segura v. United States*, 468 U.S. 796 (1984), which supported an officer's seizure of the premises for the reasonable time necessary to obtain a search warrant.

CHAPTER 13

POLICE INTERROGATION & CONFESSIONS

A. INTRODUCTION

Miranda v. Arizona, 384 U.S. 436 (1966), held that Fifth Amendment "*Miranda* warnings" must be given to all persons prior to custodial interrogation. The Supreme Court has relied on other doctrinal sources for judicial regulation of police interrogation, creating rules based on: 1) Fourteenth Amendment Due Process; 2) the Sixth Amendment right to counsel; and 3) the Court's supervisory power over the federal courts. This chapter discusses the admissibility of confessions obtained by law enforcement under various circumstances and at different times during an investigation. The following depicts the applicability of the four legal approaches to the admissibility of confessions.

Adversary proceedings begin

Prompt arraignment rules apply	**Right to counsel rules apply**

Due process/Voluntariness rules are always applicable

5th Amendment rules (*Miranda*) apply *only* when there is custodial interrogation, regardless of whether adversary proceedings have begun.

B. THE PROMPT ARRAIGNMENT RULE

The Supreme Court's regulation of the admissibility of confessions in federal courts is based on its supervisory power over all federal courts. In *McNabb v. United States*, 318 U.S. 332 (1943), the Court created an exclusionary rule for confessions obtained during the improper detention of arrestees not taken promptly to a federal judicial officer after arrest.

1. "Unnecessary Delay" Is Standard in Federal Rules

Congress incorporated the substance of *McNabb* into Rule 5(a) of the Federal Rules of Criminal Procedure in 1946, requiring that arrested persons must be presented to a judicial officer "without unnecessary delay." A confession obtained during a period of unnecessary delay is inadmissible. *Mallory v. United States*, 354 U.S. 449 (1957) warned against pre-appearance questioning that "lends itself, even if not so designed, to eliciting damaging statements." The six-hour delay in *Mallory* was held to be unnecessary, because a magistrate was available for two hours in the same building while the defendant was questioned.

2. *McNabb-Mallory* Rule Altered by Federal Statute

The *McNabb-Mallory* rule was never incorporated into Due Process doctrine and applied to the States, despite repeated requests by State defendants during the years between *McNabb* and *Miranda*. Under the *McNabb-Mallory* rule as revised by 18 U.S.C. § 3501(c), if a confession is voluntary and was obtained within six hours of arrest, it is admissible and the weight to be given the confession is left to the jury. If the confession occurred before the initial appearance but beyond six hours after the arrest *and* if the court decides that the delay was unreasonable or unnecessary, the confession is to be suppressed. *Corley v. United States*, 556 U.S. 303 (2009).

C. THE FIFTH AMENDMENT AND *MIRANDA*

The Fifth Amendment states in part that "[n]o person . . . shall be compelled in a criminal case to be a witness against himself." *Miranda v. Arizona*, 384 U.S. 436 (1966) found incommunicado interrogation "at odds with" the Fifth Amendment privilege. Unless "adequate protective devices" are used to relieve the coercion "inherent in custodial surroundings, no statement obtained from a defendant can truly be the product of his free choice." *Miranda* created a "Fifth Amendment" right to counsel in order to protect a defendant's access to the privilege during the interrogation process. *Miranda* is a constitutional rule. *Dickerson v. United States*, 530 U.S. 428 (2000), and cannot be overruled by an act of Congress.

1. *Miranda*'s Safeguards: Warnings and Waiver

The *Miranda* Court held that

> [An interrogated person in custody] must be warned prior to any questioning that he has the right to remain silent, that anything he

says can be used against him in a court of law, that he has the right to the presence of an attorney, and that if he cannot afford an attorney one will be appointed for him prior to any questioning if he so desires. Opportunity to exercise these rights must be afforded to him throughout the interrogation. After such warnings have been given, and such opportunity afforded him, the individual may knowingly and intelligently waive these rights and agree to answer questions or make a statement. But unless and until such warnings and waiver are demonstrated by the prosecution at trial, no evidence obtained as a result of interrogation can be used against him.

a. *Miranda* on Invocation of Right to Silence and Right to Counsel

On the issue of a suspect's invocation of his rights, the *Miranda* Court stated:

> If the individual indicates in any manner, at any time prior to or during questioning, that he wishes to remain silent, the interrogation must cease. [If] the individual states that he wants an attorney, the interrogation must cease until an attorney is present. At that time, the individual must have an opportunity to confer with the attorney and to have him present during any subsequent questioning. If the individual cannot obtain an attorney and he indicates that he wants one before speaking to police, they must respect his decision to remain silent. [If] authorities conclude that they will not provide counsel during a reasonable period of time in which investigation in the field is carried out, they may refrain from doing so without violating the person's Fifth Amendment privilege so long as they do not question him during that time.

b. Statements in Violation of *Miranda* Must Be Suppressed

The inadmissibility of confessions obtained in violation of these rules extends to all statements made during custodial interrogation; "no distinction" exists between inculpatory statements and statements alleged to be merely "exculpatory."

2. Rationales for *Miranda*

Two findings were at the core of the *Miranda* Court's reasoning. First, all custodial interrogation creates a "potentiality for compulsion," based on the Court's review of police manual instructions for interrogation techniques which promoted an "atmosphere of domination" by police interrogators. Second, the "human dignity" value of the Fifth Amendment could be protected only if new rules were created to limit the inherent coercion of interrogation so that confessions may be "truly [the] product of free choice." A "full opportunity to exercise the privilege" could be provided if the accused was "adequately and effectively apprised of his rights and the exercise of those rights [fully] honored."

a. Rights That Do *Not* Have to Be Disclosed Under *Miranda*

Miranda did not provide for police recitation of all rights potentially useful for a criminal defendant prior to custodial interrogation. None of the following techniques of psychological "domination" is a *Miranda* violation *per se*. For example,

- there is no right to be informed that if a defendant invokes silence or counsel rights, a cut off of questioning will follow,
- a lawyer does not have to be "present at all times to advise prisoners,"
- there is no right to contact people outside the interrogation room; and
- there is no right to defense counsel's access to a client during interrogation.

b. States and Legislatures May Create Alternative Approaches

State courts and legislatures are free to create different standards to protect the privilege, as long as they are "equally effective." The Court has not recognized any alternate rules as adequate *Miranda* substitutes, and has invalidated a Congressional attempt to overrule *Miranda* by legislation. *See Dickerson v. United States*, 530 U.S. 428 (2000).

c. When *Miranda* Warnings Are Unnecessary

However, the Court has created significant exceptions to *Miranda*. For example, the rules do not apply to

- questioning conducted by undercover police agents, *Illinois v. Perkins*, 496 U.S. 292 (1990);
- "routine booking questions," *Pennsylvania v. Muniz*, 496 U.S. 582 (1990);
- police questioning about a weapon under the "public safety exception," *New York v. Quarles*, 467 U.S. 649 (1984); or
- use of statements taken in violation of *Miranda* to impeach the defendant if she chooses to testify and the statement was not obtained in violation of Due Process. *Harris v. New York*, 401 U.S. 222 (1971).

3. *Miranda* Custody

Miranda does not require an officer to give *Miranda* warnings to everyone approached for information concerning a crime. *Miranda* applies only to "custodial interrogation," which is defined as "questioning initiated by law enforcement officers after a person has been taken into custody or otherwise deprived of his freedom of action in any significant way." If the defendant is "in custody" on one charge, *Miranda* is still required even if questioning is about another charge. *Mathis v. United States*, 391 U.S. 1 (1968).

a. Objective Test to Determine Custody

The Court uses an objective standard to determine custody based on the totality of circumstances; "the only relevant inquiry is how a reasonable [person] in the suspect's shoes would have understood [the] situation." *Stansbury v. California*, 511 U.S. 318 (1994). An individual defendant's idiosyncratic reaction to an encounter with police will not dictate a finding of custody. More importantly, a police officer's opinion about the custodial status of the interrogated person is irrelevant to the custody inquiry, as long as this opinion is not revealed to that person.

b. Advantage of Objective Test

An objective standard for custody insures that police officers will not have to "make guesses" about the existence of particular circumstances "before deciding how they may interrogate" a person. *Yarborough v. Alvarado*, 541 U.S. 652 (2004). Yarborough held that a person's "law enforcement history" and "interrogation history" are subjective experiences rather than objective facts. Officers often will not know this history, and even when they do, any conclusions they might draw about its relevance to custody are likely to be speculative.

c. Factors Relevant to Custody Determination

Under the Court's "totality of the circumstances" approach to custody, courts have identified a number of factors that may be relevant to the custody inquiry,

- the purpose of the investigation,
- the location and length of the interrogation,
- the interrogated person's awareness of her freedom to leave the scene,
- the person's actual freedom from a variety of forms of physical restraint, and
- the use of coercive interrogation methods.

(1) *J.D.B. v. North Carolina*

In *J.D.B. v. North Carolina*, 131 S.Ct. 2394 (2011), the Court held that "a child's age properly informs the *Miranda* custody analysis." The Court in *Stansbury* had stated that a child's age could affect how a reasonable person in the suspect's position "would perceive his or her freedom to leave." In other words, "a reasonable child subjected to police questioning will sometimes feel pressured to submit when a reasonable adult would feel free to go."

d. Custody Away from the Police Station

Some post-*Miranda* cases held that custody could exist outside the station house. For example, in *Orozco v. Texas*, 394 U.S. 324 (1969), the defendant was held to be in custody in his own home when he was awakened in his bedroom at 4:00 a.m. by four police officers. He was not informed that he was under arrest, but he was questioned about his presence at the scene of a homicide and about the location of his gun. On the other hand, in *Beckwith v. United States*, 425 U.S. 341 (1976), IRS agents interviewed a defendant at this home for three hours. His claim that he was in custody failed because he had consented to the interview and had been warned about the consequences of his answers and his right to consult an attorney.

e. Imprisoned Suspects

While a person at home may be regarded as being in "custody," *Miranda* warnings do not have to be administered to imprisoned defendants. In *Maryland v. Shatzer*, 559 U.S. 98 (2010), the Court observed, "Without minimizing the harsh realities of incarceration, . . . lawful imprisonment imposed upon conviction of a crime does not create the coercive pressures identified in *Miranda*." In contrast to their time in a small interrogation room removed from other inmates, inmates in the general prison population are in "their accustomed surroundings and daily routine."

f. Custody v. "General on-the-Scene" Questioning

Not every encounter between a defendant and a police officer qualifies as "custodial." *Miranda* stated:

> General on-the-scene questioning as to facts surrounding a crime or other general questioning of citizens in the fact-finding process is not affected by our holding. [In] such situations the compelling atmosphere inherent in the

process of in-custody interrogation is not necessarily present.

g. Probationer's Interview with Probation Officer Not Custodial

Certain situations are non-custodial *per se*, absent unusual circumstances. For example, in *Minnesota v. Murphy*, 465 U.S. 420 (1984), a probationer's interview with a probation officer was held to be a non-custodial event. The obligations of probationers to report to their probation officers and to be truthful with them "in all matters," upon penalty of probation revocation do not establish sufficient restraint.

h. Traffic Stops Are Typically Not Custodial

The typical "traffic stop" does not qualify as "custody." *Berkemer v. McCarty*, 468 U.S. 420 (1984). The Court explained that a temporary detention for purposes of receiving a traffic citation does not compare to the "police-dominated" atmosphere of a station house interrogation. In the typical traffic stop, a driver expects to be detained only briefly and to be questioned by no more than one or two police officers in the comparative safety of the public eye. However, the Court did recognize that some traffic stops may not fit the typical non-custodial pattern, necessitating *Miranda* warnings.

4. *Miranda* Interrogation

A suspect does not have to be advised of her *Miranda* warnings as soon as she is arrested, as long as she is advised prior to the commencement of interrogation. Volunteered statements are admissible even if the defendant is in custody when the statement was made and no *Miranda* warnings had been given. "There is no requirement that police stop a person who enters a police station and states that he wishes to confess to a crime, or a person who calls the police to offer a confession or any other statement he desires to make."

a. Why the Scope of the Interrogation Definition Matters

The *Miranda* definition of "interrogation" was a crucial concept for determining police compliance with the *Miranda* duties:

- to give warnings before interrogating persons in custody,
- to refrain from interrogating after warnings in the absence of waiver, and
- to refrain from interrogating after an invocation of rights.

b. Interrogation Defined

Rhode Island v. Innis, 446 U.S. 291 (1980) established a test for assessing whether a particular police comment or action would qualify as "interrogation." *Miranda* safeguards "come into play whenever a person in custody is subjected to either express questioning or its functional equivalent," defined as:

> any words or actions on the part of the police (other than those normally attendant to arrest and custody) that the police should know are reasonably likely to elicit an incriminating response from the suspect. The latter portion of this definition focuses primarily upon the perceptions of the suspect, rather than the intent of the police.

In this respect, the *Innis* definition of interrogation is consistent with the *Stansbury* definition of custody, because both rules avoid focusing on the police officer's intent or state of mind.

c. Rhode Island v. Innis

Facts: Innis was arrested for armed robbery, and was also suspected of a shotgun murder five days earlier. He was placed in the rear seat of a police car, and three police officers traveled with him. Innis overheard two of the officers talking to each other about how they should "continue to search for the weapon" because "a school for handicapped children [was] located nearby," and because "God forbid" that a little girl might "pick up the gun, maybe kill herself." Innis then immediately stated that he would show the officers the location of the gun, and he led them to that location.

Law: The *Innis* majority emphasized several aspects of the police dialogue that justified its conclusion that interrogation did not occur:

- the police conversation was "brief" not "evocative,"
- it was not directed to Innis but merely overheard by him,
- the police had no knowledge of any "peculiar" susceptibility of Innis to an appeal for the safety of handicapped children, and they knew of no disorientation or upset suffered by Innis at the time of arrest, and
- the incriminating response of the defendant was "unforeseeable."

d. Exceptions to Interrogation Definition

Three important *Miranda* exceptions allow police to engage in conduct that would constitute "interrogation" under *Innis* without honoring the duty to give *Miranda* warnings: 1) routine booking questions, 2) interrogators who are not known to the suspect as law enforcement officers, and 3) public safety.

(1) Routine Booking Questions

The origin of the "routine booking question" exception is the *Innis* Court's recognition that any questions "normally attendant to arrest and custody" should not count as "interrogation" under *Miranda*. *Pennsylvania v. Muniz*, 496 U.S. 582 (1990). This exception allows police to gather the biographical data needed to complete the booking process and arrange for pretrial services. The rationale is that the answers to questions about a defendant's name, address, age, and like subjects, are "reasonably related to administrative concerns" and are unrelated to the quest for incriminating statements.

(2) Undercover Officers

In *Illinois v. Perkins*, 496 U.S. 292 (1990), the Court ruled that *Miranda* warnings are not required if a person "is unaware that [she] is speaking to a law enforcement officer." This exception allows police to use undercover agents to pose as prison inmates in order to obtain incriminating statements from an unsuspecting defendant. The *Perkins* interrogation did not "implicate the concerns underlying *Miranda*," which relate to the risks of self-incrimination that are inherent in a coercive, "police-dominated atmosphere."

(3) Public Safety Exception

The "public safety exception" in *New York v. Quarles*, 467 U.S. 649 (1984), allows police to ask an arrestee a question about the location of a weapon that the arrestee may have abandoned or hidden in a public area near the scene of arrest. These questions may be asked without first providing *Miranda* warnings that could prompt the arrestee to refuse to disclose any information about the weapon. In *Quarles*, police officers had reliable information that the arrestee had recently discarded a gun somewhere in the supermarket where they arrested him. The police asked "only the question necessary to locate the missing gun" before providing the defendant with *Miranda* warnings. If a question about a weapon was "reasonably prompted by a concern for public safety" under the circumstances of the arrest, the arrestee's answer to the question is admissible evidence, as well as any weapon that is located.

5. Adequacy of *Miranda* Warnings

The prosecution must prove that the warnings were given. Police departments often provide written as well as oral warnings, and ask arrestees to sign a form to acknowledge that they received and understood them. The receipt of the warnings is the first step for government arguments for a valid *Miranda* waiver. The cases have focused on either incomplete or misleading warnings, or a recent development referred to as "question first, warn later."

a. California v. Prysock

Facts: The Court has established guidelines for the types of tolerable ambiguity in the *Miranda* warnings. In *California v. Prysock*, 453 U.S. 355 (1981), the police officer's language was as follows:

> You have the right to talk to a lawyer before you are questioned, have him present with you while you are being questioned, and all during the questioning. Do you understand this? . . . You also, being a juvenile, you have the right to have your parents present, which they are. Do you understand this? . . . You have the right to have a lawyer appointed to represent you at no cost to yourself. Do you understand this?

The defendant argued that the warnings failed to connect the right to consult counsel before questioning with the right to appointed counsel. The defendant did not realize that the "lawyer appointed to represent" him "at no cost" would be appointed before any questioning began. The defendant assumed instead that any "appointed lawyer" would be appointed after the interrogation, presumably by a judge at some proceeding in the future.

Law: The Court ruled that separate references to the right to consult counsel before questioning and the abstract right to appointed counsel sufficiently conveyed the meaning of the *Miranda* rights. What saved the *Prysock* warnings was the clarity with which the right to consult counsel was attached to the time period "prior to and during interrogation." The defendant was expected to infer that the description of the right to "appointed counsel" referred to the earlier description of the right to consult counsel before questioning. The ambiguity in the warnings was not significant. The *Prysock* Court did recognize, however, that the "right-to-counsel" warnings would be constitutionally inadequate if they expressly suggested "any limitation on the right to the presence of appointed counsel" that was different from the "rights to a lawyer in general." Specifically, "if the reference to the right to appointed counsel was linked with some future point in time after the police interrogation," the text of the warning would "not fully advise the suspect of his right to appointed counsel before" an interrogation. *Prysock* also settled that verbatim recitation of the *Miranda* warnings is unnecessary.

b. Duckworth v. Eagan

In *Duckworth v. Eagan*, 492 U.S. 195 (1989), the police told the suspect that he had a right to an attorney during interrogation and to an appointed attorney. In addition, they also told him that an attorney would be appointed for him if and when he went to court. The Court again found that the warning was sufficient, because it "simply anticipated" a question the suspect might be expected to ask after receiving *Miranda* warnings, i.e., when he will obtain an attorney.

c. Florida v. Powell

In *Florida v. Powell*, 559 U.S. 50 (2010), the Court stated that "the four warnings *Miranda* requires are invariable, but this Court has not dictated the words in which the essential information must be conveyed." For example, when police officers arrested Powell they warned him about his "right to talk to a lawyer before answering any . . . questions." They also told him that he had "the right to use of these [*Miranda*] rights at any time [he] want[ed] during th[e] interview." The Supreme Court upheld those warnings, which did not "entirely omi[t] any required information" and because they "reasonably conveyed Powell's right to have an attorney present not only at the outset of interrogation but at all times."

d. Missouri v. Seibert

Missouri v. Seibert, 542 U.S. 600 (2004) held that when police "question first and warn later," warnings that are given "midstream" between two interrogations that are "close in time and similar in content" do not "reasonably convey" the *Miranda* rights as required by *Duckworth*. Such warnings are likely to mislead the interrogated person about "the nature of his rights and the consequences of abandoning them." "[A] suspect would hardly think he had a genuine right to remain silent, let alone persist in so believing once the police began to lead him over the same ground again."

(1) When Midstream Warnings May Be Adequate

Seibert noted that midstream warnings may be adequate in some circumstances, such as those in *Oregon v. Elstad,* 470 U.S. 298 (1985), where police made a "good faith" mistake in failing to give warnings before a single comment by an officer prompted an unwarned admission by Elstad during his arrest in his home. The warnings given later at the station were "adequate," according to Seibert, because the station house interrogation was deemed to be a "new and distinct experience" for Elstad, and thus his stationhouse confession was admissible. In *Bobby v. Dixon,* 132 S.Ct. 26 (2011), the Court clarified *Seibert*: it applies only when different periods of interrogation form one continuous whole. In that situation, *Miranda* warnings at later periods are sufficient to offset the failure to warn at an earlier period of questioning.

(2) How *Dixon* differed from *Seibert*

Dixon's facts lacked the two-step interrogation technique that undermined the *Miranda* warnings in *Seibert.* In *Dixon*, there was no earlier confession to repeat because Dixon initially gave no confession. After receiving the *Miranda* warnings, "Dixon contradicted his prior unwarned statements" by confessing to murder. Thus, the police did not use an earlier admission to induce a later waiver. "Dixon declared his desire to tell police what happened . . . before the second interrogation session even began."

6. Waiver of *Miranda* Rights

The prosecution must prove not only that police administered the warnings but also that an arrestee waived her *Miranda* rights in order for any statement obtained during custodial interrogation to be admitted at trial. The *Miranda* opinion provided only one example of a hypothetical case where a waiver could be found, an express statement that an arrestee "is willing" to talk and "does not want an attorney" followed closely by an incriminating statement.

a. Nature of a *Miranda* Waiver

Miranda requires that waivers must be "voluntary, knowing and intelligent." In *Moran v. Burbine*, 475 U.S. 412 (1986), the Court summarized post-*Miranda* principles defining voluntary, knowing and intelligent waivers. "Only if the 'totality of the circumstances surrounding the interrogation' reveals both an uncoerced choice and the requisite level of comprehension may a court properly conclude that the *Miranda* rights have been waived."

b. Proving a *Miranda* Waiver

The State must prove waiver by a preponderance of the evidence. *Colorado v. Connelly*, 479 U.S. 157 (1986). A waiver may be implied through oral statements and conduct, and does not have to be in writing. *North Carolina v. Butler*, 441 U.S. 369 (1979). A waiver may be inferred from the fact that the suspect eventually makes statements to the police. *Berghuis v. Thompkins*, 560 U.S. 370 (2010). Finally, a valid waiver must include proof that an arrestee understood the *Miranda* warnings, and therefore a court may not rely on a presumption that such an understanding exists. *Tague v. Louisiana*, 444 U.S. 469 (1980). To satisfy the *Tague* burden, police sometimes administer the *Miranda* warnings and ask whether the arrestee understands her rights, thereafter seeking a written acknowledgment of the suspect's understanding.

c. Voluntary Waiver

The first key component of a waiver is its "voluntary" quality. A totality of the circumstances test includes "the duration and conditions of [detention]," the "manifest attitude of the police" toward the defendant, the "physical and mental state" of the defendant, [and] the "diverse pressures which sap or sustain" the defendant's "powers of resistance and self-control." *Colorado v. Spring*, 479 U.S. 564 (1987). A defendant trying to negate the voluntariness element will try to demonstrate that coercive police conduct caused her waiver to be the product of intimidation, coercion, or deception.

(1) *Colorado v. Spring*: Police Silence Is Not Coercion

Facts: In *Colorado v. Spring*, the police failed to tell the defendant before his waiver that they planned to ask him questions about an old murder crime as well as about the unrelated crime for which he had been arrested.

Law: The Court is unsympathetic to claims that police silence constitutes a form of coercion. The Court decided that, because the defendant had been affirmatively warned that anything he said could be used against him, he should have inferred that he was giving the police an unlimited waiver for interrogation about *all* his crimes. The *Spring* Court reserved the issue of whether sufficient "coercion" invalidates a waiver if police affirmatively misrepresent the scope of the interrogation.

(2) Defendant's Mental Condition

In another waiver ruling, the Court found that a mentally ill defendant may voluntarily waive his *Miranda* rights when there is no police overreaching. *Colorado v. Connelly*, 479 U.S. 157 (1986). The defendant approached an off-duty police officer and confessed to murder. The officer responded by reciting the *Miranda* warnings, which were repeated by an officer summoned to question the defendant who told them that he had been a patient in mental hospitals but showed no signs of mental illness during interrogation.

d. Knowing and Intelligent Waiver

The second component of a valid waiver is its "knowing and intelligent" quality. In *Spring*, the Court rejected defendant's argument that more information about the subject of the interrogation was necessary for a knowing waiver. The Court concluded that the *Miranda* warnings supplied all the information necessary for a "knowing and intelligent" waiver. Moreover, an "extension of *Miranda* would spawn numerous problems of interpretation because any number of factors could affect a suspect's decision to waive *Miranda* rights."

(1) Conditional Waiver May Be Proper

In *Connecticut v. Barrett*, 479 U.S. 523 (1987), Barrett told police after three sets of warnings that he would *talk* to them, but would not make a *written* statement without a lawyer. He then made oral admissions without police asking him for a written statement. The defendant repeatedly had said that he understood his rights, and testified about knowing that he did not have to talk without a lawyer present. That the defendant's conduct appeared "illogical" did not prevent police from obtaining a valid waiver. The defendant's "conditional waiver" of the right to silence was held to be voluntary, knowing and intelligent.

7. Invocation of *Miranda* Rights

Under *Miranda*, police officers must honor an arrestee's invocations of the right to silence, the right to counsel, or both, by "cutting off" the interrogation. If an arrestee's invocation does not satisfy these standards, police may ignore the invocation and continue to interrogate. Post-*Miranda* cases have resolved three questions about a suspect's invocation of rights:

- an invocation of counsel is different from an invocation of silence; police are barred from initiating discussions and seeking a waiver after the former but not after the latter invocation,
- police may seek a waiver after either type of invocation when the arrestee initiates a generalized discussion about the investigation with the police; and
- an invocation of either silence or of counsel must be "unambiguous."

a. Unambiguous Invocation of Rights

An adequate invocation of rights must be explicit and unambiguous, and occurs when a reasonable police officer in the circumstances would understand the statement to be a request not to talk to the police, e.g., the suspect says to the police, "Leave me alone."

(1) Davis v. United States

Facts: In *Davis v. United States*, 512 U.S. 452 (1994), Davis had waived his rights and answered questions for an hour and a half before saying, "Maybe I should talk to a lawyer." Asked to clarify his request, Davis said that he was "not asking for a lawyer," and added, "No, I don't want a lawyer."

Law: The *Davis* Court held that the initial "maybe" request for counsel did not "meet the requisite level of clarity," and the police did not have to stop questioning. *Davis* also rejected the imposition of a law enforcement "duty to clarify" an ambiguous invocation. An adequate invocation occurs when "a reasonable police officer in the circumstances would understand the statement to be a request for an attorney." An officer can ignore an invocation that is "ambiguous or equivocal in that a reasonable officer in light of the circumstances would have understood only that the suspect might be invoking the right to counsel." Requiring an "unambiguous" invocation ensured that police officers would not "be forced to make difficult judgment calls" about ambiguous invocations, and not be faced with "the threat of suppression if they guess wrong."

(2) Berghuis v. Thompkins

Facts. After receiving *Miranda* warnings, the defendant in *Berghuis v. Thompkins*, 560 U.S. 370 (2010) declined to sign a form to demonstrate that he understood his rights, and there was conflicting evidence in the record as to whether he verbally confirmed that he understood them. He was largely silent during the three-hour interrogation. He occasionally communicated by nodding his head. He gave a few limited verbal responses, such as "yeah," "no," and "I don't know."

Law: The Court held that he did not invoke the *Miranda* right to remain silent, observing that he "did not say that he wanted to remain silent or that he did not want to talk with the police" and "[h]ad he made either of these simple, unambiguous statements, he would have invoked his 'right to cut off questioning.' "

(3) Smith v. Illinois

When a defendant's invocation interrupts the police officer before all the warnings are administered, the officer should stop the interrogation as soon as the invocation is uttered. *Smith v. Illinois*, 469 U.S. 91 (1984). The rationale is that the police should not be allowed to ignore unambiguous invocations "as if the defendant had requested nothing," in the hope that later statements might create some retrospective ambiguity in the invocation.

(4) Invocation by Suspect in Custody Before Warnings

Neither *Miranda* nor *Davis* addresses the interrogation scenario in which a potential invocation is expressed by a person in custody even before the *Miranda* warnings are communicated to that person. Some lower courts recognize the validity of pre-warning invocations of the right to counsel by those in custody and assume that the unambiguous invocation requirement should apply to them. *See, e.g., Carr v. State*, 934 N.E.2d 1096 (Ind. 2010). However, courts have relied on *dicta* in *McNeil v. Wisconsin*, 501 U.S. 171 (1991), as disallowing the "anticipatory invocation" of the *Miranda* right to counsel by anyone other than a person in custody.

b. Re-Interrogation After Invocation of the Right to Silence

Michigan v. Mosley, 423 U.S. 96 (1975) governs the responsibility of police following a suspect's invocation of the right to silence.

(1) Michigan v. Mosley

Facts: Mosley told police that he did not want to answer questions about the robberies for which he was arrested. Two hours later, a different police officer told him that he was investigating a murder. After receiving a second set of warnings during questioning in another part of the station house, Mosley waived his rights and made incriminating statements.

Law: *Mosley* held that an invocation of silence does not permanently end the interrogation, if the police "scrupulously honor" the invocation. The Court began its analysis by noting the text of the governing *Miranda* rule and its policy justifications. *Miranda* had stated that if a suspect indicates "that he wishes to remain silent, the interrogation must cease; . . . any statement taken after the person invokes his privilege cannot be other than the product of compulsion, subtle or otherwise." The Court viewed this passage as leaving open the question whether, and under what circumstances, "a resumption of questioning is permissible" after an invocation of silence. Mosley's invocation of the right to silence was "scrupulously honored," which the Court explained as a combination of several factors: the invocation appeared to be limited to the robbery crimes, the subject of questioning was an "unrelated" crime, a two-hour time lapse occurred before the re-interrogation, the defendant received a second set of *Miranda* warnings, and the second interrogation was conducted by a different police officer. The Court has not explained the scope of its multi-factor holding since *Mosley*.

c. Re-Interrogation After Invocation of the Right to Counsel

Different rules apply if the suspect in custody invokes his right to counsel instead of his right to silence. The invocation of counsel is an indication by the suspect that he feels incapable of speaking to the police on his own. Because of the Court's concern that a suspect asserting his right to counsel is not as likely to change his mind for reasons other than police pressure, the Court accords the police less flexibility, i.e., after the invocation, the police cannot interrogate the suspect *unless* it is the suspect who re-initiates the contact. In *Edwards v. Arizona*, 451 U.S. 477 (1981), the Court refused re-interrogation of the defendant following an invocation of the right to counsel. *Miranda* had stated, "If the individual states that he wants an attorney, the interrogation must cease until an attorney is present." The Court accepted *Miranda*'s blanket prohibition against questioning after invocation of the right to counsel.

(1) Edwards v. Arizona

Facts: The defendant in *Edwards* had declared, "I want an attorney before making a deal." The police had cut off questioning but then returned the next morning, telling the defendant he "had to" talk to them.

Law: The Court determined that the waiver was invalid because the police initiated the second interrogation. The only proper scenario for police seeking a waiver was where the arrestee "initiates further communication, exchanges, or conversations with the police" after invocation of the right to counsel. In distinguishing *Edwards* from *Mosley*, *Edwards* cited *Mosley*'s recognition of the different "procedural safeguards" that were "triggered" by the two different invocations. Because the defendant in *Edwards* had "expressed his desire to deal with the police only through counsel," he should not be "subject to further interrogation by the authorities until counsel has been made available to him." *Edwards* specifically noted that the ban on re-interrogation after the invocation of counsel does not apply if the defendant "initiates further communication, exchanges, or conversations with the police." The rationale is that if the defendant "initiates" a discussion, then she has demonstrated a lack of desire to deal with the police only through counsel.

(2) Oregon v. Bradshaw

The Court soon decided that initiation by the suspect is not *per se* proof of a waiver. Assuming that a post-invocation "initiation" has occurred, the police must seek a valid waiver under the totality of the circumstances. *Oregon v. Bradshaw*, 462 U.S. 1039 (1983).

Facts: Shortly after invoking his right to counsel while being transferred from the police station to the jail, Bradshaw asked the escorting officer, "Well, what is going to happen to me now?" Instead of immediately answering the question, the police gave an incomplete version of the *Miranda* warnings.

Law: The definition of "initiation" split the *Bradshaw* Court. All agreed that questions "relating to routine incidents of the custodial relationship," such as a request for a drink of water or requests to use the telephone, were "bare inquiries" that do not qualify as an "initiation." The plurality held that the police officer had not violated *Edwards* by resuming the waiver-seeking process. While acknowledging that the defendant's question was "ambiguous," the police officer's response showed that the officer understood the question as "relating generally to the investigation." The officer's conduct in seeking a waiver was valid under *Edwards*. For the plurality, an "initiation" occurs whenever an arrestee engages in a "generalized discussion" of the investigation. For the dissenters, an "initiation" should be found only when an arrestee communicates explicitly about "the subject matter of the criminal investigation" in a way that invites "further interrogation."

(3) Re-Interrogation About Different Crimes

In *Arizona v. Roberson*, 486 U.S. 675 (1988), the Court ruled that *Edwards* bars re-interrogation about different crimes. The *Roberson* Court relied on several rationales to justify its use of the *Edwards* rule to govern re-interrogations on all subjects: 1) a bright line-rule barring all re-interrogations after invocation of counsel would be easy for police, prosecutors, and lower courts to interpret and apply; and 2) any invocation of counsel seeks the advice of counsel concerning questioning about any crime.

(4) Re-Interrogation After Talking to Counsel

In *Minnick v. Mississippi*, 498 U.S. 146 (1990), the defendant invoked his right to counsel after his arrest in California for a crime in Mississippi, and the arresting FBI agents allowed him to meet with counsel several times. Although his lawyer told him not to talk to anyone or to sign any waivers, Minnick was told that he "had" to talk to the Mississippi sheriff. His conversation with the sheriff led to a discussion of the crime. *Minnick* held that the *Edwards* rule bars re-interrogation of *any* kind unless counsel is present. As in *Roberson*, the *Minnick* Court valued the "clarity and certainty" of a "bright-line rule" application of *Edwards*. Only the presence of counsel after invocation provided adequate protection of the right to counsel.

(5) **If Defendant Is Released After Invocation**

In *Maryland v. Shatzer*, 559 U.S. 98 (2010), the court held that *if* a suspect is released from custody after invoking his right to counsel, the *Edwards* prohibition on police questioning lasts for fourteen days. After that time, the police may resume questioning without the suspect re-initiating the conversation. The Court reasoned that a suspect will not feel pressured if questioned again after a substantial period of time during which he is free. By contrast, if the suspect is not released from jail, the *Edwards* rules remain in effect.

8. **Uses of Either *Miranda*-Defective Evidence or Silence**

a. **When Defective Evidence Leads Police to Other Evidence**

If the police violate the *Miranda* rules and obtain a statement during custodial interrogation, that statement will be inadmissible. In *Oregon v. Elstad,* 470 U.S. 298 (1985), however, the Court rejected the need to use the Fourth Amendment "fruit of the poisonous tree" doctrine in the *Miranda* context. See Chapter 2. *Elstad* decided that the failure to give warnings before obtaining an initial confession does not invalidate a second confession, obtained after warnings, as the inadmissible fruit of the *Miranda* violation. Although *Elstad* permits the police ordinarily to remedy an initial failure to warn by subsequently giving the warnings, *Missouri v. Seibert*, 542 U.S. 600 (2004) qualified *Elstad* by holding that "midstream" warnings may be inadequate to convey *Miranda* rights in some circumstances.

(1) **Rejection of FOPT Analysis in *Miranda* Context**

The rejection of the *Wong Sun* "fruits" doctrine in the *Miranda* context was justified, because the exclusion of all non-attenuated fruits of *Miranda* violations is unnecessary to provide adequate deterrence of violations by police officers. For example, the Court held in *United States v. Patane*, 542 U.S. 630 (2004) that if police discover physical evidence based on information provided in a defendant's unwarned statement, that evidence is admissible as long as the statement was not procured by "actual coercion."

b. Impeachment with Defective Statements or with Silence

(1) Use of Defective Statements to Impeach

The "impeachment exception" to *Miranda* was established in *Harris v. New York,* 401 U.S. 222 (1971). The Court ruled that an unwarned statement was admissible during cross-examination to impeach the credibility of the defendant's testimony if the statement was not obtained in violation of Due Process, i.e., if it was given voluntarily. See Chapter 2 for further discussion.

(2) Use of Silence to Impeach

Doyle v. Ohio, 426 U.S. 610 (1976) recognized that the exercise of the "right to remain silent" in the *Miranda* warnings would be penalized at trial if a prosecutor were allowed to ask a defendant during cross-examination why she refrained, after being arrested and receiving warnings, from telling the police information that she has communicated to the jury at trial. See Chapter 2 for further discussion.

(3) Use of Silence as Evidence of Guilt

However, when a defendant is not in custody or has not received *Miranda* warnings, and he voluntarily responds to questioning by police, the use of his silence in response to another question may be used as evidence of his guilt at trial, because he failed to invoke the privilege against self-incrimination in response to the officer's question. *Salinas v. Texas*, 133 S.Ct. 2174 (2013) (plurality opinion).

D. SIXTH AMENDMENT RIGHT TO COUNSEL

The Sixth Amendment right to counsel attaches upon the commencement of adversary judicial proceedings. In *Rothgery v. Gillespie County*, 554 U.S. 191 (2008), the Court identified a short list of events that qualify as "adversary judicial proceedings," including initial appearance, formal charge, preliminary hearing, indictment or information. Once adversary proceedings are instituted, law enforcement officials or their agents may not interrogate the accused in the absence of counsel, unless the accused has validly waived that right.

1. Massiah v. United States

In *Massiah v. United States*, 377 U.S. 201 (1964), the Supreme Court held that an indicted defendant's surreptitious questioning by an undercover police agent violated the Sixth Amendment right to counsel. Years later, the Court declared that *Massiah* clearly established "that once adversary proceedings have commenced against an individual, he has a right to legal representation when the government interrogates him." *Brewer v. Williams*, 430 U.S. 387, 388 (1977).

2. Rationales for *Massiah*

The *Massiah* Court relied on three arguments to support its holding.

- Lack of access to counsel during questioning "might deny a defendant 'effective representation by counsel at the only stage when legal aid and advice would help him.' "
- Counsel's investigation and preparation are "vitally important," and defendants are therefore "as much entitled to [the] aid of counsel during that period as at the trial itself."
- If the Sixth Amendment right to consult counsel were to be meaningful, "it must apply to indirect and surreptitious interrogations as well as those conducted in the jailhouse."

3. Brewer v. Williams

Facts: On the advice of his Des Moines lawyer, Williams surrendered to police and was arraigned on an abduction charge in Davenport, while two officers traveled by car from Des Moines to retrieve Williams and escort him back for "booking" in Des Moines. Williams was suspected of murdering the victim of the abduction. His lawyer obtained the agreement of police officials that they would not question him in transit, and he would be allowed to consult with the lawyer in Des Moines before questioning. Williams received *Miranda* warnings from the Davenport police, the Davenport judge, and the Des Moines detective. Both of his lawyers also warned him against making any statements. Soon after the police car left Davenport, the detective delivered the so-called "Christian burial speech." He told Williams that he expected that they would be driving past the area where the victim's body was hidden, and that Williams might be unable to find it because "[t]hey are predicting several inches of snow for tonight." The detective reminded Williams that, "you yourself are the only person that knows where this little girl's body is." The detective opined "that the parents of this little girl should be entitled to a Christian burial for the little girl who was snatched away from them on Christmas Eve and murdered." Finally the detective said, "I do not want you to answer me. I don't want to discuss it any further. Just think about it as we're riding down the road." After thinking about it for 100 miles, Williams made incriminating statements and ultimately led the police to the body.

Law: The Supreme Court reversed the murder conviction. The violation of a *Massiah* right would require three elements: the attachment of the *Massiah* right to counsel, the failure of police to obtain a waiver of *Massiah* rights, and finally, the prohibited act of "deliberate elicitation" (equivalent to improper "interrogation") by police that produced incriminating statements. First, the Sixth Amendment right to counsel attached to Williams because the Davenport arraignment qualified as the commencement of "adversarial judicial proceedings." Second, the detective engaged in "deliberate elicitation" by making the "Christian burial speech," which was viewed as "tantamount to interrogation." *Brewer* implicitly recognized that express questioning was unnecessary for a finding of "deliberate elicitation." Third, there was no affirmative evidence of waiver before the "Christian burial speech" was delivered. Instead, Williams stated several times that he would talk to police after seeing his lawyer in Des Moines. Evidence also negated waiver, namely the defendant's "consistent reliance on the advice of counsel in dealing with the authorities," and his "express and implicit assertions of his right to counsel."

4. Deliberate Elicitation under the Sixth Amendment

Although *Rhode Island v. Innis*, 446 U.S. 291 (1980) observed that the concepts of "deliberate elicitation" under the Sixth Amendment and "interrogation" under the Fifth Amendment are "not necessarily interchangeable, since the policies underlying the two constitutional protections are quite distinct," the Court has not identified any differences between *Miranda* "interrogation" and "deliberate elicitation" under *Massiah* where defendants are questioned by police. If there is no deliberate elicitation by the police or police agents, there is no Sixth Amendment violation.

a. Questioning by Undercover Police Agents

One distinction between the Fifth and Sixth Amendments relates to the treatment of persons who are questioned by undercover police agents. The *Perkins* exception to *Miranda* allows the "interrogation" by undercover agents of persons in custody. *Massiah* does not allow the "deliberate elicitation" of incriminating statements by undercover agents from persons who possess Sixth Amendment rights, regardless of whether the suspect is incarcerated at the time of questioning.

(1) Deliberate Elicitation by Active Undercover Agent

"Deliberate elicitation" exists when an undercover informant-cellmate is not a "passive listener" and joins as an active participant in conversations with the defendant despite instructions to the informant "not to initiate any conversation with [the defendant] about the crime." *United States v. Henry*, 447 U.S. 264 (1980).

(2) No Deliberate Elicitation by Passive Undercover Agent

By contrast, the Court held that "deliberate elicitation" did not occur in *Kuhlmann v. Wilson*, 477 U.S. 436 (1986), when a police informant placed in the defendant's cell merely listened to a defendant's statements, without making comments to stimulate incriminating conversations; this behavior does not resemble police interrogation and does not need to be barred by the Sixth Amendment. *Kuhlmann* decided that the defendant failed to prove that "the police and their informant took some action, beyond merely listening, that was designed deliberately to elicit incriminating remarks."

(3) Deliberate Elicitation Statements Permitted for Offenses Other Than Crime to Which Sixth Amendment Had Attached

Maine v. Moulton, 474 U.S. 159 (1985) affirmed that statements obtained through "deliberate elicitation" by undercover agents are admissible at a trial on offenses *other than* the crime to which the Sixth Amendment right already has attached. The *Moulton* majority described this scope limitation as a "sensible solution" to the problem of the government's need to continue to investigate "the suspected criminal activities" of indicted defendants. *Moulton* also clarified the scope of *Massiah*'s prohibition of "deliberate elicitation" by holding that it applies to situations where the defendant initiates a meeting with an undercover police agent as well as to situations where the agent initiates a meeting with the defendant.

5. Waiver

The waiver standards for *Miranda* and *Massiah* rights are so similar that the *Miranda* warnings serve as an adequate method for informing a defendant of *Massiah* rights. In *Patterson v. Illinois*, 487 U.S. 285 (1988), the Court interpreted the "key inquiry" in both "formulations" of waiver to be whether "the accused, who waived his Sixth Amendment rights during postindictment questioning, [was] made sufficiently aware of his right to have counsel present during the questioning, and of the possible consequences of a decision to forgo the aid of counsel?"

a. Patterson v. Illinois

Facts: The defendant in *Patterson* had received *Miranda* warnings after arrest and had not invoked the right to counsel. After being informed of his indictment and given another set of *Miranda* warnings, he signed a waiver and made statements that were held to be admissible.

Law: Patterson's post-indictment *Miranda* warnings adequately informed him of both his *Miranda* and *Massiah* rights, and his *Miranda* waiver adequately established a *Massiah* waiver as well. The third and fourth *Miranda* "right-to-counsel" warnings satisfied the first component of the *Patterson* waiver formulation to make the defendant "sufficiently aware of his right to have counsel present during the questioning." *Patterson* also determined that the second *Miranda* warning about the consequences of waiving the privilege described implicitly "the possible consequences of a decision to forgo the aid of counsel."

6. Invocation of Sixth Amendment Right

When a defendant in custody is questioned by police after the initiation of "adversary judicial proceedings," she may invoke her Sixth Amendment right to counsel. *Montejo v. Louisiana*, 556 U.S. 728 (2009). The legal consequences of that invocation depend on whether the suspect is in custody when the invocation occurs. Regardless of whether a suspect has requested or obtained a lawyer, the police may question and seek a waiver from any suspect who is *not* in custody. "When a defendant is not in custody, he is in control, and need only shut his door or walk away to avoid police badgering."

a. Invocation by Suspect in Custody

If the suspect is in custody and the police have informed him of his *Miranda* rights, a suspect who asserts his right to counsel is protected by the *Edwards v. Arizona* rules previously discussed. If the suspect re-initiates contact with the police following the invocation, the police may seek a waiver and question him.

b. Invocation Applies Only to Charged Offenses

The invocation of the Sixth Amendment right to counsel applies only to the offenses that have been charged. (The previously discussed Fifth Amendment rule in *Arizona v. Roberson,* 486 U.S. 675 (1988) prohibits the questioning of arrestees for *any* crime, once the *Miranda* right to counsel is invoked.) The Court refused to extend *Roberson* to the Sixth

Amendment context in *McNeil v. Wisconsin*, 501 U.S. 171 (1991). Because the Sixth Amendment right to counsel is "offense-specific," the invocation of the *Massiah* right to counsel cannot bar questioning for crimes to which the Sixth Amendment has not yet attached, i.e., where adversary proceedings have not begun for that charge.

(1) What Constitutes "Charged Offenses"?

The police may continue to question a defendant who invokes the Sixth Amendment right to counsel about offenses that have not been charged, as long as those uncharged offenses do not constitute the "same offense" in the Double Jeopardy context. *Texas v. Cobb*, 532 U.S. 162 (2001). Reaffirming the concept that the Sixth Amendment right to counsel is "offense specific," the Court formally adopted the definition of "offense" from the Double Jeopardy context, i.e., "where the same act or transaction constitutes a violation of two distinct statutory provisions, the test to be applied to determine whether there are two offenses or only one, is whether each provision requires proof of a fact which the other does not." See Chapter 29.

c. Summarizing and Comparing Invocation Standards

(1) Unequivocal Invocation

As with the Fifth Amendment doctrine under *Miranda*, a defendant may invoke her right to counsel under the Sixth Amendment. The invocation must be unequivocal and the defendant must reinitiate communications with her police interrogators in order to waive her rights.

(2) Effect of Invocation

A *Massiah* defendant in custody will be provided with *Miranda* warnings that function as "*Massiah* warnings" under *Patterson v. Illinois*. If a defendant who has been to court (and therefore entitled to counsel) invokes the right to counsel in response to such warnings, both *Miranda* and *Massiah* rights to cut off police questioning will arise. The *Miranda* right will provide the defendant with the *Roberson* protection to "cut off" questioning about all crimes, while the *Massiah* right will provide the redundant *Edwards* protection with a "cut off" of questioning about only the charged crime. However, if a defendant who has been to court fails to invoke the right to counsel in response to the warnings, then neither *Miranda* nor *Massiah* "cut off" rights will arise. Only if she is in custody and affirmatively has invoked the *Massiah* right to counsel, will the *Massiah* right provide her with the *Edwards* "cut off" right.

(3) Timing and Scope of Invocation

However, there are differences between Sixth and Fifth Amendment invocations of the right to counsel.

- A Sixth Amendment invocation may occur even prior to *Miranda* warnings.
- *McNeil* indicates that the consequences of a Sixth Amendment invocation require that the police may nevertheless continue questioning the suspect about uncharged offenses.

7. Impeachment with Defective Statements

Statements taken in violation of Massiah may be used to impeach the defendant if she chooses to testify, as long as the statement was not obtained in violation of Due Process. *Kansas v. Ventris*, 556 U.S. 586 (2009). See Chapter 2 for further discussion.

E. DUE PROCESS

Before the decisions in *Miranda* and *Massiah*, the admissibility of a defendant's statement was tested by determining whether it was "voluntary." If the statement was not voluntary, then its admission into evidence was barred by the Due Process Clause of the Fourteenth Amendment. In order to be admissible in evidence today, a statement of the defendant must not only comply with the requirements of the Fifth and Sixth Amendments, it must also be voluntary to satisfy the Due Process requirements of the Fourteenth Amendment.

1. Why the Voluntariness Approach Is Still Important

Part of the reason for Due Process's vitality is that the Fifth and Sixth Amendment doctrines contain gaps that can be filled only by reference to Due Process rules. For example, *Miranda* does not apply to undercover investigations, to impeachment evidence, or to defendants who have waived their *Miranda* rights. *Massiah* is relevant only at or after the start of adversary judicial proceedings when a defendant has been charged with crimes. The most significant Due Process decisions in the post-*Miranda* era involve defendants whose confessions could not satisfy the Fifth and Sixth Amendment doctrines.

a. Impeaching Defendant with Statements Violating *Miranda*

The standard of voluntariness is also important with respect to the requirements of *Miranda*. A *Miranda* violation may make a statement inadmissible, but only in the prosecution's case-in-chief. However, the prosecution may never make use of an involuntary confession. If a confession is involuntary, the confession cannot even be used for impeachment or cross-examination. See Chapter 2 for further discussion.

2. Early Voluntariness Standards

Beginning in the 1930s, the Court's definition of coercion included police brutality, and physical and psychological torture. The early cases looked at voluntariness issues in three ways to express concern about:

- confessions of doubtful reliability,
- confessions obtained with dubious police practices, even if reliability was not a concern (due to corroborating evidence), and
- confessions where the defendant's free choice was significantly impaired even if the police did not use offensive tactics.

3. The Current Voluntariness Standard

Colorado v. Connelly, 479 U.S. 157 (1986) altered the judicial approach to these issues. The Court held that, while the defendant's free choice is relevant, its importance depends on the police having engaged in overreaching the suspect, evaluated by the totality of circumstances. The Court also stated that the issue of reliability is governed by the jurisdiction's evidentiary standards rather than by the Due Process Clause.

a. Mincey v. Arizona

The Court followed a traditional case-by-case approach to reach its finding of involuntariness in *Mincey v. Arizona*, 437 U.S. 385 (1978), where a police officer questioned a wounded arrestee for three hours while he was hospitalized in intensive care. The officer took advantage of Mincey's physical trauma by interrogating him in his vulnerable state, and also repeatedly violated *Miranda* by ignoring Mincey's three invocations of his right to counsel. Thus, the evidence of involuntariness consisted of police "relentlessness," of *Miranda* violations, and of Mincey's condition. Building from earlier cases, a defendant's personal vulnerabilities thus continued to be a foundation for a Due Process violation.

b. Colorado v. Connelly

Facts: The police knew only that the defendant had been a patient in several mental hospitals in the past, and knew nothing of the auditory hallucinations that led him to confess; his symptoms of mental illness were manifested only the day after his confession during an interview with appointed counsel.

Law: The Court concluded that "coercive police activity is a necessary predicate to a finding of involuntariness." Even if a defendant's free will is "overborne" by his mental illness, this does not make his confession involuntary in the absence of police coercion. At the time of his unsolicited confession, the defendant was given *Miranda* warnings, and "appeared to understand fully the nature of his acts" when he waived his rights. By contrast, if the police had politely questioned Connelly knowing that he was insane, they would have overreached him by exploiting a situation even though they did not create it.

c. Arizona v. Fulminante

Facts: In *Arizona v. Fulminante*, 499 U.S. 279 (1991), a group of inmates had threatened the defendant with violence because of rumors that he had killed a child. The informant-inmate played the role of sheriff, bargaining for Fulminante's confession with a promise to provide protection from the other inmates.

Law: This promise carried weight, in the Court's view, because the informant-inmate was pretending to be an organized crime figure. The majority treated this promise as a "credible threat of violence," and viewed the defendant's situation as a frightening one. His failure to confess to the informant could have resulted in attacks by the threatening inmates. Affirming the totality-of-the-circumstances analysis, the Court treated the defendant's individual frailties as relevant to its finding that the confession was involuntary.

4. Police Conduct Must Overbear the Suspect's Will

As noted in *Fulminante*, direct or implied promises by the police must be evaluated as part of the totality of circumstances. The promise must have been "sufficiently compelling to overbear the suspect's will in light of . . . circumstances." The Court has found Due Process violations when

- the police threatened to take the suspect's wife into custody if he did not confess, *Rogers v. Richmond*, 365 U.S. 534 (1961), and

- the suspect was told that she could lose her welfare payments and custody of her children if she did not confess, *Lynumn v. Illinois*, 372 U.S. 528 (1963).

5. Suspect's Personal Characteristics

Assuming that the police have engaged in overreaching conduct, courts also consider the particular characteristics of the suspect in order to evaluate his ability to resist the coercive police pressure. The common factors present in both traditional voluntariness as well as *Miranda* waiver cases include the defendant's:

- age, *Fare v. Michael C.*, 442 U.S. 707 (1979), *Gallegos v. Colorado*, 370 U.S. 49 (1962);
- intelligence, *Culombe v. Connecticut*, 367 U.S. 568 (1961);
- education, *Crooker v. California*, 357 U.S. 433 (1958);
- criminal experience, *Haynes v. Washington*, 373 U.S. 503 (1963);
- mental condition, *Colorado v. Connelly*;
- intoxication on alcohol or drugs, *Townsend v. Sain*, 372 U.S. 293 (1963);
- physical injury and coercion, *Brown v. Mississippi*, 297 U.S. 278 (1936); *Payne v. Arkansas*, 356 U.S. 560 (1958);
- threats to others, see *Lynumn v. Illinois*, 372 U.S. 528 (1963);
- length of interrogation and number of interrogators, *Reck v. Pate*, 367 U.S. 433 (1961), *Ashcraft v. Tennessee*, 322 U.S. 143 (1944); and
- other circumstances, e.g., *Spano v. New York*, 360 U.S. 315 (1959) ("false friend" technique condemned).

CHAPTER 14

IDENTIFICATION PROCEDURES

A. IDENTIFICATION PROCEDURES

An eyewitness to a crime may be asked to testify that, prior to trial, she has identified the defendant as the perpetrator of the crime. The event at which such an identification was made is frequently called a "pretrial confrontation." In addition, a police officer who was present at the pretrial confrontation may be asked to testify at trial about the pretrial identification made by the eyewitness, i.e., an out-of-court identification. In addition, the eyewitness may be asked to identify the defendant in the presence of the jury. Such testimony is known as an "in-court identification."

1. Dangers from Confrontations

The dangers inherent in pretrial confrontations were noted in *United States v. Wade*, 388 U.S. 218 (1967): "mistaken identification," "the degree of suggestion inherent in the manner in which the prosecution presents the suspect to witnesses for pretrial identification," and the unlikelihood that anyone who has picked the accused in a line-up will retract the identification later.

2. Challenging Testimony About Out-of-Court Confrontations

There are three possible and distinct challenges to an out-of-court identification.

- The identification may be challenged on the basis of the Sixth Amendment right to counsel rule requiring that defense counsel be present at the pretrial confrontation.
- The out-of-court identification may be challenged on the basis of Fourteenth Amendment Due Process, which excludes a pretrial confrontation between the defendant and the eyewitness that is so impermissibly suggestive as to give rise to a very substantial likelihood of misidentification.

- The third challenge is based on the idea that the identification is the fruit of an earlier illegality such as an illegal arrest, search or confession. Similar to a Sixth Amendment violation, the in-court identification will be permitted only if intervening events served to remove the prior "taint." See Chapter 2.

If the defendant is successful in either of the first two challenges, proof of the out-of-court identification is not admissible in the prosecution's case-in-chief. Furthermore, if there were a Sixth Amendment violation, an in-court identification by the eyewitness will not be permitted by the court unless the prosecution has proven by clear and convincing evidence that the in-court identification is not tainted by the out-of-court identification. Similarly, a Fourteenth Amendment violation which meets the Due Process test will also exclude an in-court identification, but the prosecution is not permitted to "rehabilitate" the identification.

3. Applicable Legal Theories for Challenging Identification Procedures

	Pre-Adversary Proceedings	At or after Adversary Proceedings Begin
Physical Identification	Due process	Sixth Amendment Due process
Photo Identification	Due process	Due process

B. SIXTH AMENDMENT RIGHT TO COUNSEL

If adversary judicial criminal proceedings have been initiated against the defendant, the defendant is entitled to have a lawyer present at any State-sponsored pretrial confrontation with an eyewitness. The reason for this rule is two-fold:

- to enable the defense at trial to challenge the credibility of the witness' in-court identification, and
- to eliminate unfair pretrial confrontations resulting in identifications of persons as the perpetrators of crime when, in fact, they are not. *Kirby v. Illinois*, 406 U.S. 682 (1972).

IDENTIFICATION PROCEDURES

1. When "Adversary Judicial Criminal Proceedings" Begin

In *Rothgery v. Gillespie County*, 554 U.S. 191 (2008), the Court identified a short list of events that qualify a "adversary judicial proceedings," including initial appearance, formal charge, preliminary hearing, indictment or information. The defendant's initial appearance triggers the attachment of the right to counsel because at such a proceeding the "government's commitment to prosecute is sufficiently concrete" and the "accusation [there] prompts arraignment and restriction on the accused's liberty to facilitate the prosecution."

a. Identification at Preliminary Hearing Is Illegal

In *Moore v. Illinois*, 429 U.S. 1061 (1977), an identification of an unindicted and unrepresented defendant at a preliminary hearing was held to violate the defendant's Sixth Amendment right to counsel.

2. Exclusion of Testimony About Pretrial Identifications without Counsel

When defense counsel can show that the pretrial confrontation required the presence of defense counsel because adversary judicial criminal proceedings had begun but defense counsel had not been present, any proof that an identification was made of the defendant at that pretrial confrontation is not admissible. *United States v. Wade*. Even if the confrontation was fairly conducted, the out-of-court identification must still be excluded. This is a *per se* exclusionary rule in that no proof of an out-of-court identification may be presented to the jury. *Gilbert v. California*, 388 U.S. 263 (1967). It is possible, however, that the witness may still be able to identify the defendant in court.

a. Scope of Exclusion

Neither the eyewitness who made the identification nor persons who were present when the eyewitness made the identification, may testify in court that an out-of-court identification was made. The type of pretrial identification where the right to counsel applies includes any lineup, showup, walk-in or other type of identification process where the defendant is required to submit to a physical identification. *Moore v. Illinois*.

b. No Right to Counsel at Photographic Display

There is no right to have counsel present when an eyewitness is shown a photographic display which includes a photo of the defendant, even where the photographic display is shown to the eyewitness after the defendant has been indicted. *United States v. Ash*, 413 U.S. 300 (1973).

3. Waiver of Right to Counsel

The accused may waive the right to have counsel present at a pretrial confrontation. The waiver must be knowing, voluntary and probably will be deemed more effective if it is written.

4. Exclusion of In-Court Identification Testimony

Once the court determines that there was a Sixth Amendment violation in the pretrial confrontation, testimony about that confrontation is excluded from evidence. At this point the "fruit of the poisonous tree" doctrine of *Wong Sun v. United States*, 371 U.S. 471 (1963) becomes applicable to the in-court identification. See Chapter 2.

a. Independent Source for the In-Court Identification

The court will not permit the eyewitness to make even an in-court identification unless the prosecution can demonstrate, by "clear and convincing evidence," that the in-court identification will be based on the eyewitness's observations of the defendant at the crime scene and not at the pretrial confrontation. *United States v. Wade*. Certain factors should be considered by the court in deciding whether to permit the eyewitnesses to make an in-court identification. These factors are the same as those set forth in *Neil v. Biggers*, discussed below.

5. Role of Counsel at Lineup

While the defendant has the right to counsel at a pretrial lineup after a formal charge, the role of counsel is unclear. The majority opinion in *United States v. Wade* implies that, at best, defense counsel might point out unfair aspects of the lineup to the police, and suggest corrective measures. *Wade* also stresses that counsel's presence puts her in a position to decide whether it is tactically wise to bring out the details of the lineup identification in order to cast doubt on an in-court identification.

C. DUE PROCESS

A second challenge to an out-of-court identification is based on the Due Process Clause of the Fourteenth Amendment which is separate and distinct from the Sixth Amendment approach. A Due Process violation may exist even where the pretrial confrontation took place before adversary judicial criminal proceedings began, and it may also exist even though defense counsel was present at the pretrial confrontation. If the pretrial confrontation violated Due Process, then proof that the defendant was identified at the pretrial confrontation is not admissible in evidence nor may the witness identify the defendant at trial. This is a *per se* exclusionary rule.

1. Stovall v. Denno

The Fourteenth Amendment challenge arises from the decision of the Supreme Court in *Stovall v. Denno*, 388 U.S. 293 (1967). The Court held that a pretrial confrontation violates the Due Process Clause if it is "unnecessarily suggestive and conducive to irreparable mistaken identification." To decide whether there was a Due Process violation, the Supreme Court held that the "totality of the circumstances" had to be considered. Showups (in which the eyewitness is shown a single suspect) were condemned in *Stovall*.

a. The Nature of a Suggestive Lineup

In the companion case of *United States v. Wade*, the Court stated that a suggestive physical lineup would occur when

> all in the lineup but the suspect were known to the identifying witness, [when] the other participants in a lineup were grossly dissimilar in appearance to the suspect, [when] only the suspect was required to wear distinctive clothing which the culprit allegedly wore, [when] the witness is told by the police that they have caught the culprit after which the defendant is brought before the witness alone or is viewed in jail, [when] the suspect is pointed out before or during a lineup, and [when] the participants in the lineup are asked to try on an article of clothing which fits only the suspect.

b. State Action Required

One of the purposes of the Due Process approach to identifications is to deter improper police behavior so that the police would fear that their conduct actions would lead to the exclusion of identifications as unreliable. Private confrontations therefore do not give rise to the same considerations as police-initiated identifications. Consequently, the suggestibility of confrontations is not a legitimate issue unless there is State action involved.

2. Due Process Violation Requires Reliability

In its decision in *Neil v. Biggers*, 409 U.S. 188 (1972), the Court changed the test for determining whether a pretrial confrontation violated Due Process. In *Neil*, the Court held that even though a showup may have been suggestive, the in-court and out-of-court identifications are still admissible where there was "no substantial likelihood of misidentification." An out-of-court identification was held not to violate Due Process if under the totality of the circumstances the identification was reliable. Whereas the emphasis in *Stovall* was on the suggestiveness of the confrontation, *Neil* focused on the reliability of the identification itself.

a. The Timeliness of the *Neil* Decision

Because the trial in *Neil* preceded the date of the decision of the Supreme Court in *Stovall*, the exclusionary rule of *Stovall* was not applicable to the case and there was some uncertainty whether the test should be applied to pretrial confrontations which took place after *Stovall*. This uncertainty ended in 1977, when the Supreme Court held in *Manson v. Brathwaite*, 432 U.S. 98 (1977) that the test previously announced in *Neil* was to be used in determining whether a pretrial confrontation violated Due Process even when the identification took place after the date of the decision in *Stovall*.

b. Relationship between Suggestiveness and Reliability

As *Stovall*, *Neil*, and *Manson* indicate, the suggestiveness of an identification procedure by itself does not require suppression of eyewitness evidence, even if the suggestiveness increases the risk of mistaken identification. Suggestiveness becomes problematic only when it is unnecessary, which in turn requires an analysis of all the reliability factors. A preliminary judicial inquiry into the reliability of an eyewitness identification is mandated *only* when the identification was procured under unnecessarily suggestive circumstances arranged by law enforcement. *Perry v. New Hampshire*, 132 S.Ct. 716 (2012).

(1) Perry v. New Hampshire

In *Perry*, the Court used the *Stovall* facts to explain the application of its new test: there was no due process violation even though the defendant was the only person presented to the victim for identification in a show-up in the victim's hospital room and even though the defendant was presented wearing handcuffs, because the suggestive show-up used was necessary: the victim was the only eyewitness and it was not certain that she would survive long enough for the identification to be conducted under less suggestive conditions.

(2) Other Methods for Testing Reliability

Perry also described alternative devices to test reliability, regardless of whether law enforcement has engaged in improper activity: expert testimony, "counsel at postindictment lineups, vigorous cross-examination, protective rules of evidence [FRE 403], and jury instructions on both the fallibility of eyewitness identification and the requirement that guilt be proved beyond a reasonable doubt."

3. Due Process Standard for Admitting Out-of-Court Identification

There is a two-part test to determine whether trial testimony about an *out-of-court* identification violates Due Process. The first part of the test is: whether the pretrial identification procedure was unnecessarily suggestive? If it was not, then proof about the out-of-court identification is admissible at trial. However, if the pretrial confrontation was unnecessarily suggestive, the second part of the test requires the trial court to assess whether that suggestiveness created a very substantial likelihood of misidentification at trial. In other words, was the suggestiveness outweighed by the reliability of the identification, based on the five *Neil* factors, discussed below? Expert eyewitness identification testimony is admissible on problems like cross-racial identification, identification after long delays or under stress, and psychological phenomena.

4. Due Process Standard for Admitting In-Court Identification

For an *in-court* identification by a witness at trial, if the unnecessary suggestiveness of the pretrial confrontation outweighed the reliability of that identification, a trial court must ask itself whether the out-of-court identification was so unnecessarily suggestive as to create a very substantial likelihood of *irreparable* misidentification by the witness in the trial court, using the same *Neil* factors, discussed below.

5. Types of Identification Procedures Under Due Process

a. Showup Identification

A "showup" is a one-on-one presentation of the suspect to the eyewitness. An identification based upon a showup is constitutionally acceptable if under the totality of circumstances it does not present a substantial likelihood of irreparable misidentification. For example, in *Stovall*, a hospital room showup of a suspect to a witness for identification was justified by the risk that the witness might not otherwise have an opportunity to make a proper identification, so long as the totality of circumstances did not suggest a substantial risk of misidentification. Even a station house showup may be upheld under the totality of the circumstances.

b. Photograph Identification

Photographic lineups are used when the suspect is not yet in custody. Even when a suspect is in custody, a physical identification may not be conducted because physical lineups are usually difficult to manage. It is sometimes difficult to find persons of the same race, age, height and weight who are willing to participate in a lineup. Furthermore, facilities to conduct a physical lineup are not always available. For these reasons it is far easier for the police to conduct a photographic lineup.

(1) Types of Photo Lineups

Photo lineups are of several types. The first is the single photo of a suspect which is shown to a witness. The second type of photo lineup is like a physical lineup where the police have a suspect in mind and display her photograph with several additional photos of similar looking people. The third use of photographs is the so-called "mug book" view. Here, the police have no firm suspect in mind and show a victim a book of many mug shots with the hope that the culprit is among the photos. The most circumspect identification is where a single photo is presented. Where this occurs, courts assume suggestiveness and then inquire as to the totality of circumstances to see if the identification was otherwise reliable. *Manson v. Brathwaite*.

c. Physical Lineup

A physical lineup consists of presenting the defendant and several other similar looking persons to the witness for identification. This is to be distinguished from the showup where only the defendant is presented. In determining the validity of a lineup, the question is one of unnecessary suggestiveness. If the lineup is suggestive, then the *Neil* five-factor test must be considered in determining whether an identification is reliable despite suggestiveness in the identification procedure.

6. Determining Unnecessary Suggestiveness

To determine the possible unnecessary suggestiveness of a lineup, the courts have looked to numerous factors such as the circumstances of the lineup, matters which occur prior to the lineup, and the number of lineups. *See Foster v. California*, 394 U.S. 440 (1969).

7. Determining the Reliability of Identification

Where the proof shows unnecessary suggestiveness in the physical or photo lineup or in the showup, the court must then inquire from the totality of the circumstances whether the resulting identification was reliable. The courts look to numerous elements included within the five-factor *Neil* test to determine reliability.

a. Opportunity to View

The first reliability factor is the opportunity of the witness to view the criminal at the time of the crime. Here, the courts look to the lighting conditions, the amount of time for the view, and the degree of view by the victim.

b. Witness's Degree of Attention

The second factor is the witness's degree of attention. Courts consider whether the witness was a victim or casual observer as well as the training of the witness.

c. Prior Description of Criminal

The third reliability factor is the accuracy of the witness's prior description of the criminal. Somewhat related is any discrepancy between the defendant's appearance at the time of the crime and at the time of identification.

d. Witness's Certainty

The fourth factor is the level of certainty of the witness at the confrontation. The level can run from nonexistent to virtual certainty. It is highly relevant whether the witness has previously observed other physical or photographic displays and has or has not picked out someone else.

e. Time between Crime and Confrontation

The final reliability factor is the time between the crime and confrontation. This is also a variable, but the other factors appear to be given more weight.

8. Additional Reliability Factors

Other courts have recognized additional concerns to include in the evaluation of an identification's reliability. For example in *State v. Henderson*, 27 A.3d 872 (N.J. 2011), the New Jersey Supreme Court added the following reliability considerations to the *Neil* list:

- Stress: Did the event involve a high level of stress?
- Weapon focus: Was a visible weapon used during a crime of short duration?

- Duration: How much time did the witness have to observe the event?
- Distance and Lighting: How close were the witness and perpetrator? What were the lighting conditions at the time?
- Witness Characteristics: Was the witness under the influence of alcohol or drugs? Was age a relevant factor under the circumstances of the case?
- Characteristics of Perpetrator: Was the culprit wearing a disguise? Did the suspect have different facial features at the time of the identification?
- Memory decay: How much time elapsed between the crime and the identification?
- Race-bias: Does the case involve a cross-racial identification?

9. Burden of Proof

a. Prosecution Must Prove Circumstances of Pretrial Identification

The prosecution appears to have the burden of proving the circumstances under which a pretrial identification was made. The court must first determine whether the pretrial identification was impermissibly suggestive and, if it was, the court must then decide whether the procedure created a substantial risk of irreparable misidentification. *Simmons v. United States*, 390 U.S. 377 (1968).

b. Prosecution Must Prove That In-Court Identification Is Not Tainted

If the pretrial identification is suppressed, the prosecution must establish by clear and convincing evidence that any in-court identification is not tainted. *Moore v. Illinois*. Even if this is established to the satisfaction of the trial court, the defendant may still challenge the identification procedures before the jury. *See Watkins v. Sowders*, 449 U.S. 341 (1981).

CHAPTER 15

PRETRIAL RELEASE

A. GENERAL PRINCIPLES

A defendant's pretrial release from custody typically is in exchange for a pledge of something of value that the defendant will appear in court and will comply with the court's orders in a pending criminal case. Bail is the Anglo-American criminal justice system's answer to the issue of what is to be done with an accused, whose guilt has not been proven, during the time period between arrest and trial.

1. The Purposes of the Pretrial Release Decision

The use of bail is to accommodate the individual defendant's interest in pretrial liberty (consistent with the presumption of innocence) and society's interest in assuring that the accused is present for trial. In each case a judge decides whether to grant pretrial release, and if so, what monetary amount and/or conditions of release will assure the defendant's presence. Instead of focusing on whether an accused could afford an amount imposed by the court, defense counsel emphasize that the facts of the defendant's situation demonstrate that the likelihood of appearance at trial would be increased by the imposition of nonfinancial conditions of release, e.g., that the accused not commit another crime during release, or the use of a curfew.

a. Ensuring Defendant's Presence at Trial

The traditional rationale for the use of money bail and/or conditions imposed upon defendants pending trial is to ensure their appearance at trial. During the 1960s and 1970s, "bail reform" meant that nonmonetary information increasingly became an important part of the pretrial release process, in order:

- to avoid discrimination against accused persons who could not afford the monetary amount imposed for their release, and
- to reemphasize the rationale of appearing for trial.

b. Protecting Public Safety

By the 1980s, the nature of "bail reform" changed. Increasing numbers of persons released pending trial were committing crimes—either against specific witnesses in the pending case, against others in the community, or both. The nature of reform began to focus not on whether an accused would appear in court, but on whether and under what circumstances an accused legally could be detained and not released at all pending trial in order to prevent the accused from committing crimes.

2. The Constitutional and Statutory Standards

a. Eighth Amendment Prohibition Against Excessive Bail

The Eighth Amendment states that "[e]xcessive bail shall not be required." *U.S. Const. amend. VIII.* While state constitutions at least implicitly recognize the fundamental nature of the right to bail by their express prohibition of excessive bail, *United States v. Salerno,* 481 U.S. 739 (1987) found that there is no federal constitutional right to bail, holding that the Eighth Amendment is not violated by the use of pretrial detention due to the dangerousness of the defendant.

b. What Is "Excessive Bail"?

The Eighth Amendment prohibition on excessive bail has traditionally been interpreted to prohibit a judge from setting bail higher than reasonably necessary to assure a defendant's appearance at trial. In *Stack v. Boyle*, 342 U.S. 1 (1951), the Court stated that bail set at a figure higher than an amount reasonably calculated to fulfill the purpose of assuring that the defendant will stand trial and, if found guilty, submit to sentence, is excessive under the Eighth Amendment. That prohibition is not directly applicable to the states, but a comparable standard may be required as a matter of Due Process of law and Equal Protection of the laws.

c. Fourteenth Amendment Equal Protection and Due Process

The Equal Protection approach to the issue of excessive bail is that the defendant is being detained solely on account of the economic inability to afford the monetary bail set by the court. The Due Process argument is two-fold: 1) the defendant is being punished without a trial and in violation of the presumption of innocence; and 2) continued pretrial detention prevents adequate trial preparation and could result in ineffective assistance of counsel.

d. State Constitutions

A judge's discretion to make pretrial release available is limited, because most state constitutions expressly guarantee pretrial release before conviction. Constitutional concerns about pretrial release concentrate on whether there is a right to release and, if so, whether the conditions of release are excessive. A judge's discretion in deciding whether to grant or deny release is not absolute, however. Several limited legislative or judicial exceptions exist to the general right of pretrial release. For example, in states that use capital punishment, the denial of bail occurs in capital cases if the prosecution can show that the proof is evident or the presumption is great that the defendant is guilty. The denial of bail also is authorized in cases in which a prisoner has escaped and is recaptured, as well as in cases of criminal contempt.

e. Statutory Qualifications

In response to a growing problem of defendants committing crimes during the period of pretrial release, some state legislatures and the Congress have enacted laws prohibiting pretrial release due to a defendant's criminal history or to the nature of the pending charges. See 18 U.S.C. §§ 3141–3150 for the Bail Reform Act of 1984.

B. TYPES OF RELEASE

1. Why the Type of Release Matters

The types of release described below may be strategically important both to the defendant and to the outcome of the defendant's case.

a. Defendant's Perspective

From the defendant's perspective, personal recognizance or an unsecured bond is the least intrusive because the defendant does not have to expend any funds that could be used for other purposes such as hiring defense counsel.

b. Prosecutor's Perspective

Prosecutors are likely to consent to these types of release for defendants who are charged with minor property crimes and have extensive ties to the community. Otherwise, prosecutors will prefer that a defendant be required to post at least 10% of the cash bond that is set.

c. Judicial Perspective

Judges may want to emphasize the importance of the bail that is set by requiring the defendant to post the entire amount of the cash bond.

d. Consequences of Defendant's Failure to Appear

If the defendant does not appear as scheduled for a court appearance, the defendant will be obligated to pay the full amount of the unsecured appearance bond, the cash bond, or the percentage bond. The defendant also may be prosecuted for the offense of bail jumping. If a young defendant does not appear for court, the loyal parents face the possibility of losing their home (as well as their child).

2. Categories of Release

a. Personal Recognizance

Upon acquiring control over the person of the defendant, the court allows the defendant to be at liberty in return for a written promise to return and to comply with the orders of the court throughout the case. Because the defendant has this duty anyway and the only thing the defendant pledges is the surrender of liberty which is already under the power of the court, a release on personal recognizance is not a contractual undertaking for a consideration in the classical sense. Release on personal recognizance has long been a practice in the courts for good reason. If the defendant has ties to the community (e.g., the time she has resided in the current place, with whom the defendant lives, full-time or part-time employment, economic dependence on another person or on governmental compensation, ownership of property in the area, possession of a telephone line, etc.) and will likely return to court without the imposition of liability or other conditions, the requirement of a monetary amount for release accomplishes none of the purposes of bail but may impose a substantial hardship upon persons of limited resources. Perhaps for this reason, the law not only acknowledges the power of the courts to release a defendant on recognizance but indeed mandates a defendant to release in this manner (as, for example, in the federal Bail Reform Act) unless the court finds that something more is required to insure the defendant's appearance in court.

b. Unsecured Bond

An unsecured bond is a pledge by the defendant alone to be liable for a specified sum if the defendant should breach a material condition of release. Unlike the release on personal recognizance, the unsecured bond is a contractual undertaking in the true sense. The unsecured bond undoubtedly has an advantage over the release on personal recognizance in the case of a defendant of means who has long-term ties to the community. The bond gives the defendant a financial stake in obeying the orders of the court and thus helps insure the defendant's appearance. On the other hand, the theoretical civil liability of an indigent defendant upon an unsecured bond provides no real stake in the proceedings.

c. Release on Nonfinancial Conditions

The court has the power to attach nonfinancial conditions to the basic bond agreement that the defendant will be responsive to the orders of the court. Courts often impose the least onerous conditions that will insure the presence of the defendant in court. Such conditions may include but are not limited to placing the defendant in the custody of a person or agency, placing restrictions upon travel, association or place of abode, or requiring confinement during specified hours.

d. Cash Bond

A defendant may be released from custody by depositing cash in the amount of the bail with the court. The money is deposited by the clerk in an escrow account, and is available for forfeiture or for application to indebtedness at the conclusion of the case. A major advantage of the cash bond is that it gives the defendant an immediate stake in the court proceedings. The cash may be returned only if upon compliance with the terms of the bond. The defendant thus faces an immediate financial loss, rather than future civil liability, as would be true under an unsecured bond. A further advantage of the cash bond is that it creates a visible asset which can be assigned to counsel for a fee.

e. Percentage Bond

Instead of a total cash bond, a court may permit the defendant to deposit only a percentage of the total amount of the bond. The money deposited is generally handled in the same way as a full cash bond. However, a portion of the deposit is kept by the court for operating costs. The percentage bond can be used effectively to permit the release from custody of defendants of limited means and still provide adequate assurance that they will appear in court.

f. Property Bond

Property bonds are often set when young defendants are arrested and their parents are willing to post the equity in their home as collateral. The pledging of real property or of stocks and bonds as security for a bail bond is permitted. The proposed pledge of security must be justified by a detailed statement filed with the court. If the pledge is of real estate, it is recorded as a lien. Upon the failure of the defendant to comply with the terms of the bond, the security may be forfeited in whole or in part. On the other hand, if the defendant is discharged from the obligations of the bond, the stocks or bonds are returned to their owner, and any lien on real estate is released.

g. Surety Bond

The court may require the bond of a defendant to be underwritten by one or more sureties. The surety is undertaking an indebtedness to insure the conduct of another. Unlike the surety offering security for a property bond, the surety on a surety bond is not required to create an encumbrance on property, and enforcement of the obligation is essentially the same as any other civil action for debt. The officers before whom bail may be taken ascertains that the amount deposited is no less than the amount fixed by the court. Surety bonds are still used in the federal system and in some state courts. The use of "bail bondsmen" lost favor in the 1970s when it became apparent that bondsmen and some defense attorneys were swapping referrals in exchange for services and kickbacks. Some states began to phase out the use of bonding companies and now leave the task of finding absent defendants to law enforcement personnel.

h. Guaranteed Arrest Bond Certificate

A guaranteed arrest bond certificate is a printed card or certificate of an association (e.g., Automobile Club) obligating the association and a licensed surety to guarantee the appearance in court of the member whose signature appears on the certificate and to pay any fine or forfeiture imposed upon the member, not to exceed a certain amount of money, e.g., five hundred dollars. The certificate may not be accepted for certain violations, such as the laws regulating motor carriers or for the offense of driving under the influence of an intoxicant.

C. RELEASE UNDER THE FEDERAL BAIL REFORM ACT

The Bail Reform Act of 1984 is an example of a legislature's attempt to regulate the pretrial release process. The Act governs release determinations in federal courts, and serves as a reference for defining various types of pretrial release. Assuming that the accused is not a flight or safety risk, the federal statute *mandates* a recognizance bond or an unsecured appearance bond. 18 U.S.C. § 3142(b).

1. Scope

In most criminal cases, the issue of pretrial release is the first important decision for a judge. Prior to the judge's involvement, a person accused of a minor offense may be released according to the terms of a release schedule providing for specific ranges of monetary bail for specific misdemeanors. If a defendant accused of a felony has been interviewed by a pretrial services official prior to the initial appearance in court, the official will have compiled a report for the judge about the defendant. The official also may have recommended a form of pretrial release for the particular defendant.

a. Pretrial Service Agency

With a view toward whether either type of release is appropriate, the pretrial service agency's activities will provide the judge with information about the defendant's assets, ties to the community, and prior record of appearing in court in response to any previous criminal charges. The official's work also will save time for the judge who probably has scores of other cases awaiting decisions. Pretrial services agencies reach a conclusion about the advisability of recommending a recognizance release by calculating points on the basis of several aforementioned factors.

b. How the Agency Does Its Work

The total pretrial release points are computed by subtracting the negative points from the positive points. For example, suppose that a total of eight verified points is necessary for a release recommendation. Positive points may be given for residency longevity in the area, employment, property ownership, and lack of recent criminal convictions. Negative points are given for recent criminal convictions, as well as the person's failure to appear when charged with criminal offenses. No one is eligible for personal recognizance if she is charged with or convicted of escape from custody, has any outstanding bench warrants issued, or has a detainer filed.

2. How the Statute Works

a. Offender and Offense Characteristics

In a felony prosecution, if a judge decides that a recognizance or unsecured release will not reasonably assure the defendant's presence at trial, the judge must decide about releasing the accused based on the facts about the specific defendant and the charges that have been brought against the defendant. Specifically, under 18 U.S.C. § 3142(g), the judge must consider several factors about the defendant and the charged offense in order to tailor conditions for release:

- the nature and circumstances of the offense, e.g., crime of violence, drug offense, family dispute,
- the weight of the evidence against the accused at this early point in the case,
- the history and characteristics of the defendant, including not only the information already discussed for a recognizance release but also the defendant's history of drug or alcohol abuse, criminal history, and physical and mental condition,
- whether the defendant was on some type of release such as parole, probation or appeal for some other offense at the time of the current offense or arrest, and
- whether conditions will reasonably assure the defendant's appearance. 18 U.S.C. § 3142(c).

b. Fact-intensive Determination

The nature of the inquiry is fact-intensive. For example, multiple defendants charged with the same offense may receive different treatment from the court in its evaluation of the release conditions that can reasonably assure each defendant's appearance at the next proceeding. Or, a series of individual defendants each charged with the same offense may receive vastly different types of release conditions—some may be released on personal recognizance, others with cash bond, and still others may be released only if a bonding company is willing to "post bond" for the defendant.

c. Conditions of Release

As the fourteen conditions in 18 U.S.C. § 3142(c)(1)(B) suggest, in addition to the boilerplate conditions of not committing additional offenses and avoiding contact with the victim or persons known to engage in criminal activities, a defendant may be instructed not to leave the jurisdiction, to find employment, comply with a curfew, contact a pretrial services official on a daily basis, etc. Pretrial release decisions are rarely subject to appeal, because most courts regard the issue of release as moot following disposition of the case by a guilty verdict, a guilty plea or an acquittal. If the court concludes that there are no conditions short of detention that will minimize either the risk of the defendant's failure to appear or the safety of the community or any person, the court may order a detention hearing.

D. PREVENTIVE DETENTION

Like some state statutory regulation of pretrial release, the Bail Reform Act of 1984 not only governs pretrial release decisions but also pretrial detention determinations. Detention is authorized if the prosecution persuades the court that the defendant poses *either* a danger to the community or to any other person *or* a danger of not appearing for trial.

1. Constitutionality of Preventive Detention

Preventive detention is constitutional, violating neither Due Process nor the Eighth Amendment, as long as that detention (1) serves a compelling state interest; (2) does not impose punishment before an adjudication of guilt; and (3) is implemented in a fair, non-arbitrary manner. *United States v. Salerno*, 481 U.S. 739 (1987).

a. Due Process

Preventive detention does not violate Due Process, because it is a regulatory measure imposed to regulate the "pressing societal problem" of defendants on pretrial release endangering the community by continuing to engage in criminal activity. The *Salerno* Court found that the Congress did not intend to punish individuals through preventive detention. The regulatory goal of preventing danger to the community outweighed a defendant's liberty interest. The legislation is limited to specific categories of individuals arrested for specific categories of serious crimes, both of which are likely to pose a danger to the community.

b. Excessive Bail

Preventive detention due to dangerousness is not "excessive bail" under the Eighth Amendment. The Court found that excessive bail applies only to cases that qualify for bail where the traditional concern is prevention of flight. Detention, on the other hand, is constitutionally permitted when a different compelling interest (the protection of the community) exists.

2. Eligibility for Detention

18 U.S.C. § 3142(f) of the Bail Reform Act provides eligibility requirements for preventive detention based on the defendant's current charge or the defendant's prior conduct. A defendant who meets these eligibility criteria poses a flight or safety risk, and the trial judge must consider whether the risk can be minimized by releasing the defendant under the conditions previously described. If the risk can be minimized, the court tailors conditions to the risks posed by the defendant. However, if the risk cannot be minimized, the court holds a detention hearing.

3. Detention Hearing

The issue at the detention hearing is whether, given the offense and offender factors already discussed, there are conditions to minimize the particular risk, or whether instead the defendant should be detained prior to trial without an opportunity for pretrial release because the accused is a safety or flight risk.

a. Burden of Proof

The government has the burden of proof by a preponderance of the evidence to show that the defendant is a flight risk. The burden of proof is on the Government to prove by clear and convincing evidence that the defendant should be detained prior to trial as a result of the defendant being a safety risk. 18 U.S.C. § 3142(f).

b. Rebuttable Presumptions

To aid the prosecution in sustaining its burden of proof at the detention hearing, the statute establishes two rebuttable presumptions upon which the prosecution may rely. However, a court may still order detention even if neither of the statutory presumptions applies.

(1) Presumption of Dangerousness

A rebuttable presumption of dangerousness arises when a judge finds that a defendant is charged with a violent crime, capital offense, or a drug felony with a maximum term of ten years imprisonment *and* within five years of the finding, the defendant was convicted of or released from prison for a similar offense. 18 U.S.C. § 3142(e).

(2) Presumption of Dangerousness and Flight

A rebuttable presumption of both dangerousness and risk of flight occurs when a defendant is charged with a drug felony with a maximum term of ten years imprisonment *or* with the use or possession of a firearm during the commission of any violent crime or drug trafficking crime, *and* there is a finding of probable cause that the defendant committed the offense charged.

CHAPTER 16

RIGHT TO COUNSEL

A. THE CONSTITUTIONAL RIGHT TO COUNSEL

In 1938, the Supreme Court held that *federal* criminal defendants who could not afford an attorney had a constitutional right to have criminal defense counsel appointed for them under the Sixth Amendment. *Johnson v. Zerbst*, 304 U.S. 458 (1938). Twenty-five years later, the Court held in *Gideon v. Wainwright*, 372 U.S. 335 (1963) that this same Sixth Amendment right to appointed criminal defense counsel is "fundamental and essential," and also applies to criminal defendants charged with a felony in State court criminal proceedings.

1. Rationale for the Right to Counsel

In *Gideon*, the Court noted that the right to counsel is a necessity due to the State's belief that attorneys are essential to the public's prosecutorial interest. Defendants who can afford attorneys hire them. A fair and impartial system can be a reality only if indigents face their accusers with the assistance of an attorney.

2. Indigent Standards for Appointing Counsel

Because the Supreme Court has never defined the meaning of "indigency" for the Sixth Amendment purposes, each jurisdiction defines this constitutional entitlement, usually by statute or court rule, in its own way.

a. How Courts Determine Whether an Accused Is Indigent

Courts consider such factors as income, property owned, outstanding obligations and the number and ages of her dependents. If the trial court finds that defendant is indigent, it must appoint counsel unless defendant waives counsel. The court may terminate the appointment upon proof that defendant is financially able to hire counsel.

b. Methods of Appointing Counsel for Indigents

Federal and State courts use different types of service-delivery systems to provide counsel for indigent defendants: public-defender programs; contract-attorney programs; or simply by means of an appropriate judge assigning the indigent's defense to a private attorney by order of appointment. Unfortunately, heavy caseloads and inadequate funding for indigent-defense programs have often produced poor representation.

c. No Choice of Appointed Counsel

Indigent defendants do not have the right to choose the defense attorney who will be appointed to represent them, *Wheat v. United States*, 486 U.S. 153 (1988), because a defendant has no right to a "meaningful attorney-client relationship" with appointed counsel. *Morris v. Slappy*, 461 U.S. 1 (1983). Nonetheless, a judge may use judicial discretion to appoint the particular attorney desired by an indigent defendant, if that attorney is available, if she is willing to accept the appointment, and if she is also agreeable to accepting the (typically low) compensation made available for provision of such appointed services. When a defendant facing a death sentence requests that his appointed counsel be replaced, the correct standard is for the trial court to use its discretion and determine whether the "interests of justice" justify the request. *Martel v. Clair*, 132 S.Ct. 1276 (2012).

3. When the Right to Appointed Counsel Attaches

Because the Sixth Amendment text applies to "all criminal prosecutions," not simply to "all criminal trials," the Supreme Court has held that the right to appointed counsel attaches prior to trial, at any "critical stage of the criminal prosecution" after the "initiation of adversary judicial criminal proceedings—whether by way of formal charge, preliminary hearing, indictment, information, or arraignment." *Kirby v. Illinois*, 406 U.S. 682 (1972).

a. Defining a Critical Stage of a Criminal Prosecution

A critical stage is when "potential substantial prejudice to the defendant's rights inheres in the particular confrontation," and "the ability of counsel [can] help avoid that prejudice." *United States v. Wade,* 388 U.S. 218 (1967). In application to specific proceedings, the Court has found the right to counsel to apply, for example, when a criminal defendant appears at her preliminary hearing, at a guilty-plea hearing, and at a sentencing proceeding.

b. Defendant's Initial Appearance In Court

Rothgery v. Gillespie County, 554 U.S. 191 (2008) strongly suggested that where a first appearance involves no more than making an *ex parte* probable cause determination, giving notice of the charges, and setting bail, that first appearance does *not* constitute a "critical stage" requiring counsel. The right to counsel attached at the first appearance "to allow for adequate representation at any critical stage before trial, as well as the trial itself."

c. "Day in Jail" Rule

Despite the Sixth Amendment's declaration that an accused has the right to the assistance of counsel, the holdings of the Supreme Court do not extend the right so far. Specifically, a person charged with and convicted of a misdemeanor but not jailed has no right to counsel. An indigent defendant charged with a misdemeanor cannot be imprisoned in jail or prison for *any* period of time unless she had the opportunity (subject to waiver) to have appointed counsel. *Argersinger v. Hamlin*, 407 U.S. 25 (1972), *Argersinger* also requires appointment of counsel for defendants who receive suspended sentences (i.e., cases where imprisonment is imposed but may or may not actually occur), rather than actual, immediate incarceration, because such a sentence may ultimately result in incarceration. *Alabama v. Shelton*, 535 U.S. 654 (2002).

d. Actual (Not Merely Potential) Imprisonment Requires Counsel

The so-called "day in jail" rule does not mean that an indigent defendant has a right to counsel when she is charged with an offense conviction of which *could* result in potential imprisonment. *Scott v. Illinois*, 440 U.S. 367 (1979).

e. Uncounseled Conviction to Enhance Later Sentence

A valid uncounseled misdemeanor conviction, with no sentence of imprisonment, may be relied upon to enhance the sentence for a subsequent offense, even one that entails imprisonment. *Nichols v. United States*, 511 U.S. 738 (1994).

4. Right to Counsel

a. During Criminal Proceedings

Once the adversary process begins, an indigent defendant has the right to counsel at the following stages of a criminal case:

- initial appearance, *Rothgery v. Gillespie County*, 554 U.S. 191 (2008)
- preliminary hearings, *Coleman v. Alabama*, 399 U.S. 1 (1970),
- arraignments, *Hamilton v. Alabama*, 368 U.S. 52 (1961),
- felony trials, *Gideon v. Wainwright*, 372 U.S. 335 (1963),
- misdemeanor trials where imprisonment is imposed, *Scott v. Illinois*, 440 U.S. 367 (1979),
- sentencing, *Mempa v. Rhay*, 389 U.S. 128 (1967), and
- appeals as a matter of right, *Douglas v. California*, 372 U.S. 353 (1963).

b. During Proceedings Related to Criminal Case

- custodial interrogation, *Miranda v. Arizona*, 384 U.S. 436 (1966), and
- post-adversarial lineups, *Kirby v. Illinois*, 406 U.S. 682 (1972).

5. No Right to Counsel

a. During Criminal Proceedings

- *ex parte Gerstein* hearings, *Gerstein v. Pugh*, 420 U.S. 103 (1975),
- grand jury proceedings, *United States v. Mandujano*, 425 U.S. 564 (1976), and
- discretionary appeals, *Ross v. Moffitt*, 417 U.S. 600 (1974).

b. During Proceedings Related to Criminal Case

- photo identification, *United States v. Ash*, 413 U.S. 300 (1973),
- handwriting samples, *Gilbert v. California*, 388 U.S. 263 (1967),
- pre-adversarial lineup or showup identification, *Kirby v. Illinois*, 406 U.S. 682 (1972),
- *habeas corpus* proceedings, and
- probation and parole hearings, *Gagnon v. Scarpelli*, 411 U.S. 778 (1973).

6. Retained Counsel

In contrast to indigent defendants, a criminal defendant who possesses sufficient financial resources to retain private criminal defense counsel has the right to be represented at trial by any criminal defense attorney she chooses to employ. *United States v. Gonzalez-Lopez*, 548 U.S. 140 (2006).

a. Minimum Requirements for Retained Counsel

Retained counsel must be admitted to practice law in the place where the criminal proceedings are to occur, unless the trial court exercises discretion to grant counsel special admission to the Bar of that jurisdiction for the limited purpose of representing defendant in that criminal proceeding ("*pro hac vice* admission"). The trial court's authority is discretionary, because "the Constitution does not require that because a lawyer has been admitted to the bar of one State, he or she must be allowed to practice in another." *Leis v. Flynt*, 439 U.S. 438 (1979).

B. WAIVER OF THE RIGHT TO COUNSEL

1. Knowing and Intelligent Waiver

A criminal defendant may waive her Sixth Amendment right to counsel, provided that such waiver is made knowingly and intelligently. A court must engage in precautions before approving a waiver of the right to counsel, i.e., the defendant has assured the court on the record that she fully understands the significance and consequences of such a waiver. *Johnson v. Zerbst*, 304 U.S. 458 (1938).

a. What Constitutes a Valid Waiver

A defendant must understand "the nature of the charges, the statutory offenses included within them, the range of allowable punishments thereunder, possible defenses to the charges and circumstances in mitigation thereof, and all other facts essential to a broad understanding of the whole matter." *Von Moltke v. Gillies*, 332 U.S. 708 (1948).

(1) Advice for a Valid Waiver

The Court also has discussed what is *not* required for a waiver. *Iowa v. Tovar*, 541 U.S. 77 (2004). To waive counsel in order to plead guilty, a defendant is *not* required to be advised by the trial court "specifically:

- . . . that 'waiving the assistance of counsel in deciding whether to plead guilty [entails] the risk that a viable defense will be overlooked', and
- . . . 'that by waiving his right to an attorney he will lose the opportunity to obtain an independent opinion

on whether, under the facts and applicable law, it is wise to plead guilty.' "

b. What Qualifies as an Intelligent Waiver

A waiver of counsel is intelligent when the defendant "knows what he is doing and his choice is made with eyes open." But the Court has rejected any "formula or script to be read to a defendant who states that he elects to proceed without counsel. The information a defendant must possess in order to make an intelligent election . . . will depend on a range of case-specific factors, including the defendant's education or sophistication, the complex or easily grasped nature of the charge, and the stage of the proceeding." *Id.*

2. Representing Oneself

Despite the "strong presumption" against defendants' waivers of the Sixth Amendment right to counsel, and despite the Supreme Court's admonition that such waivers can only be accepted if made knowingly and intelligently, the Court has nonetheless permitted defendants to waive counsel and represent themselves in appropriate circumstances.

a. *Pro Se* Representation in Federal and State Court

In 1942, the Supreme Court ruled in a federal case that "the Constitution does not force a lawyer upon a defendant. He may waive his Constitutional right to assistance of counsel. . . ." *Adams v. United States ex rel. McCann*, 317 U.S. 269 (1942). The Supreme Court later extended the right to proceed *pro se* to criminal defendants being tried in State court criminal proceedings. *Faretta v. California*, 422 U.S. 806 (1975).

b. Deciding Whether to Grant a Request for Self-Representation

Before invoking the right to self-representation, the defendant must make an unequivocal request that also must be timely. In response, the trial court holds a hearing to determine whether the defendant is competent to make the decision to completely or partially waive the right to counsel, and whether to appoint standby counsel.

c. Competency to Proceed *Pro Se*

The standard for waiving the right to counsel is the same as the competency standard for standing trial. *Godinez v. Moran*, 509 U.S. 389 (1993). *Indiana v. Edwards*, 554 U.S. 164 (2008) recognized a trial court's authority to deny *pro se* representation in cases where the defendant's mental illness interferes with self-representation, even when the defendant is mentally competent to stand trial and understands the disadvantages of self-representation described in *Faretta*. For the waiver to be intelligent and knowing, the defendant's "technical legal knowledge" is irrelevant. *Faretta*.

d. Standby Counsel

In *Faretta*, the Supreme Court acknowledged that "a State may—even over objection by the accused—appoint a 'standby counsel' to aid the accused if and when the accused requests help, and to be available to represent the accused in the event that termination of the defendant's self-representation is necessary." In *McKaskle v. Wiggins*, 465 U.S. 168 (1984), the Supreme Court offered guidance on the proper role of standby counsel. Against his periodic wishes, McKaskle's standby criminal defense attorneys made motions, questioned witnesses, and conducted colloquies with the judge. The Court recognized that "the *Faretta* right must impose some limits on the extent of standby counsel's unsolicited participation."

(1) Scope of Standby Counsel's Assistance

The *pro se* defendant is entitled to preserve actual control over the case he chooses to present to the jury. The *Faretta* right is eroded "if standby counsel's participation over the defendant's objection effectively allows counsel to make or substantially interfere with any significant tactical decisions, or to control the questioning of witnesses, or to speak instead of the defendant on any matter of importance." In addition, the trial court cannot permit standby counsel's participation without the defendant's consent "to destroy the jury's perception that the defendant is representing" herself. *Id.*

C. INEFFECTIVE ASSISTANCE OF COUNSEL

In 1932, the Supreme Court concluded that a criminal defendant's Sixth Amendment right to counsel includes the right to the "effective" assistance of counsel. *Powell v. Alabama,* 287 U.S. 45 (1932). A defendant whose counsel is unable to provide effective representation is in no better position than one who has no counsel at all.

1. Scope of the Right to Effective Assistance

The right to effective assistance applies not only to trial, but also to guilty pleas, sentencing, and a first appeal of right. Conversely, if there is no right to counsel, no right to effective assistance exists. *Pennsylvania v. Finley*, 481 U.S. 551 (1987). The standard of review applied to all types of ineffectiveness claims does not vary with the status of counsel as retained or court-appointed. *Cuyler v. Sullivan*, 446 U.S. 335 (1980). Whether a defendant has a right to effective assistance of counsel during state post conviction proceedings is still an open question after *Martinez v. Ryan*, 132 S.Ct. 1309 (2012). The remedy for ineffective assistance is automatic reversal of the conviction.

2. *Per Se* Ineffectiveness

The question that is raised when a criminal defendant claims that her defense counsel was guilty of "extrinsic ineffectiveness" is whether some factor or factors *extrinsic* to counsel's actual performance created a permissible inference of Sixth Amendment ineffectiveness. Such claims focus commonly, for example, on counsel's age, her inexperience overall or in criminal cases, disability, personal or emotional problems, alcoholism or substance abuse problems, problems with the law, insufficient preparation time, or disciplinary issues with the Bar.

a. United States v. Cronic

Facts: In *United States v. Cronic*, 466 U.S. 648 (1984), the Supreme Court established criteria for evaluating when claims of extrinsic ineffectiveness establish ineffective assistance of counsel. After appointment, Cronic's trial-inexperienced, young, real estate attorney had only twenty-five days to prepare a complicated case that the prosecution had investigated for four and one-half years and which involved thousands of documents and hundreds of checks.

Law: On appeal, the Court refused either to make an inference of ineffective assistance or to accept a hypothetical basis for finding ineffectiveness, concluding that ordinarily a defendant can "make out a claim of ineffective assistance only by pointing to specific errors made by trial counsel." Every attorney has a "first jury trial," twenty-five days is adequate preparation time, and real estate experience in a white collar crime trial may be "useful." The criteria make it almost impossible for a criminal defendant to make a successful claim.

Exception: The *Cronic* Court recognized exceptions to the general rule that ineffectiveness cannot ordinarily be established extrinsically. Besides a complete denial of counsel at a critical stage of the trial, "if counsel entirely fails to subject the prosecution's case to a meaningful adversarial testing, then there has been a denial of Sixth Amendment rights that makes the adversary process itself presumptively unreliable."

(1) Frequency of Successful *Per Se* Claims

Despite the exceptions, rarely does an appellate court reverse a conviction due to extrinsic ineffectiveness. For example, extrinsic ineffectiveness did not exist when defense counsel conceded his client's guilt of the murder with which he was charged. A "concession of . . . guilt does not rank as a 'fail[ure] to function in any meaningful sense as the Government's adversary.'" *Florida v. Nixon*, 543 U.S. 175 (2004).

b. Comparing *Per Se* Ineffectiveness v. Actual Ineffectiveness

Allegations of a defense counsel's failures at specific points (e.g., failure to introduce mitigating evidence, waiver of closing argument) may raise issues of *actual* ineffectiveness under *Strickland* (discussed in the next section), but not under *Cronic*. Similarly, a trial court's order denying a defendant the opportunity to consult with his attorney during a fifteen-minute recess taken while the defendant was continuing to testify was not extrinsic ineffective assistance because the order did not amount to "[a]ctual or constructive denial of the assistance of counsel altogether." *Perry v. Leeke*, 488 U.S. 272 (1989).

3. Actual Ineffectiveness Assessed as of the Time of Representation, Given the Government's Case

In a companion case to *Cronic*, *Strickland v. Washington*, 466 U.S. 668 (1984), the Supreme Court established the criteria for ineffective assistance of counsel when claims of *actual* episodes of ineffectiveness are alleged. Counsel's action or inaction as to a particular matter must be judged both in the context of her total representation at the time of representation and the strength of the government's evidence. In other words, the effectiveness of the representation is based on what defense counsel encountered at the time of representation, rather than evaluating in retrospect what counsel should have done.

a. *Strickland v. Washington*: Defective Performance *and* Prejudice to the Defendant

Facts: In *Strickland*, defendant Washington ignored his counsel's advice, and pleaded guilty to all offenses for which he was indicted, including three counts of first-degree murder. During Washington's guilty-plea colloquy, in which he "accepted responsibility for the crimes," the trial judge told him that he respected people who admitted their criminal responsibility "but that he was making no statement at all about his likely sentencing decision." The trial judge sentenced Washington to death at his capital sentencing hearing. Washington's counsel admitted to having done little preparation for the capital sentencing hearing: his client discussed his background, and he spoke by phone with Washington's wife and mother. He did not otherwise seek out character witnesses or request a psychiatric examination, since the conversations with his client gave no indication that Washington had psychological problems. He also decided to rely on the plea colloquy for evidence about Washington's background and his claim of emotional stress, in order to prevent the prosecutor from cross-examining defendant at a sentencing hearing. "Counsel also excluded from the sentencing hearing other evidence he thought was potentially damaging," e.g., he did not request preparation of a presentence report which would have included his client's criminal history. On the basis of the record, the Supreme Court concluded that Washington had *not* proved ineffective assistance of counsel.

Law: The Court's standard involves a fact-sensitive analysis which measures the quality and impact of counsel's representation under the circumstances of the individual case. The federal constitutional standard for reviewing an allegation of ineffective assistance of counsel involves:

- a finding of an error in counsel's performance, and
- prejudice resulting from that error which had an adverse effect on the outcome, i.e., but for counsel's unprofessional errors, a reasonable probability exists that the result of the proceeding would have been different or that the defendant would have chosen a different course of action.

Strickland v. Washington, 466 U.S. 668 (1984); *Hill v. Lockhart*, 474 U.S. 52 (1985). The two parts of the test are independent of one another. A defendant must show *both* that her defense counsel performed deficiently *and* that the deficient performance actually prejudiced her defense.

b. The Performance Prong

No one specific task by defense counsel qualifies counsel as effective. The Court rejected an approach using a "checklist for judicial evaluation of attorney performance." Instead, as the *Strickland* Court stressed, "the proper standard for attorney performance is that of reasonably effective assistance," based on the totality of circumstances. "Even the best criminal defense attorneys would not defend a particular client in the same way." Adequate performance is virtually unchallengeable, as reviewing courts are highly deferential to counsel's actions.

(1) Mandatory Duties of an Effective Counsel

The Court did define general duties that defense counsel *must* undertake on behalf of the client. "[C]ounsel owes the client a duty of loyalty, a duty to avoid conflicts of interest." Counsel has a duty to advocate the defendant's cause, to consult with the defendant on important decisions, to inform the defendant about important developments in the case, and to use her skills and knowledge in order to "render the trial a reliable adversarial testing process."

(2) Advice to Client

In *Kentucky v. Padilla*, 559 U.S. 356 (2010), the Court concluded for the first time that in order to satisfy the performance prong of Strickland, "counsel must inform her client whether his plea carries a risk of deportation." Counsel advised Padilla incorrectly that he did not have to worry about his immigration status because he had been in the country so long. The Court stated that when an area of law such as immigration law is not clear, defense counsel must at least advise the client about the risk of adverse immigration consequences. The Court stated that when the deportation consequences are clear, the duty to give correct advice is "equally clear."

(3) Comparing Counsel's Lack of Diligence v. Strategic Decisions

In general, a defendant is likely to establish incompetency where counsel's alleged errors of omissions or commission are attributable to a lack of diligence. For example, in *Evitts v. Lucey*, 469 U.S. 387 (1985), counsel's failure to follow a simple court rule about filing a statement of appeal with an appellate brief constituted ineffective assistance of counsel rather than an exercise of judgment. By contrast, *Burger v. Kemp*, 483 U.S. 776 (1987) held that counsel's strategic decision not to mount an extensive investigation into the defendant's background in search of mitigating circumstances was supported by the attorney's reasonable professional judgment which is afforded a heavy measure of deference. *Bobby v. Van Hook*, 558 U.S. 4 (2009). The crucial factor is how far a court is willing to go in assuming that counsel's actions are strategic, in accord with the general presumption of competence.

(4) Lack of Diligence for Failure to Investigate Facts

In *Wiggins v. Smith*, 539 U.S. 510 (2003), defense counsel's decision in a capital case not to expand the penalty phase investigation beyond a presentence investigation report and a social services report was below prevailing professional standards in the State at the time of trial. Standard practice included preparation of a social history report. Counsel's decision was unreasonable, because counsel knew from the social services report about defendant's alcoholic mother and his problems in foster care. A reasonably competent attorney would have known that those leads would assist in making an informed choice among possible defenses. Similarly, in *Rompilla v. Beard*, 545 U.S. 374 (2005), trial counsel failed to present mitigating evidence in the penalty phase about the defendant's childhood, mental capacity and health, and alcoholism, even when the "capital defendant's family members and the defendant himself have suggested that no mitigating evidence is available." Defense counsel was bound to make reasonable efforts to review material that she knows the prosecution will probably rely on as evidence of aggravation at the sentencing phase of trial. Accord, *Porter v. McCollum*, 558 U.S. 30 (2009) (failure to conduct any mitigation investigation, including failure to uncover and present evidence of defendant's mental health or impairment, family background, or military service "did not reflect reasonable professional judgment").

(5) Lack of Diligence for Failure to Investigate Law

In *Hinton v. Alabama*, 134 S.Ct. 1081 (2014), defense counsel's mistaken belief that state law allowed him to request and receive limited funding for expert witnesses was held to be "a quintessential example of unreasonable performance." Defense counsel's ignorance on a point of law was both fundamental to the case and could have been resolved with a cursory investigation into the relevant statutes. The case was remanded to determine whether the errors prejudiced the outcome of the trial. In *Kimmelman v. Morrison*, 477 U.S. 365 (1986), the Court held that defense counsel's failure to conduct pretrial discovery constituted deficient performance, when it was based on the mistaken belief that the prosecution takes the initiative on discovery issues.

(6) Strategic Decisions for Counsel v. Decisions for Defendant

A defendant is most likely to establish defective performance by proving a lack of diligence rather than an exercise of judgment. Decisions such as whether to investigate, whether to file a motion to dismiss the charge or to suppress evidence, whether to raise substantive defenses objecting to evidence, *Wainwright v. Sykes*, 433 U.S. 72 (1977) or selecting witnesses are for counsel because they involve matters requiring the superior ability of trained counsel in assessing strategy. Decisions within the client's control are simply described as involving "fundamental rights," such as decisions as to guilty plea, jury trial, appeal, and the defendant testifying. *Brookhart v. Janis*, 384 U.S. 1 (1966); *Jones v. Barnes*, 463 U.S. 745 (1983). While strategic choices are not regarded as constituting deficient performance, defense counsel *is* subject to an ineffectiveness claim when such choices are made after less than complete investigation. *Rompilla v. Beard* suggested, however, that a reasonable lawyer is not required to look "for a needle in a haystack, when [she] truly has reason to doubt there is any needle there."

(7) Strategic Decisions: Capital Cases

In capital cases, the Supreme Court has stated that counsel must consider both the guilt and penalty phases in determining how best to proceed. When counsel informs the defendant of the strategy counsel believes to be in the defendant's best interest and the defendant is unresponsive, counsel's strategic choice is not impeded by any blanket rule demanding the defendant's explicit consent.

(8) Strategic Decisions in *Strickland*

In *Strickland*, applying the performance prong to the facts was not difficult, because the Court viewed counsel's decisions as strategic. "Although counsel understandably felt hopeless about respondent's prospects, . . . nothing in the record indicates . . . counsel's sense of hopelessness distorted his professional judgment. Counsel's strategy choice was well within the range of professionally reasonable judgments, and the decision not to seek more character or psychological evidence than was already in hand was likewise reasonable."

(9) Other Strategic Decision Examples

If counsel's strategy satisfies the *Strickland* standard, that is the end of the matter; no tenable claim of ineffective assistance would remain.

- Defense counsel was not presumptively ineffective by failing to obtain client's express approval of a strategy to concede guilt to a capital offense and focus on urging mercy during the penalty phase. *Florida v. Nixon*, 543 U.S. 175 (2004).
- After the guilt phase, defense counsel's recommendation that the client withdraw his insanity defense was not deficient performance; the recommendation instead was based on counsel's reasonable belief that the insanity defense was doomed because medical testimony had already been rejected and the defendant's parents were unavailable to testify. *Knowles v. Mirzayance*, 556 U.S. 111 (2009).
- Defense counsel's strategic advice to his client to enter a plea to felony murder without challenging the admissibility of one confession was reasonable, because two witnesses heard another confession. *Premo v. Moore*, 131 S.Ct. 733 (2011).
- The failure to present certain forensic evidence does not constitute ineffective assistance of counsel. A competent attorney may choose a strategy that did not require using blood evidence experts since "counsel is entitled to balance limited resources in accord with effective trial tactics and strategies." Although the strategy did not work out as hoped, it was not an unreasonable or unprofessional strategy, viewed objectively. *Harrington v. Richter*, 131 S.Ct. 770 (2011).

c. The Prejudice Prong

To apply the prejudice standard, a court must assess the strength or weakness of the prosecution's case and the importance of defense counsel's error, analyzed under the law at the time of counsel's conduct. For example, if the evidence against the defendant is overwhelming, a conviction will be affirmed no matter how fundamental counsel's error. Reviewing courts examine the totality of circumstances. Recall that *Strickland* ruled that a defendant must show both that her defense counsel performed deficiently *and* that the deficient performance actually prejudiced her defense.

(1) Prejudice May Be Presumed in Three Circumstances

Prejudice may be presumed or proved by the defendant. *Strickland* stated that prejudice may be presumed when:

- there is an actual or constructive denial of counsel, such as counsel being asleep for long periods, or counsel is not a member of the bar,
- the state interferes with the lawyer's assistance, such as when there is a late appointment of counsel or the judge denies the defense counsel the right to cross-examine witnesses, and
- defense counsel is burdened by an actual conflict of interest (though it may be waived).

(2) Proof of Prejudice by the Defendant

If prejudice is not presumed, the defendant must show that trial errors prejudiced the defendant by depriving her of a fair trial. To prove prejudice, a defendant must show a reasonable probability that, but for defense counsel's errors the results of the case would have been different. "A reasonable probability is a probability sufficient to undermine confidence in the outcome." In death penalty cases, the defendant must prove that absent the error, her sentence would have been something other than death.

(3) Nature of Prejudice Proof

"[T]he 'prejudice' component of the *Strickland* test . . . focuses on the question whether counsel's deficient performance renders the result of the trial unreliable or the proceeding fundamentally unfair. Unreliability or unfairness does not result if the ineffectiveness of counsel does not deprive the defendant of any substantive or procedural right to which the law entitles him." *Lockhart v. Fretwell,* 506 U.S. 364 (1993). An argument that focuses "solely on mere outcome determination, without attention to whether the result of the proceeding was fundamentally unfair or unreliable, is defective."

(4) Prejudice in *Strickland*

As with the performance prong, *Strickland* established a presumption against a finding of prejudice. Applying the standard to the facts, the Court concluded that defendant Washington had not in fact been prejudiced by his counsel's conduct. The Court explained that "[g]iven the overwhelming aggravating factors, there is no reasonable probability that the omitted evidence would have changed the conclusion that the aggravating circumstances outweighed the mitigating circumstances and, hence, the sentence imposed."

(5) No Prejudice in Post-*Strickland* Cases

In decisions after *Strickland*, the Court has found no prejudice to exist where:

- defense counsel threatened to withdraw if his client perjured himself at trial, *Nix v. Whiteside*, 475 U.S. 157 (1986),
- defense counsel failed to make an objection in a capital sentencing hearing that would have (then) been supported by a decision that was subsequently overruled, *Lockhart v. Fretwell*,
- defense counsel failed to request a jury instruction, *Berghuis v. Thompkins*, 560 U.S. 370 (2010),
- defense counsel's closing argument at the penalty phase of a capital murder trial was weak, *Smith v. Spisak*, 558 U.S. 139 (2010),
- defense counsel failed to investigate and present sufficient mitigating evidence during the penalty phase, *Wong v. Belmontes*, 558 U.S. 15 (2009), and
- defense counsel had misinformed his client of his parole eligibility date in explaining to him the consequences of his contemplated guilty plea, *Hill v. Lockhart*, 474 U.S. 52 (1985) (but for counsel's deficient performance, there is a reasonable probability that defendant would not have pleaded guilty and would have insisted on trial).

(6) Prejudice in Post-*Strickland* Cases

In *Porter v. McCollum*, the Court found that the defendant was prejudiced by his counsel's deficient performance:

> This is not a case in which the new evidence would barely have altered the sentencing profile presented to the sentencing judge. * * * The judge and jury at Porter's original sentencing heard almost nothing that would humanize Porter or allow them to accurately gauge his moral culpability. They learned about Porter's turbulent relationship with [the victim], his crimes, and almost nothing else. Had Porter's counsel been effective, the judge and jury

> would have learned of the kind of troubled history we have declared relevant to assessing a defendant's moral culpability.

The Court has also concluded that defense counsel's failure to object to a legal error that affected the calculation of a prison sentence, resulting in additional incarceration, is clearly prejudicial to a defendant. "[A]ny amount of actual jail time has Sixth Amendment significance." *Glover v. United States*, 531 U.S. 198 (2001).

d. Ineffective Assistance in Plea Bargaining

Defense counsel may be ineffective if she fails to properly inform the defendant of a beneficial plea agreement offered by the prosecution, or if she incorrectly advises the defendant on the state of the law, leading the defendant to reject a beneficial plea agreement. *Missouri v. Frye*, 132 S.Ct. 1399 (2012); *Lafler v. Cooper*, 132 S.Ct. 1376 (2012).

(1) Duty to Advise Correctly about Plea Offer

Counsel's assistance is prejudicially ineffective where the defendant shows that 1) but for the ineffective advice of counsel there is a reasonable probability that the plea offer would have been accepted and brought before the court, 2) that the court would have accepted its terms, and 3) that the conviction or sentence would have been lesser than under those imposed after trial. The proper remedy is for the prosecution to re-offer the plea and, if the defendant accepts it, the trial court can decide how to amend the original sentence.

e. Ineffective Assistance in Federal *Habeas Corpus* Proceedings

The Antiterrorism & Effective Death Penalty Act of 1996 ("AEDPA") provides, in part that "[a]n application for a writ of habeas corpus on behalf of a person in custody pursuant to the judgment of a State court shall not be granted with respect to any claim that was adjudicated on the merits in State court proceedings unless the adjudication of the claim . . . resulted in a decision that was contrary to, or involved an unreasonable application of, clearly established Federal law, as determined by the Supreme Court of the United States." 28 U.S.C. § 2254(d)(1).

(1) Unreasonable v. Incorrect State Court Decisions

The fact that a State court may have made an *incorrect* constitutional ruling on an ineffectiveness inquiry does not suffice under the AEDPA provision to entitle a defendant to *habeas corpus* relief. *Williams v. Taylor*, 529 U.S. 362 (2000). As *Williams* stated, "an *unreasonable* application of federal law is different from an *incorrect* application of federal law . . . Congress specifically used the word 'unreasonable,' and not a term like 'erroneous' or 'incorrect. . . .' " Thus, it is insufficient to conclude that counsel's decision was erroneous or incorrect; counsel's judgment must also have been unreasonable.

The Court has repeated its distinction between an unreasonable and an incorrect State court decision in *Woodford v. Visciotti*, 537 U.S. 19 (2002). The Court in *Woodford* concluded that, while the California Supreme Court may have *incorrectly* concluded that a capital defendant whose defense counsel failed to introduce available mitigating evidence was not prejudiced given the severity of the aggravating factors also in evidence, such a conclusion was not unreasonable. Again, in *Bell v. Cone*, 535 U.S. 685 (2002), the Court concluded that a Tennessee appellate court did not act unreasonably in concluding that defense counsel at a capital sentencing hearing was not ineffective:

- for failing to present sufficient mitigating evidence, and
- by waiving final argument.

(2) Incorrect *and* Unreasonable State Court Decisions

However, the Court has not always justified incorrect State court decisions relating to ineffective assistance of counsel as not unreasonable, for AEDPA purposes. For example, in *Rompilla v. Beard*, 545 U.S. 374 (2005), the Court found that the Pennsylvania Supreme Court had acted incorrectly and objectively unreasonably in concluding that defense counsel in a capital case were not ineffective when they failed to make reasonable efforts to obtain and review critical material relating to a prior conviction that counsel knew the prosecution would probably rely upon as evidence of aggravation at the sentencing phase of trial.

f. When Ineffective Assistance Claims Can Be Brought

In *Massaro v. United States*, 538 U.S. 500 (2003), the Supreme Court unanimously concluded that "an ineffective assistance of counsel claim may be brought in a collateral proceeding under

§ 2255, regardless of whether the petitioner could have raised the claim on direct appeal." The Supreme Court rule is the majority rule in the States as well. In a federal habeas proceeding, collateral proceeding counsel's ineffectiveness may excuse the procedural default. *Martinez v. Ryan*, 132 S.Ct. 1309 (2012).

D. CONFLICTS OF INTEREST

The constitutional right to effective assistance of counsel entitles the defendant to the "undivided loyalty" of counsel. The defendant loses the full benefit of the adversary process when counsel's decisions are influenced by obligations owed to other persons. The situation producing the most frequent conflict claims is the representation of more than one codefendant by the same attorney.

1. Conflicts When One Attorney Represents Multiple Defendants

Although codefendants may start out with identical concerns, a divergence of interests may develop at almost every point in the progress of the litigation. One defendant may receive an attractive plea bargain, while the other may receive a less attractive offer or none at all. Co-defendants may raise conflicting defenses, or have different levels of culpability, which may affect defense counsel's closing arguments or approach to sentencing. One defendant's decision to testify may highlight the lack of testimony from the other.

2. Conflicts When One Attorney Represents a Defendant and a Third Party

A lawyer also may be placed in a conflict situation when there is a professional relationship with both the defendant and a third party who has some interest in the case. Or, a conflict arises when someone with an interest in the case pays the legal fees of defense counsel. *Wood v. Georgia*, 450 U.S. 261 (1981).

3. Conflict of Interest as Ineffective Assistance of Counsel

A criminal defense attorney's conflict of interest by representing a defendant can amount to ineffective assistance of counsel. *Glasser v. United States*, 315 U.S. 60 (1942). When there are conflicting interests, "the evil . . . is in what the advocate finds himself compelled to *refrain* from doing, not only at trial but also as to possible pretrial plea negotiations and in the sentencing process." *Holloway v. Arkansas*, 435 U.S. 475 (1978) (emphasis in original).

a. Holloway v. Arkansas

Facts: Trial counsel in *Holloway* was appointed to represent three co-defendants, each of whom was charged with one count of robbery and two counts of rape, arising out of the same criminal episode. Prior to and during trial, counsel's motions for the appointment of separate counsel for the three co-defendants were denied. Although counsel stated that he would not be able to cross-examine the co-defendants on behalf of other co-defendants due to his conflict of interest, the court instructed him to simply put his clients on the stand and let each tell his story without any questioning at all. Defense counsel followed the trial court's instruction.

Law: The Supreme Court reversed, agreeing that the defendants' Sixth Amendment rights to conflict-free counsel were violated, but the Court did not establish a *per se* rule against joint representation. However, the Court stated that, when trial counsel timely alerts the trial court to the risk of a conflict of interest, the trial judge must "either . . . appoint separate counsel or . . . take adequate steps to ascertain whether the risk was too remote to warrant separate counsel."

(1) Remoteness-of-Risk Hearing

When faced with a possible conflict, a court can hold a remoteness-of-risk hearing to determine whether or not the risk of conflict is real. The hearing must include a thorough, meaningful inquiry into any and all potential for conflict. Where counsel raises the potential conflict issue but the trial court fails to either grant the motion or hold a hearing, reversal of a defendant's conviction is "automatic," even without a showing of prejudice. *Mickens v. Taylor*, 535 U.S. 162 (2002).

b. Cuyler v. Sullivan

Cuyler v. Sullivan, 446 U.S. 335 (1980) addressed the issue left open in *Holloway*: when does an alleged conflict of interest, *not* raised prior to or during trial, amount to ineffective assistance of counsel? The Court concluded that the timing of when the issue was raised required a different approach. "[A] defendant who raised no objection at trial must demonstrate that an actual conflict of interest adversely affected his lawyer's performance." In *Holloway*, the Court had concluded that a trial court's failure to adequately respond to defense counsel's motion for separate counsel automatically required a reversal of the defendant's conviction without showing, as *Cuyler* required, that "an actual conflict of interest" existed which "adversely affected [the defendant's] lawyer's performance."

c. Waiver of Conflict of Interest

A trial judge has the discretion to refuse waivers of conflicts of interest in both actual and potential conflict situations, without violating a defendant's Sixth Amendment right to her counsel of choice. In *Wheat v. United States*, 486 U.S. 153 (1988), the Court held that a defendant may waive a conflict of interest with regard to her attorney and a trial judge must recognize a presumption in favor of a defendant's counsel of choice, but that presumption may be overcome by a demonstration of either an actual conflict or a serious potential for conflict.

E. THE *GRIFFIN-DOUGLAS* DOCTRINE

The government has a constitutional obligation to redress the consequences of indigency in the criminal justice system.

1. Indigent's Right to Transcript and an Appeal

In *Griffin v. Illinois*, 351 U.S. 12 (1956), the Supreme Court concluded that an indigent prisoner appealing from his conviction in State court had a Fourteenth Amendment right (under both the Due Process and Equal Protection Clauses) to a free trial transcript where such transcripts were a practical necessity for success on appeal. In *Douglas v. California*, 372 U.S. 353 (1963), the Court held that indigent defendants convicted at trial have a Fourteenth Amendment right (again, under both the Due Process and Equal Protection Clauses) to the assistance of counsel on a first appeal where the State has granted them the right to appeal (contrasted with situations where appeal is only discretionary).

2. Adequate Opportunity for Indigents to Present Claims Fairly

In *Ross v. Moffitt*, 417 U.S. 600 (1974), the Court changed the focus of the standard. Instead of focusing on whether an indigent defendant could obtain the same sort of services that a non-indigent defendant could or would receive, the Court concluded that "[t]he duty of the State under our cases is not to duplicate the legal arsenal that may be privately retained by a criminal defendant in a continuing effort to reverse his conviction, but only to assure the indigent defendant an adequate opportunity to present his claims fairly."

a. No Right to Counsel for Discretionary Appeals

Applying this less-demanding test, *Ross* ruled that indigents undertaking State discretionary appeals (as opposed to appeals as of right) and appeals to the United States Supreme Court (which are also discretionary and not of right) are not entitled to the appointment of counsel, even though a non-indigent would have the resources and, hence, could retain such appellate counsel. "Unfairness results only if indigents are singled out by the State and denied meaningful access to the appellate system because of their poverty."

b. Right to Counsel for Appeals of Right

Halbert v. Michigan, 545 U.S. 605 (2005) held that there is a constitutional entitlement to appointed counsel on an appeal as of right when a convicted defendant has pleaded guilty or *nolo contendere*. "Halbert's case is framed by two prior decisions of this Court concerning State-funded appellate counsel, *Douglas* and *Ross*. The question before us is essentially one of classification: With which of those decisions should the instant case be aligned? We hold that *Douglas* provides the controlling instruction." "[I]ndigent defendants pursuing first-tier review in the Court of Appeals are generally ill equipped to represent themselves."

c. Meaningful Access to Expert Services

Other post-*Ross* Supreme Court decisions raising *Griffin-Douglas* doctrine issues have focused on what constitutes "meaningful access to justice." For example, in *Ake v. Oklahoma*, 470 U.S. 68 (1985), the Court held that an accused was entitled to have access to a psychiatrist and a psychiatric examination when raising an insanity defense. Such services are a necessary, basic tool when the issue of sanity is raised at trial or sentencing. Thus, indigent defendants have the right to expert services under *Griffin-Douglas* in order to have "an adequate opportunity to present their claims fairly within the adversary system."

d. Transcripts

Indigent defendants also have constitutional rights relating to transcripts and filing fees, involving:

- a trial transcript for use in a collateral attack upon a conviction, *United States v. MacCollom*, 426 U.S. 317 (1976),
- a transcript of a *habeas corpus* proceeding to be used on appeal from a denial of *habeas* relief, cf. *Eskridge v. Washington State Bd. of Prison Terms and Paroles*, 357 U.S. 214 (1958), or in filing a second *habeas* petition, *Gardner v. California*, 393 U.S. 367 (1969), and

- a transcript of a preliminary hearing to be used in preparing for trial, *Roberts v. LaVallee*, 389 U.S. 40 (1967).

Transcripts for use on appeal have generally been required where they were the usual and preferable means of presenting a claim of the type asserted by the indigent defendant. Where the grounds of appeal make out a colorable need for a transcript, the burden is on the prosecution to establish the adequacy of a less costly alternative. *Mayer v. City of Chicago*, 404 U.S. 189 (1971). Courts will look more closely at alternatives, however, where a transcript is no longer available through no fault of the prosecution. *Norvell v. Illinois*, 373 U.S. 420 (1963).

e. Filing Fees

Filing fees for appeals and post-conviction proceedings do not apply to indigent defendants. *Burns v. Ohio*, 360 U.S. 252 (1959); *Smith v. Bennett*, 365 U.S. 708 (1961).

CHAPTER 17

PROSECUTORIAL DISCRETION

A. GENERAL PRINCIPLES

Courts recognize that prosecutors have broad discretion about when and whether to pursue criminal prosecutions.

1. Separation of Powers

The separation of powers doctrine is said to require broad discretion because prosecutors act as the executive branch's delegate to help discharge a chief executive's constitutional responsibility to "take Care that the Laws be faithfully executed." *United States v. Armstrong*, 517 U.S. 456 (1996).

2. Judicial Intervention Inappropriate

Courts also have repeatedly noted that "the decision to prosecute is particularly ill-suited to judicial review." *Wayte v. United States*, 470 U.S. 598 (1985). Prosecutors possess *discretion* (rather than an obligation or duty) to investigate and to prosecute and are not legally bound to do either, i.e., they cannot be judicially ordered to investigate or prosecute anyone. Among the discretionary factors that are not readily susceptible to judicial analysis are "the strength of the case, the prosecution's general deterrence value, the Government's enforcement priorities, and the case's relationship to the Government's overall enforcement plan."

a. No Interference with Decision Not to Prosecute

Courts generally refuse to interfere with prosecutors' decisions *not* to prosecute, based upon the separation of powers doctrine. Courts believe that judicial review of the decision (not) to prosecute would be unwise, even under an abuse of discretion standard. See, e.g., *Inmates of Attica Correctional Facility v. Rockefeller*, 477 F.2d 375 (2d Cir. 1973).

b. Discretion to Select from among Multiple Statutes

When a person's conduct violates more than one criminal statute, the prosecution may charge him under either statute without regard to the severity of the penalty, as long as the prosecution is not discriminatory. *United States v. Batchelder*, 442 U.S. 114 (1979).

3. Probable Cause as a Lynchpin to Discretionary Challenges

As long as probable cause exists to believe that the defendant has committed an offense, the prosecutor has broad but not unfettered discretion about whether to investigate or prosecute, which charges to bring as well as when and where to bring them, and whether to seek immunity or a plea bargain.

4. Pretrial Diversion as Alternative to Prosecution

In addition to a significant measure of discretion with respect to who and when to investigate and who, what, and whether to charge, prosecutors in many jurisdictions also possess substantial authority to divert accused persons into pretrial diversion programs that have been established in their jurisdiction. Typically, the successful completion by an accused of the conditions set upon entry into the diversion program results in the dismissal of whatever pending charges that led to the diversion. Failure to meet those diversion requirements results in the prosecutor's office taking the defendant to trial.

B. SELECTIVE PROSECUTION

As a result of the wide discretion prosecutors have in prosecuting criminal cases, the potential exists for abuse of that discretion. Misuse of that discretion especially occurs when a prosecutor purposefully chooses to pursue a case because of the defendant's race, religion, or other arbitrary classification. Such prosecutorial conduct, known as selective prosecution, denies an accused equal protection of the law. A defendant asserts selective prosecution as a constitutional defense; the claim is not relevant to the defendant's guilt or innocence, but instead is addressed to a constitutional defect in the institution of the prosecution, without regard to the specific facts of the charged offense.

1. Yick Wo v. Hopkins

In *Yick Wo v. Hopkins*, 118 U.S. 356 (1886), the Supreme Court first recognized that equal protection standards apply to prosecution of crimes. Wo, a Chinese native, operated a laundry business in San Francisco for more than twenty years. When he attempted to renew his license to do business, the board of fire wardens told him that was violating a new city ordinance prohibiting laundries in wooden buildings. He was arrested after refusing to pay the fine for violating the ordinance. When the Supreme Court decided in his favor, it noted that of the 320 San Francisco laundries, 310 were housed in wooden buildings. Of 280 people who applied for licenses from the fire warden, all 80 non-Chinese received a license, even though their laundries were in wooden structures, and all 200 Chinese applicants were denied. The Court held that Yick Wo's imprisonment was illegal, inferring that the ordinance's intent was discriminate against the Chinese and not simply to regulate the laundries for the public safety.

2. Oyler v. Boles

The conscious exercise of some selectivity in criminal enforcement is not in and of itself a constitutional violation. In *Oyler v. Boles*, 368 U.S. 448 (1962), the defendant moved for dismissal of the recidivist charges against him because others who could have been charged with being a recidivist were not. The Court held that it was unknown whether the prosecution's failure to bring recidivist charges against others who were eligible was due to a lack of knowledge of their prior offenses or the result of a deliberate policy of prosecuting only certain persons. As a result, the Court refused to find an equal protection violation. Even if available statistics do imply a policy of selective enforcement, the selectivity must be deliberately based upon an arbitrary classification such as race or religion.

3. Wayte v. United States

In *Wayte v. United States*, 470 U.S. 598 (1985), the defendant refused to register for the military draft and also wrote letters to various officials indicating his intent to continue his course of conduct. The United States Department of Justice obtained the names of those who had either reported themselves or were reported by others for failing to comply with draft registration requirements. Following repeated attempts to persuade him to register, Wayte and a dozen others were prosecuted for willfully failing to register. Unlike Wayte, approximately 670,000 other non-registrants were never indicted. The Supreme Court required a two-part showing for a successful selective prosecution challenge. First, a defendant must establish that similarly situated persons who broke the same law were not prosecuted. Second, the defendant must show that the prosecution's decision to prosecute was based on impermissible considerations, such as race, religion, political beliefs, or the desire to prevent the exercise of other constitutional rights.

4. United States v. Armstrong

The Supreme Court has defined a stringent standard for a defendant to satisfy in order to merit discovery and an evidentiary hearing on the selective prosecution claim. In *United States v. Armstrong*, 517 U.S. 456 (1996), the defendants were charged with cocaine offenses and sought governmental disclosure about the race of defendants in cocaine prosecutions for the previous three years. The government must grant discovery to the defendant only after he has made a preliminary showing of "some evidence" that similarly situated persons of a different race were not prosecuted for the same offense.

5. United States v. Bass

The summary reversal in *United States v. Bass*, 536 U.S. 862 (2002) illustrates the weight of the defendant's burden, even in death penalty cases. The lower court had held that the defendant had made a credible showing that similarly situated persons of a different race were not prosecuted based on nationwide statistics showing that the "United States charges blacks with a death-eligible offense more than twice as often as it charges whites" and that the United States "enters into plea bargains more frequently with whites than it does with blacks." The Court's response was that:

> Even assuming that the [*United States v.*] *Armstrong* requirement can be satisfied by a nationwide showing (as opposed to a showing regarding the record of the decisionmakers in respondent's case), raw statistics regarding overall charges say nothing about charges brought against similarly situated defendants. And the statistics regarding plea bargains are even less relevant, since respondent was offered a plea bargain but declined it. Under *Armstrong*, therefore, because respondent failed to submit relevant evidence that similarly situated persons were treated differently, he was not entitled to discovery.

6. Elements of a Selective Prosecution Claim

To prove an Equal Protection violation from selective prosecution, a defendant must prove that

- others similarly situated are generally not prosecuted for the offense,
- selection of the defendant was intentional or purposeful, and
- the claimant's selection was based on an "arbitrary classification," e.g., race or religion.

The success of proving this claim is rare because of the need to show both a discriminatory purpose and a discriminatory effect on the defendant. It is very difficult to obtain information about a comparison of non-prosecuted offenders known to the police to show disparate treatment. Further, because prosecutors do not maintain records of the motives behind their charging decision, circumstantial evidence through statistical disparities (if they exist) is the sole method for proving discriminatory intent.

C. VINDICTIVE PROSECUTION

Due Process prohibits a prosecutor from using criminal charging discretion to penalize a defendant's proper exercise of constitutional or statutory rights, e.g., reindicting a defendant on more serious charges as retaliation.

1. Actual Vindictiveness

The Court in *Blackledge v. Perry*, 417 U.S. 21 (1974), held that a prosecutor violated Due Process by bringing a more serious charge against a defendant who pursued a statutory right of appeal from a conviction on a lesser charge for the same conduct. While the defendant did not show actual vindictiveness by the government, the Court found a Due Process violation due to the possibility that the increased punishment posed a "realistic likelihood of vindictiveness." The prosecution was unable to identify specific reasons for increasing the charges.

2. Presumption of Vindictivenss

A presumption of vindictiveness arises when a defendant is reindicted following a trial, but only if there has been an increase in the number or severity of the charges.

a. Thigpen v. Roberts

In *Thigpen v. Roberts*, 468 U.S. 27 (1984), the defendant was convicted in a district court of several misdemeanors growing out of an automobile accident where a passenger was killed. The defendant appealed, but while his appeal was pending he was indicted for manslaughter. Although a second prosecutor was responsible for the increased charge, the Court had little trouble finding that such an increased charge was prohibited by the possibility of vindictive action by the state in response to the defendant's exercise of his right to appeal.

b. North Carolina v. Pearce

In *North Carolina v. Pearce*, 395 U.S. 711 (1969), after the defendant's conviction was reversed on appeal, on retrial for the same charge, he received a longer sentence. On these facts, the court as in *Blackledge* applied a rebuttable presumption of vindictiveness. The Court then identified objective information to rebut the presumption and to justify the increased sentence, i.e., the additional time was the result of information unavailable to the judge at the time of the first sentencing proceeding.

c. **Rebutting the Presumption**

A presumption of vindictiveness also can be rebutted by objective evidence that the prosecution was proper. Suppose a defendant initially is convicted of assaulting a victim but the conviction is reversed. Because it was impossible to prosecute the defendant for the victim's death until the person died, the defendant may be charged with homicide if the victim died after the start of the defendant's first trial.

d. **Presumptions Usually Do Not Arise in a Pretrial Context**

In *Bordenkircher v. Hayes*, 434 U.S. 357 (1978), the Court found no presumption of vindictiveness from explicit threats made by a prosecutor during plea negotiations that he would seek more serious charges against a defendant who rejected the prosecutor's offer. Likewise, no presumption existed when added charges were filed after the defendant requested a jury trial. *United States v. Goodwin*, 457 U.S. 368 (1982). In *Goodwin*, the Court explained that because defendants commonly invoke procedural rights before trial that impose some burden on prosecutors, e.g., jury trial demands, it is unrealistic to presume that the prosecutor's response is an effort to penalize the defendant.

3. **Elements of a Vindictive Prosecution Claim**

To win a vindictive prosecution claim under Due Process, a defendant has the burden of showing either actual vindictiveness by the prosecution, or the facts give rise to a rebuttable presumption of vindictiveness.

CHAPTER 18

PRELIMINARY PROCEEDINGS

A. INITIAL APPEARANCE

Most jurisdictions require that the arresting officer bring the accused before the nearest available judge without unnecessary delay. *See, e.g.*, Fed.R.Crim.P. 5(a)(1)(A). The period of delay in federal courts usually is measured from the time the accused is arrested on federal charges.

1. Delay between Arrest and Initial Appearance

An unreasonable delay between arrest and the initial appearance may violate due process. In evaluating an allegation of unreasonable delay, courts analyze the amount of time that passes as well as how and why the delay occurred. Confessions obtained during periods of unnecessary delay *prior to* the initial appearance may be inadmissible. For example, under 18 U.S.C. § 3501, delay is one of several statutory factors considered to decide whether a confession was given voluntarily during the period of unreasonable delay. See Chapter 13.

2. Federal Rules Governing Initial Appearance

Federal Rule of Criminal Procedure 5(d) is typical of most rules setting the procedures for the initial appearance in court. At the initial appearance, the judge must inform the accused about:

- the charges,
- the right to remain silent,
- the right to request or retain an attorney,
- the fact that any statement made may be used against the accused,
- the general circumstances under which the accused may secure pretrial release,

- the right to a preliminary hearing, and
- a reasonable time to consult with an attorney.

a. Proving Identity of the Accused

While the court is not required to conduct any preliminary inquiry, it is customary and desirable at the outset that the court determines that the correct person is before the court. The court should inquire whether the person is actually the person who is accused of committing the offense charged and that the defendant is actually before the court, either in person or by counsel.

b. Notice to the Defendant of the Charge

The court must give the defendant notice of the charges by informing the defendant in open court, by either reading or stating the substance of the charge. A defendant who has counsel prior to the initial appearance normally waives a formal reading of the charge, because counsel has previously ascertained the charge.

c. Entering a Plea to the Charge

After the court gives the accused notice of the charges, procedural rules may require that the court ask the accused to enter a plea to those charges. Most defendants enter a plea of not guilty to felony charges, in part because defense counsel knows little about the charges at the time. If a defendant chooses to stand mute, the court, by rule or its inherent authority, enters a not guilty plea on the defendant's behalf.

d. Counsel for the Accused at the Preliminary Hearing

Under rules like Fed.R.Crim.P. 44(a), the right of the accused to be represented by counsel begins at the initial appearance. However, the initial appearance is not regarded as a "critical stage" at which the Sixth Amendment grants a right to counsel. On the other hand, an accused's request for counsel at the initial appearance precludes subsequent police interrogation about the charged offense but does not prohibit police interrogation about other crimes. See Chapter 13.

B. *GERSTEIN* HEARING

In *Gerstein v. Pugh*, 420 U.S. 103 (1975), the Supreme Court held that "the Fourth Amendment requires a judicial determination of probable cause as a prerequisite to extended restraint of liberty following arrest." A *Gerstein* hearing is necessary prior to the continued detention of an accused who was arrested *without* either a prior judicial determination of probable cause such as an arrest warrant or the return of a grand jury indictment. Because of the similarity between the timing of the initial appearance and the timing of a *Gerstein* hearing following a warrantless arrest, a judge may conduct both proceedings at the time of the initial appearance.

1. Nature of the *Gerstein* Hearing

The only issue determined at a *Gerstein* hearing is whether there is probable cause to believe that the accused committed an offense. *Gerstein* requires a "fair and reliable determination of probable cause." The hearing is nonadversarial in nature, with the accused having no right to counsel, to be present, or to question witnesses. Hearsay and written testimony are admissible. When a court determines that there is no probable cause, release from custody is the proper remedy but that finding does not foreclose a later prosecution. The absence of a prompt decision about further detention does not invalidate a later conviction.

2. Timing of the *Gerstein* Hearing

The determination of probable cause ordinarily must occur within 48 hours of the warrantless arrest. *County of Riverside v. McLaughlin*, 500 U.S. 44 (1991). This is not to say that the probable cause determination in a particular case passes constitutional muster simply because it is provided within 48 hours. Such a hearing may nonetheless violate *Gerstein* if the arrested individual can prove that the probable cause determination was delayed unreasonably.

3. Burden Shifts When the Initial Appearance Exceeds 48 Hours After Arrest

When the probable cause determination does not occur within 48 hours, the burden shifts to the prosecution "to demonstrate the existence of a bona fide emergency or other extraordinary circumstance. The fact that . . . it may take longer than 48 hours to consolidate pretrial proceedings does not qualify as an extraordinary circumstance. Nor, for that matter, do intervening weekends." *Gerstein.*

4. Examples of Unreasonable Delay in Conducting the *Gerstein* Hearing

Examples of unreasonable delay are delays for the purpose of gathering additional evidence to justify the arrest, a delay motivated by ill will against the arrested individual, or delay for delay's sake. In evaluating whether the delay in a particular case is unreasonable, however, courts allow a substantial degree of flexibility. Courts cannot ignore the often unavoidable delays in transporting arrested persons from one facility to another, handling late-night bookings where no magistrate is readily available, obtaining the presence of an arresting officer who may be busy processing other suspects or securing the premises of an arrest, and other practical realities.

C. PRELIMINARY HEARING

Although *Gerstein* held that there is no constitutional right to a preliminary hearing, court rules like Fed.R.Crim.P. 5.1, statutory enactments and court decisions provide for preliminary proceedings involving felony charges. If a preliminary hearing is held, the defendant has a right to the assistance of counsel at this "critical stage" of the proceedings. *Coleman v. Alabama*, 399 U.S. 1 (1970) describes several collateral benefits of counsel's participation, e.g., discovery, perpetuation of testimony.

1. Purpose of Preliminary Hearing

The traditional purpose of a preliminary hearing, or examining trial, is to determine whether there is probable cause for the defendant's charge to be presented to the grand jury or transferred to the trial docket when a grand jury is not used. The required "probable cause" is that an offense was committed and that the accused committed it. Without a finding of probable cause, the accused is released from custody.

a. Timing of Preliminary Hearing

The preliminary hearing occurs shortly after arrest. In many jurisdictions, the timing of the preliminary hearing depends on whether the defendant is still in custody at the initial appearance when the hearing is scheduled. Under Fed.R.Crim.P. 5.1(c), the hearing must occur "no later than 14 days after the initial appearance if the defendant is in custody and no later than 21 days if not in custody."

b. Nature of Preliminary Hearing

Unlike a *Gerstein* hearing or the initial appearance, the preliminary hearing is a formal, adversarial proceeding to determine probable cause. The preliminary hearing interrelates with other aspects of the criminal process—arrest, pretrial release, prosecutorial discretion, the grand jury, and the trial itself. For example, information disclosed at the preliminary hearing may influence a judicial decision to set conditions for pretrial release. Or, it may serve as a review of a prosecutor's decision to charge the accused at all or with a particular offense.

c. Scope of the Preliminary Hearing

Fed.R.Crim.P. 5.1(e) permits the defendant to cross-examine adverse witnesses at the preliminary hearing. On the other hand, because the rules of evidence usually are inapplicable at a preliminary hearing, *see, e.g.,* Fed.R.Evid. 1101(d)(3), the right of defendant's cross-examination is not as valuable because the government may introduce proof through hearsay testimony. Another effect of the inapplicability of the evidence rules is that a defendant cannot "object to evidence on the ground that it was unlawfully acquired." Fed.R.Crim.P. 5.1(e).

2. Functions of the Preliminary Hearing

The primary function of a preliminary hearing is screening cases. The prosecutor must prove that there is probable cause to believe that a crime was committed and that the defendant committed the crime charged. Preliminary hearings save accused persons from the humiliation and anxiety involved in a public prosecution.

a. Screening Cases

For the prosecution, the preliminary hearing provides an opportunity for the termination of weak or groundless charges without lengthy preparation and trial time. With the opportunity to discover the nature of its own evidence early in the prosecution, the government is able to conform the charge(s) to its proof before trial. In cases originating by a "private" complaint obtained by a citizen where no police investigation has occurred, the preliminary hearing provides an immediate forum for testing the strength of the case until further investigation can be conducted.

(1) Does the Screening Function Work?

Whether the screening function is successful depends upon:

- the extent of screening by the prosecutor before the case reaches the preliminary hearing stage,
- whether the prosecutor bypasses the preliminary hearing by first obtaining an indictment,
- whether the prosecutor at the preliminary hearing presents all the key witnesses or relies largely on the testimony of the arresting or investigating officer, and
- the practical impact of the judge's finding of no probable cause.

b. Pretrial Discovery

In practice, the preliminary hearing may provide defense counsel with a valuable discovery technique. In meeting the evidentiary standard for sending the case to the grand jury, the prosecutor necessarily provides the defense with some discovery of the prosecution's case. Defense counsel may obtain even more discovery by cross-examining the prosecution's witnesses at the hearing and by subpoenaing other potential trial witnesses to testify as defense witnesses at the hearing.

(1) Does the Discovery Function Work?

The extent of the discovery depends upon whether:

- the prosecution relies entirely upon hearsay reports and thereby limits the witnesses it presents,
- the probable cause standard is satisfied by presenting a minimal amount of testimony on each element of the offense,
- the prosecutor follows a general practice of presenting most or all of the government's case,
- the defense is limited, in both cross-examination of prosecution witnesses and in the presentation of its own witnesses, to direct rebuttal of material presented by the prosecution.

(2) Importance of Discovery

The importance to the defense of the limited discovery accessible through the preliminary hearing depends in large part on the availability of alternative discovery procedures. For example, if prior statements of prospective witnesses and the arresting officer's report are readily accessible, the hearing's discovery potential may be relatively unimportant. On the other hand, if state law and practice provide for little pretrial discovery, the preliminary hearing may serve as the primary discovery device. Similarly, if discovery does not occur until after the critical time for plea negotiations, the preliminary hearing may serve as the main discovery device for the large percentage of cases resolved by guilty pleas.

c. Future impeachment

Extensive cross-examination of prosecution witnesses at the preliminary hearing may be of value to the defense even though there is little likelihood of successfully challenging the prosecution's showing of probable cause and little to be gained by way of discovery. The skilled interrogation of witnesses can be a vital impeachment tool for use in cross-examination later at trial. Witnesses are more likely to make damaging admissions or contradictory statements at the preliminary hearing because they are less thoroughly briefed for that proceeding than they are for trial.

d. Perpetuation of Testimony

Preliminary hearing testimony traditionally has been admissible at trial as substantive evidence under the "prior testimony" exception to the hearsay rule, where the witness is unavailable to testify. The preliminary hearing perpetuates the testimony of witnesses so that it may be used even if the witness dies, disappears or otherwise becomes unavailable to testify. The Sixth Amendment Confrontation Clause permits admission of testimonial (such as prior testimony from a preliminary hearing) hearsay. Preliminary hearing testimony is admissible as substantive evidence at trial if: 1) it was given under oath; 2) the declarant is unavailable to testify at trial; and 3) a reasonable opportunity, whether exercised or not, for cross-examination on substantially the same issues was afforded the opposing party at the preliminary hearing.

e. Pretrial Release

Where conditions of pretrial release are set at the initial appearance on the basis of sketchy facts, the preliminary hearing provides the judge with the first extensive examination of the facts of the individual case. The testimony may persuade the court to modify the terms of release, or impose other terms or conditions of pretrial release. The hearing also insures that an accused who has been unjustifiably charged will be promptly released from custody.

f. Plea Bargaining

A preliminary hearing may be an "educational experience" for the defendant who is unpersuaded by defense counsel's opinion that the prosecution has such a strong case that a negotiated plea is in the defendant's best interest. Conversely, the proof at the hearing may be insufficient on the charged offenses, requires reduction of excessive charges, and thereby serves as a check against the prosecutorial practice of "overcharging" (by the number of charges and/or the severity of charges) in anticipation of plea negotiations.

3. Waiver of Preliminary Hearing

A defendant may waive a preliminary hearing. Waiver rates vary substantially among jurisdictions and sometimes exceed 50%, even in places that provide quite extensive hearings. Despite the aforementioned advantages of the hearing, defense counsel may consider a waiver where the hearing presents a substantial danger to the defense. The prosecutor will oppose a defense waiver and insist upon a hearing under special circumstances, e.g., where either there appears to be a need to perpetuate testimony because a particular witness is likely to become unavailable, or a particular witness's testimony is "shaky" and there would be some value in placing him under oath.

4. Dispositions Following Preliminary Hearing

At the close of the prosecution's case at a preliminary hearing, defense counsel should move to dismiss the charges, based upon the failure of the proof to establish:

- that an offense was committed,
- that the accused committed an offense, and
- where the offense took place, for jurisdictional purposes.

a. Probable Cause Finding

If the evidence presented at the preliminary hearing establishes probable cause to believe that the defendant has committed the offense, the court refers the case to the grand jury for possible indictment or to the court for trial following the filing of an information on any charge supported by probable cause.

b. No Probable Cause Finding

If the court does not find probable cause to refer the charge, it may nevertheless find probable cause as to some other offense. In this situation, the court may permit the prosecution to amend the charge if substantial rights of the defendant are not prejudiced. If the evidence at the preliminary hearing fails to establish probable cause, the defendant is discharged from the jurisdiction of the court. However, dismissal of the charge due to the insufficiency of the evidence at a preliminary hearing does not bar a subsequent prosecution or indictment arising out of the same transaction.

c. Plea Bargaining

Frequently, after the judge denies defense counsel's motion for a dismissal based upon the above grounds, counsel will move the court to reduce the original charge to a lesser offense, e.g., from a felony to a misdemeanor, have the accused plead guilty to the reduced charge, and thereby dispose of the case. If a court permits a guilty plea to an amended charge that is a lesser included offense of the original charge, double jeopardy probably will prevent the prosecution from later reinstituting the original charge against the accused. See Chapter 29.

5. What Completely Preempts the Preliminary Hearing?

Most courts have held that there is no necessity for a preliminary hearing after a grand jury first has returned an indictment. If the only purpose of the preliminary hearing is to determine whether there is probable cause for holding the accused to answer further, this is a logical rule because the grand jury has decided the issue of probable cause and there is no need for a court duplicate that determination. Thus, where an accused is first arrested after indictment, rather than on an arrest warrant, the accused is not entitled to a preliminary hearing. 18 U.S.C. § 3060(e) states that no preliminary hearing is required for an arrested person if at any time subsequent to the initial appearance of that person and prior to the date fixed for the preliminary examination, an indictment is returned.

CHAPTER 19

GRAND JURY PROCEEDINGS

A. INTRODUCTION

A grand jury may consider charges against an accused:

- after a preliminary hearing, regardless of whether there was a finding of probable cause at that hearing, or
- when the prosecution wants to proceed in secret, in which case the indictment issued by the grand jury may be the first occurrence in a case known by the public or by the named defendant.

1. Comparing Preliminary Hearings with Grand Jury Proceedings

a. Similarities

Both the preliminary hearing and the grand jury review test the government's case for the quantum of proof required to proceed to trial, although each usually requires only proof of probable cause (as opposed to proof beyond a reasonable doubt) that a crime has been committed and that a particular defendant committed the crime.

b. Differences

Preliminary hearings and grand jury proceedings differ, however, in important respects. For example, preliminary hearings are public, while grand jury proceedings are secret. Preliminary hearings are adversary proceedings in which the defense can challenge the prosecution's case but grand juries normally hear only the prosecution's case, and prospective defendants and defense counsel are excluded. Judges preside over preliminary hearings, while grand jury proceedings occur without judicial participation. Finally, judges determine the sufficiency of the evidence in preliminary hearings, while grand jurors (citizens of the local community) make this determination in grand jury proceedings.

2. Grand Jury History

The grand jury is an ancient common law entity that originated as a body of local residents who helped look into possible crimes. This investigative function of a grand jury has been characterized as a *sword* to root out crime. By the time of the American Revolution, however, the grand jury assumed another function—as a *shield* to protect citizens against malicious and unfounded prosecutions. The dual functions of the grand jury are considered separately in this chapter.

3. Constitutional Requirement for a Grand Jury to Indict a Defendant

In the federal system, the view that the grand jury acts as a "shield" or "screen" against improper prosecutions is embodied in the Fifth Amendment to the United States Constitution, which provides: "No person shall be held to answer for a capital, or otherwise infamous crime, unless on a presentment or indictment of a Grand Jury. . . ." The Fifth Amendment phrase "infamous crimes" is construed to apply to all felonies. However, this provision is one of the few parts of the Bill of Rights that have not been applied to the states through the Fourteenth Amendment. See Chapter 1.

a. Presentment

A presentment is a formal charging document issued by a grand jury when the prosecutor's office did not initiate the grand jury's consideration of the defendant's case.

b. Indictment

An indictment is the more common charging instrument, issued by the grand jury for cases brought to its attention by the prosecutor. Both documents have the same legal effect, with both having been approved by the grand jury.

4. State Grand Jury Practice

The Supreme Court has held that the States are not required to abide by the grand jury requirement imposed on the federal courts. *See Hurtado v. California*, 110 U.S. 516 (1884). About half the States have their own constitutional provisions or statutory requirements for grand jury indictment. The other half have either eliminated grand juries and permit prosecution by a verified document known as an information, or allow the prosecutor to choose between a grand jury indictment and an information. Even the states using grand juries may have rules like the federal rules, permitting defendants to waive the right to indictment and proceed by information. Fed.R.Crim.P. 7(b). (An information is a charge drawn up by the prosecutor and not submitted to a grand jury, although it may or may not be screened by a judicial officer).

B. SIZE AND SELECTION OF THE GRAND JURY

1. Size of Grand Jury

Grand juries in individual jurisdictions differ greatly in their composition and selection processes. At common law, the grand jury was comprised of twenty-three persons, twelve of whom had to agree in order to hand down an indictment for a criminal offense. Today, federal grand juries consist of between sixteen and twenty-three jurors, twelve of whom must agree to indict the defendant for any charge. Fed.R.Crim.P. 6(a)(1). Other jurisdictions use smaller grand juries, although all grand jury jurisdictions require that an indictment be based on the concurrence of at least a majority (rather than a unanimous view) of the grand jurors empaneled to review the charges.

2. Selecting Grand Jurors

The process of selecting grand jurors begins with the court's summoning a number of persons qualified to serve as grand jurors. The qualifications for grand jury service are set out in each jurisdiction's statutes and normally include requirements that the prospective grand juror be a citizen of the jurisdiction; reside there; be over eighteen years of age; have no felony convictions; and be a person of honesty, intelligence, and good demeanor.

a. Dismissing Grand Jurors

Purging the grand jury is the process of narrowing the number of qualified grand jurors to the number of jurors who will actually serve. The process eliminates otherwise qualified grand jurors who have legitimate excuses for not serving, such as health problems, or family obligations.

b. Defense Objection to the Selection of Grand Jurors

Generally, the courts have recognized only two proper grounds for objecting to the composition of the grand jury:

- one or more of the grand jurors failed to meet the statutory qualifications for service, or
- the process for selecting grand jurors violated constitutional standards.

Defense counsel does not participate in the selection of the grand jury. Thus, any deficiencies in the composition of the grand jury must be raised when the defendant is brought to trial (objections cannot be raised for the first time on appeal). A timely pretrial objection allows the trial court to void the indictment and compel the prosecutor to present the case to a lawfully constituted grand jury. Challenges to the composition of the grand jury are made by a motion to dismiss or quash the indictment returned by the grand jury.

3. Equal Protection Motion to Dismiss for Excluding Potential Jurors

Although the states are not required to use grand juries, if they choose to do so, the Fourteenth Amendment Equal Protection Clause requires that no state may deliberately and systematically exclude individuals because of race, gender, or national origin. *Taylor v. Louisiana*, 419 U.S. 522 (1975). The defendant challenging his own indictment does not have to be a member of the excluded group. See *Campbell v. Louisiana*, 523 U.S. 392 (1998). However, a grand jury witness cannot challenge the selection of the grand jury. *Blair v. United States*, 250 U.S. 273 (1919).

The basic elements of an Equal Protection challenge to the grand jury are the same as required for challenges to the trial jury. (The Supreme Court has not determined whether the Sixth Amendment requirement that the jury be drawn from a "fair cross-section of the community" applies to grand juries). Constitutional infirmities in the composition of a grand jury may invalidate a conviction even though the trial jury was legally constituted and guilt was established beyond a reasonable doubt. *Vasquez v. Hillery*, 474 U.S. 254 (1986).

C. SCOPE OF GRAND JURY INVESTIGATION

Once the grand jury is selected and impaneled, the judge will charge the grand jury. This charge may include the prosecution's burden of proof (probable cause) for an indictment to issue, the obligation of the grand jury to indict even if its members do not like the legal basis for the indictment, and the requirement that the grand jurors maintain the secrecy of its proceedings. Once the judge has charged the grand jury, the grand jury independently conducts its investigation of alleged criminal offenses. Unlike preliminary hearings, the judge does not preside over grand jury proceedings.

1. Prosecutor's Relation to the Grand Jury

In the absence of the judge, the prosecutor focuses the grand jury's attention by submitting an indictment, which is a written accusation of crime prepared by the prosecutor. Prosecutors exert substantial influence over the grand jury by selecting the:

- witnesses subpoenaed by the grand jury,

- the evidence heard by the grand jury,
- documents it will examine, and
- the laws to be considered by the grand jury.

The prosecutor also instructs the grand jurors about the amount of proof for a specific charge necessary to indict a defendant, as well as prepares indictments for the grand jury foreperson to sign.

2. The Grand Jury's Role After Hearing Evidence

If the grand jury agrees that the evidence indicates that a specific person has committed a crime, it will return a "true bill" of indictment upon which the accused will face trial. If the grand jury concludes that the evidence does not warrant a trial, it will return "no true bill." The grand jury's refusal to return a true bill does not preclude the prosecutor from resubmitting the indictment to another grand jury. Until the actual trial begins, double jeopardy generally does not protect the accused from undergoing successive grand jury investigations.

3. The "Runaway" Grand Jury

Although the prosecutor may direct the grand jury's attention to the submitted indictments, the prosecutor may not limit the scope of the grand jury's investigation of other crimes because grand juries are often charged to inquire into all felonies, misdemeanors and violations of penal laws committed within its jurisdiction. A grand jury that goes beyond the indictments prepared by the prosecutor and launches its own investigation is often referred to as a "runaway" grand jury. The charges returned by such a grand jury are referred to as presentments rather than indictments, because they are drawn up at the grand jury's initiative.

D. GRAND JURY SECRECY

Unlike most stages of a criminal prosecution, grand jury proceedings are conducted in secret. The Supreme Court in *United States v. Procter & Gamble Co.*, 356 U.S. 677 (1958) explained that the secrecy requirement is designed to serve five important objectives:

- to prevent the escape of those whose indictment may be contemplated,
- to insure the utmost freedom to the grand jury in its deliberations, and to prevent persons subject to indictment or their friends from importuning the grand jurors,
- to prevent subornation of perjury or tampering with the witnesses who may testify before the grand jury and later appear at the trial of those indicted by it,

- to encourage free and untrammeled disclosures by persons who have information with respect to the commission of crimes, and
- to protect the innocent accused who is exonerated from disclosure of the fact that he has been under investigation, and from the expense of standing trial where there was no probability of guilt.

1. Federal Rules About Grand Jury Secrecy

Fed.R.Crim.P. 6(e) contains complex secrecy provisions, including:

- exceptions to the general rule of secrecy,
- procedures for seeking court-approved disclosures,
- closure of judicial proceedings to avoid disclosure of grand jury matters, and
- sealing grand jury records to prevent violations of secrecy requirements.

2. Grand Jury Secrecy in the States

Grand jury secrecy requirements vary among jurisdictions, but generally the prosecutor and the grand jurors are prohibited from disclosing grand jury testimony except when authorized by court order. Most jurisdictions do not impose an obligation of secrecy upon grand jury witnesses, and the Supreme Court has held that a state may not prohibit grand jury witnesses from disclosing their own testimony after the term of the grand jury has ended. *Butterworth v. Smith*, 494 U.S. 624 (1990).

E. THE GRAND JURY AS A "SHIELD"

The grand jury protects "the innocent against hasty, malicious, and oppressive prosecutions." When a grand jury refuses to indict because there is insufficient evidence, the grand jury protects the person "from an open and public accusation of crime, and from the trouble, expense, and anxiety of a public trial." *Ex parte Bain*, 121 U.S. 1 (1887).

1. Sufficiency of the Evidence

The majority view is that the shielding function of the grand jury, while attractive rhetoric, is illusory in practice. Statistics show that grand juries rarely refuse to indict, an understandable result in light of the fact that grand jury proceedings are not adversarial. When a properly constituted grand jury returns an indictment, courts will not review the adequacy of evidence presented to a grand jury.

a. Costello v. United States

Costello v. United States, 350 U.S. 359 (1956), allowed a grand jury to rely exclusively on hearsay evidence as the basis for an indictment. Justice Burton's famous concurrence tried to leave open the possibility that an indictment may be quashed "if it is shown that the grand jury had before it no substantial or rationally persuasive evidence." *Costello*'s assumptions seem to be that prosecutors rarely seek indictments supported primarily by incompetent evidence, and that grand jurors can recognize when competent evidence for a trial of the charges is lacking.

b. United States v. Calandra

In *United States v. Calandra*, 414 U.S. 338 (1974), a grand jury witness was asked questions about records that had been seized previously and illegally in a search of his office. The Supreme Court held that the exclusionary rule cannot be invoked by a grand jury witness to prevent questions based on unconstitutionally seized evidence. The *Calandra* rule extends to evidence obtained in violation of the Fifth Amendment privilege against self-incrimination. *United States v. Blue*, 384 U.S. 251 (1966). See Chapter 2.

2. No Duty to Present Exculpatory Evidence to Federal Grand Jury

United States v. Williams, 504 U.S. 36 (1992), held that under no circumstances could a federal court dismiss an indictment on the ground that the prosecutor failed to present exculpatory evidence to the grand jury. Requiring the grand jury to weigh inculpatory and exculpatory evidence would alter the grand jury's historical role. The federal courts have no inherent authority to impose upon a prosecutor a duty to present the defendant's version of the facts in a non-adversarial setting, and such a procedure would threaten to alter the grand jury from an investigative proceeding to a mini-trial on the merits.

a. States' Rejection of *United States v. Williams*

Despite *Williams*, many state courts that have confronted the issue have imposed a duty on prosecutors to disclose exculpatory evidence to the grand jury in the unique cases where the prosecutor has evidence in her file of the target's guilt and also evidence negating guilt that is genuinely exculpatory. Most courts rejecting the *Williams* approach have also ignored the standard that imposed a requirement on prosecutors to disclose evidence that "reasonably tends to negate the guilt of the accused." Instead, most state courts have imposed a limited duty on the prosecutor to inform the grand jury of evidence which *directly* negates the guilt of the accused and is clearly exculpatory.

F. THE GRAND JURY AS A "SWORD"

The grand jury can exercise its broad investigative powers on the basis of "tips, rumors, evidence offered by the prosecutor, or [the jurors'] own personal knowledge." *United States v. Dionisio*, 410 U.S. 1 (1973). Simply on the basis of the prosecutor's speculation or the hint of suspicion about possible criminal activity, the grand jury can call anyone to testify. The breadth of a grand jury inquest is indeed large: any aspect of a person's life that might shed light on some criminal activity by somebody is within the proper scope of a grand jury investigation.

1. Grand Jury Subpoena *ad Testificandum* for Witness Testimony

Unlike suspects or witnesses who are questioned by the police, an individual subpoenaed to appear before the grand jury has no general right to remain silent or to refuse to cooperate. While compliance with a subpoena may be inconvenient and burdensome, every person has a "historically grounded obligation" to appear and give evidence before the grand jury. As such, the grand jury had no need to explain the basis for its subpoenas. In the absence of a constitutional provision such as the Fifth Amendment privilege against self-incrimination or a common law communication privilege, the witness "must appear before the grand jury to answer the questions put to him," or risk being punished for contempt. *Branzburg v. Hayes*, 408 U.S. 665 (1972).

a. Claiming the Fifth Amendment Privilege to Avoid Testifying

Any witness appearing before a grand jury may assert the Fifth Amendment privilege against self-incrimination. The privilege applies to statements that are in themselves incriminating and also to statements that "furnish a link in the chain of evidence needed to prosecute. . . ." *Hoffman v. United States*, 341 U.S. 479 (1951). Because of the multitude of federal and state criminal statutes and broad conspiracy statutes, the prosecution would have a difficult time showing that a question cannot possibly have a tendency to incriminate.

b. Fifth Amendment Rights Regarding Testimony

(1) No *Miranda* Warnings Required

A target of the investigation has no right to receive *Miranda* warnings. *United States v. Mandujano*, 425 U.S. 564 (1976).

(2) Witness Waiver of Fifth Amendment Rights

A witness who discloses any incriminating fact waives the Fifth Amendment privilege as to all details about that fact. In *Rogers v. United States*, 340 U.S. 367 (1951), a grand jury witness testified that she was the local Communist Party treasurer. She denied having custody of other records because she had turned them over to someone else but she refused to identify that person. The Supreme Court held that once the witness had disclosed incriminating information about her activities, she could not invoke the privilege against self-incrimination to avoid disclosure of the details. However, a witness can validly claim the privilege if the answer calls for information beyond the "subject" of the prior testimony. Defense attorneys must use extreme caution when advising their clients about what questions to answer during their grand jury testimony.

c. Sixth Amendments Rights Regarding the Grand Jury

The Supreme Court has indicated, though never explicitly held, that a witness before a grand jury has no Sixth Amendment right to be represented by counsel. A grand jury witness's rights may be substantially prejudiced after answering grand jury questions, but the witness may not have an attorney, appointed or retained. A witness who is unfamiliar with the law or who is the target of a probe may be particularly in need of counsel when an investigation becomes accusatory. After a witness has received immunity, the witness risks contempt for refusing to answer questions and certainly could use the advice of counsel.

d. Immunity Grants to Witnesses Who Refuse to Testify

The contempt sanction makes the grand jury subpoena particularly useful in obtaining statements from persons who will not voluntarily furnish information to the police. Even when a witness invokes the privilege against self-incrimination, the prosecutor may seek an immunity order from the judge overseeing the grand jury granting the witness immunity and thus force an answer. The common types of immunity are transactional and use/derivative use.

(1) Transactional Immunity

One type of immunity is transactional immunity, which immunizes the grand jury witness from prosecution based upon any transaction about which he is questioned and testifies.

(2) Use/Derivative Use Immunity

The immunity used by statute in federal courts is use/derivative use immunity. Its scope is narrower than transactional immunity, because the witness may still be prosecuted. However, the witness's grand jury testimony and any information derived from that testimony cannot be used against the witness in that criminal prosecution. *See, e.g.*, 18 U.S.C. § 6002 (constitutionality of this federal statute upheld in *Kastigar v. United*, 406 U.S. 441 (1972)). *Murphy v. Waterfront Commission of New York Harbor*, 378 U.S. 52 (1964) held that a state witness who has been granted use/derivative use immunity from state prosecution may not be compelled to give incriminating testimony under federal law as well as under state law.

(3) Contempt for Refusal to Testify

If an immunized witness refuses to testify, the court may issue an order to the witness requiring him to show cause why he should not be held in contempt of the court's immunity order. The witness risks being jailed for civil contempt, which he can end simply by testifying, or for criminal contempt that carries a sentence for a time certain, e.g., six months. A witness held in civil contempt cannot be jailed past the end of the current grand jury's term, but may be subject to being held in contempt again by refusing to testify to another grand jury.

(4) Perjured Testimony Trumps Any Immunity Grant

Regardless of the type of immunity order issued by the court, a witness may be prosecuted for perjury based upon his grand jury testimony.

e. Physical Characteristics Unprotected by Fifth Amendment

United States v. Dionisio, 410 U.S. 1 (1973) held that voice exemplars and handwriting samples do not invade any privacy right, because they relate to physical characteristics "constantly exposed to the public." *Dionisio* also found that a grand jury subpoena to appear is not a seizure in the Fourth Amendment sense. The Court noted the distinction between an arrest or stop and the "compulsion exerted" by a subpoena. Similarly, handwriting samples do not violate the Fifth Amendment. *United States v. Mara*, 410 U.S. 19 (1973).

2. Grand Jury Subpoena *Duces Tecum* for Documents or Objects

The grand jury also may issue a subpoena *duces tecum*, which is a command to a person to produce writings or objects described in the subpoena. Without proof of probable cause, people may be summoned to appear to bring documents or other tangible objects with them. A grand jury subpoena *duces tecum* is typically issued by a court clerk at the request of the prosecutor or the grand jury. A court does not ordinarily review the issuance of the subpoena unless a witness moves to have it quashed or modified. The subpoena is not a court order. However, unless the subpoena is withdrawn or quashed, failure to comply with a court's order to comply with a subpoena is punishable as contempt.

a. Fifth Amendment Rights and Subpoena *Duces Tecum*

The Fifth Amendment applies to a subpoena *duces tecum* when three conditions are met:

- the government seeks to "compel" compliance with its demand that the defendant produce documents or tangible items,
- the produced, compelled material is "testimonial" in nature,
- the material "incriminates" the person required to produce it. This requirement of "personal self-incrimination" implicates the "collective entity rule," discussed below.

(1) Is Compliance with the Subpoena Compelled or Voluntary?

The first requirement of compulsion is clearly met when a subpoena *duces tecum* orders the defendant to produce documents. A subpoena does not compel the preparation of a document; it compels only the production of the document. When the government seeks documents previously created by the defendant, the act of creation is deemed to have been voluntary, not compelled.

(2) Is Compliance Testimonial?

Because the Fifth Amendment prohibits compelling a person to be a witness against himself, its protections are limited to "testimonial" evidence, which requires a communicative act. The act of producing voluntarily created documents is deemed "testimonial" in a manner *unrelated* to the contents of the document. See *United States v. Doe*, 465 U.S. 605 (1984). The act of producing a document has certain testimonial (communicative) aspects, i.e., the act of production communicates that the documents exist, that they in the possession of the person producing them, and that they are the documents described in the subpoena.

(3) Is Compliance Incriminating?

As with a person's testimony, a defendant's production of existing documents within the subpoena categories can provide a prosecutor with a lead to incriminating evidence or a link in the chain of evidence needed to prosecute.

b. Motion to Quash Subpoena *Duces Tecum* Based on Fifth Amendment

A person served with a subpoena *duces tecum* may file a motion to quash the subpoena on Fifth Amendment grounds. The prosecutor can defeat the motion to quash by showing that when the subpoena issued, it was aware that the documents sought were in existence, the documents were in the recipient's possession, and were the documents described (also known as authentication) in the subpoena. If the prosecutor cannot establish all three grounds, the court will grant the subpoena recipient's motion. At that time, the prosecutor will have to decide whether to seek a judicial grant of immunity for the production of the documents, forcing the recipient to disclose the documents, although the prosecution cannot tell the fact finder their source.

c. Example of the Act of Production: *United States v. Hubbell.*

United States v. Hubbell, 530 U.S. 27 (2000) provided an application of the act of production doctrine. As part of a plea agreement, the defendant promised to provide the government with information relevant to its investigation. The prosecutor served defendant with a grand jury subpoena for the production of eleven categories of documents. After defendant appeared before the grand jury and invoked his Fifth

Amendment privilege, the prosecutor obtained an order granting him use/derivative use immunity. Defendant then produced the documents.

(1) Prosecutors Used Immunized Documents to Prosecute

The *Hubbell* prosecutor used the documents' contents in an investigation that led to defendant's indictment for other offenses. The trial court dismissed the indictment on the ground that the prosecutor's use of the subpoenaed documents violated the law on immunity, because all of the evidence he would offer against defendant at trial was derived either directly or indirectly from the testimonial aspects of the immunized act of producing the documents.

(2) Supreme Court Criticism of the Prosecutors

The Supreme Court held that under a grant of use/derivative use immunity, a prosecutor must prove that evidence proposed for use against a defendant is derived from a legitimate source wholly independent of that testimony, unless he can show prior knowledge of the existence or location of the documents. The Court noted, too, that the compelled testimony relevant in the case was not in the contents of the documents produced, but in the act of producing those documents. Even if the act of production would not be used as proof at trial, the prosecutor still had made "derivative use" of the testimonial aspect of the act of producing the documents in obtaining the indictment and preparing for trial.

d. Fifth Amendment, Subpoenas, and Whose Rights Are Violated

Couch v. United States, 409 U.S. 322 (1973) held that a taxpayer's rights were not violated by enforcing a subpoena directed to her accountant and requiring production of the taxpayer's records possessed by the accountant. Similarly, a taxpayer cannot shield her accountant's papers by giving them to her lawyer. *Fisher v. United States*, 425 U.S. 391 (1976).

e. Fifth Amendment, Subpoenas, and the Collective Entity Doctrine

A corporation or other collective entity cannot claim the Fifth Amendment privilege to avoid producing potentially incriminating documents for a grand jury's investigation. See, e.g., *Bellis v. United States*, 417 U.S. 85 (1974) (partnership); *United States v. White*, 322 U.S. 694 (1944) (unincorporated association); *Hale v. Henkel*, 201 U.S. 43 (1906) (corporation). By contrast, a corporate employee may claim Fifth Amendment protection to avoid giving oral testimony. *Curcio v. United States*, 354 U.S. 118 (1957).

(1) Braswell v. United States

Braswell v. United States, 487 U.S. 99 (1988) shows the interplay of the act of production doctrine and the collective entity rule, and exemplifies the idea that corporations and other entities have no Fifth Amendment privilege. A corporate officer was served with a subpoena to produce corporate records and to testify concerning certain corporate transactions. The Supreme Court found a distinction between an individual and a corporation, with the latter having no right to refuse to submit its books and papers for an examination.

(2) Rights of the Custodian of Corporate Records

The custodian of records of any collective entity such as a corporation cannot claim the privilege on behalf of the corporation against a compelled act of production. The custodian has no privilege as to the corporate records, even though the act of production may amount to personal incrimination. In an attempt to "protect" the custodian's Fifth Amendment rights, the Court stated that the prosecution cannot inform the jury about who produced the document (*de facto* use immunity). However, the prosecutor can still prove that the documents came from the custodian's organization, thereby allowing the trial jury to infer that the custodian knew about the documents.

f. Comparing Grand Jury Subpoenas and Trial Subpoenas

There is a distinction between challenges to a subpoena *duces tecum* for trial and a subpoena *duces tecum* in a grand jury proceeding. The distinction is grounded in how a grand jury operates compared with a trial court. In issuing a subpoena, it is presumed that a grand jury acts within the legitimate scope of its authority.

(1) Relevancy

United States v. R. Enterprises, 498 U.S. 292 (1991) held that the burden is on the recipient of the subpoena to show that there is "no reasonable possibility that the category of material the Government seeks will produce information relevant to the general subject of the grand jury's investigation." By contrast, the trial standard places the burden on the prosecution to show that the material sought is relevant to the investigation, the things sought are described with particularity, and they cover only a reasonable period of time.

(2) Reasonableness

With a grand jury subpoena, the prosecution does not have to make a threshold showing of relevancy. All that the prosecution needs to show (as a matter of sustaining a burden of production) in response to a motion to quash on reasonableness grounds is that there is a grand jury investigation, the general nature and subject matter of the investigation (without having to give, e.g., statutory citations), and that the subpoenaed documents bear a general relation to the subject matter of the investigation. The burden of proof then switches to the recipient. A blanket denial or assertion of unreasonableness by the recipient does not meet the burden of proof.

g. Required Records Exception

When the government requires records to be maintained for an administrative purpose, those records must be disclosed and neither their content nor the act of producing them is protected by the Fifth Amendment. *Shapiro v. United States*, 335 U.S. 1 (1948). Thus, if a statute requires record-keeping, a person may be penalized for failing to keep the records, for failure to turn them over, and for any untruthful information found in the records.

CHAPTER 20

CHARGING INSTRUMENT

A. INDICTMENT V. INFORMATION

An indictment is a written criminal charge made by a grand jury. An information is a similar charge made by the prosecutor. In most states, all felony criminal charges are brought by indictment or information, which is the jurisdictional document in the trial court. An indictable offense is any offense, felony or misdemeanor, for which the punishment at common law was infamous, *i.e.*, a crime punishable by imprisonment at hard labor in a penitentiary.

1. Nature of the Charge

The indictment or information is brought in the name of the sovereign, and concludes that the offense was against the peace and dignity of the sovereign. A number of other formalities are required by rules of court. A prosecutor's failure to satisfy these requirements does not deprive a court of jurisdiction. These standards are for the purpose of:

- giving the defendant adequate notice of the charge,
- protecting the defendant from surprise in the course of a criminal prosecution.

2. Notice of the Charge

The purpose of an indictment or information is to give the defendant fair notice of the charge in order to prepare a defense and to invoke double jeopardy protections if appropriate. The validity of the charge does not depend upon whether a more satisfactorily framed or more detailed document could have been returned. The document must state an offense that is within the power of the court to adjudicate.

a. Recidivist Charge

A defendant is entitled to notice of being charged as a recidivist before the trial of the underlying substantive offense. A separate indictment meets this requirement, as does a separate count in the indictment charging the substantive offense to which it refers. It is common practice for the indictment to specify the nature, time and place of the prior conviction.

B. CONTENT OF THE CHARGE

An indictment or information generally contains a caption setting forth the name of the court and the names of the parties. While the requirement of a caption is not strictly jurisdictional, it is an acceptable way of indicating jurisdictional requirements. The following describe other aspects of the typical charging instrument.

1. Parties

An indictment or information designates the parties to it. The sovereign is named as the party plaintiff. The defendant must be designated by name or other description that will permit his identification with reasonable certainty.

2. Legal Citations

Some court rules require that an indictment or information contain a citation to the applicable provision of law which the defendant is charged with violating. However, an error or omission in the citation may not be grounds for relief unless the defendant has been misled resulting in prejudice to the defendant.

3. Signature

Generally, an indictment must be signed by the foreperson of the grand jury. An information must be signed by the prosecuting attorney. However, the absence of a required signature is not a jurisdictional defect.

4. Witnesses

Court rules may require that the names of the witnesses supporting an indictment or information be listed thereon. In the case of an indictment, only the witnesses who testify before the grand jury need be recorded, while all witnesses relied upon must be enumerated on an information. The failure to endorse the names of witnesses usually does not affect the validity of the pleading.

5. Surplusage

Unnecessary allegations in an indictment or information may be disregarded as surplusage. They need not be proved by the prosecutor to sustain a conviction. Upon motion by the defendant, surplusage frequently may be stricken from the indictment or information by the court.

6. Official Forms

Official forms for an indictment or information have been adopted by many state courts. Naturally, courts regard an indictment in compliance with the official forms as a sufficient charging document.

C. DEFECTS ON THE FACE OF THE CHARGING PAPER

The indictment or information must comply with certain statutory and constitutional requirements. When failure to comport with some of those requirements is apparent by looking at the document, such errors are collectively referred to as technical defects that appear on the "face" of the indictment or information. A defense attorney, examining an indictment or information for the first time, should look for apparent physical errors in the document itself.

1. Defining the Charge

An indictment or information is sufficient if it contains a "plain, concise and definite written statement of the essential facts constituting the offense charged. . . ." Fed.R.Crim.P. 7(c)(1). The offense may be pleaded alternatively in successive counts. In the case of an information, the facts usually must be stated to be upon the knowledge, information and belief of the prosecuting attorney or to be based upon a verified complaint.

a. Examples of Charging Defects

Courts give charging instruments a "common sense" construction. States may permit the use of conclusory language, e.g., "John Doe murdered Jane Roe on January 1, 2012." The omission of details or the absence of allegations of all of the elements of the offense may generally be overlooked, especially when the indictment includes a citation to the applicable statute that was violated. Errors or variances often may be corrected by amendment at any time before verdict, and those that cannot be corrected may normally be overcome by a new indictment or information.

2. Bill of Particulars to Obtain More Information About the Charge

Defendants often file a motion for a bill of particulars to provide fuller disclosure about the nature of the charge when they perceive that a charging document is incomplete. However, the availability of a bill of particulars does not cure an indictment that omits an essential element of the offense.

a. Russell v. United States

In *Russell v. United States*, 369 U.S. 749 (1962), the indictment charged the defendant with refusing to answer questions submitted by a congressional subcommittee. However, it was not a crime to refuse to answer irrelevant questions and the charging document failed to identify the subject of the inquiry which was crucial in deciding whether the defendant was justified in refusing to answer. The Court held that the indictment's fatal defect could not be cured by providing information in a bill of particulars, because the defendant had a right to have an adequately informed grand jury return the indictment rather than have the indictment effectively rewritten by the prosecutor.

b. United States v. Resendiz-Ponce

On the other hand, *United States v. Resendiz-Ponce*, 549 U.S. 102 (2007) held that an indictment for attempted re-entry into the United States after being deported was sufficient when it identified the time and place of the defendant's criminal activity, as well as the criminal statute that was violated. Unlike *Russell*, guilt under the pertinent statute did not depend "crucially upon . . . a specific identification of fact." Because the indictment complied with Fed.R.Crim.P. 7(c)(1), an allegation in the indictment of any overt act committed during the illegal re-entry was unnecessary.

D. DUPLICITY AND MULTIPLICITY

Despite the presence of official forms for indictments in many states, prosecutors may create problems for themselves by drafting their own indictments. Constitutional problems can arise from duplicitous or multiplicitous indictments.

1. A Duplicitous Charge

A duplicitous indictment charges two or more distinct offenses in a single count. Duplicity may prevent the jury from deciding guilt or innocence on each offense separately and may obscure the specific charges on which the jury convicted the defendant. Duplicitous indictments may also violate constitutional protections such as the defendant's right to notice of the charges and the prevention of exposure to double jeopardy in a subsequent prosecution. The rule prohibiting duplicitous indictments is a rule of pleading, and the defect is therefore not fatal to the indictment, which may be corrected by requiring the prosecution to elect the basis upon which it will proceed or by making a corrective instruction to the jury. A court, however, may dismiss a duplicitous indictment that is prejudicial to the defendant.

2. A Multiplicitous Charge

A multiplicitous indictment charges a single offense in several counts. Multiplicity may violate constitutional double jeopardy provisions by resulting in multiple sentences for a single offense, or otherwise may prejudice the defendant by suggesting to the jury that the defendant committed more than one crime. If each count of the indictment requires proof of facts that the other counts do not require, the offenses are not the same, and the indictment is not multiplicitous. As with duplicitous indictments, the rule prohibiting multiplicity is a pleading rule that is not fatal to the indictment. A court, however, may require the prosecution to elect the count on which it will proceed if the multiplicity is apparent before trial. If the problem surfaces during trial, the court will instruct the jury on the proper charges and may order the prosecution to dismiss or consolidate multiplicitous counts.

a. Legislative Intent

In determining whether an indictment is multiplicitous, courts must consider whether the legislature clearly intended to provide for the possibility of multiple convictions and punishments for the same act. For example, in *United States v. Woodward*, 469 U.S. 105 (1985), the Court held that an indictment was not multiplicitous because there was no indication that Congress intended not to allow separate punishments for the distinct offenses of making false statements to a federal agency and intentionally failing to report transporting over $5,000 into the country.

E. JURISDICTIONAL REQUIREMENTS

A defendant may move to dismiss an indictment or information because of lack of jurisdiction. Jurisdiction relates to several concepts. A court may lack jurisdiction over the subject matter. Examples include a felony tried in a court of inferior jurisdiction, a crime occurring outside the state, or a federal crime tried in state court. The court may also lack jurisdiction over the defendant.

1. Jurisdiction of the Sovereign over the Offense

A state only has jurisdiction of offenses committed within its borders. Some part of the criminal transaction must have occurred within the geographical boundaries of the state.

a. Comparing Jurisdiction with Venue

This jurisdictional concept is often confused with venue that refers to the local jurisdiction of where an offense is tried. So long as a criminal act has been committed in the state, jurisdiction over the offense does not depend upon the physical presence of the actor at the time of its commission. Neither does the consummation elsewhere of a criminal act that was commenced in the state deprive that state of jurisdiction over the offense. Likewise, there is no requirement that the consequences of a criminal act occur in the state in order to give it jurisdiction over the offense. The one indispensable element necessary for jurisdiction over the offense is the commission of some portion of the criminal transaction within the physical boundaries of the state.

b. Concurrent and Exclusive Jurisdiction

The jurisdiction of a state to define and punish offenses is limited only by the state and federal constitutions. Within its constitutional sphere of action, the federal government may assert exclusive jurisdiction over particular offenses and thereby deprive the state of jurisdiction. However, unless the federal government has clearly preempted state action in this manner, jurisdiction over offenses is presumed to be within the police powers reserved to the states. Unless federal legislation regulating a particular crime manifests a clear intention to preempt the field, the offense is considered to be within the concurrent power of both sovereignties. Some offenses committed within the state are not crimes because the crime is against the federal government and not against the state. Some offenses committed in the state may be punished by both the state and federal government, e.g., bank robbery. Where the location of the crime is within the state, exclusive jurisdiction over the land may be that of the federal government and thus preclude state prosecution of an act committed on federal land. It is within the power of the federal government to assimilate state criminal laws into the federal law governing such enclaves. On the other hand, the federal government may define and punish offenses committed in a federal enclave which are entirely at odds with the law of the state in which the enclave is situated.

2. Jurisdiction over the Person

Jurisdiction over a person is essentially the physical power of a sovereignty to subject the person to its will. As a general rule, personal jurisdiction exists whenever a person is found within the boundaries of the state or is otherwise within the reach of its judicial process. The person need not be a resident or a citizen to be subject to the personal jurisdiction of a sovereignty. So long as the person participated in the commission of some criminal act in the state, his physical absence from the state when it was committed does not preclude the exercise of personal jurisdiction over him thereafter.

3. Waiver of Jurisdiction

Personal jurisdiction is the physical power of the sovereign over a person, and thus may be conferred by waiver or consent. However, subject matter jurisdiction is the power of the court over the subject matter of the action and cannot be created or waived by parties to the action. Venue, or local jurisdiction, can be waived.

4. Venue

Assuming that a court has jurisdiction over a certain class of cases, the prosecution must prove that the necessary elements of the crime charged were perpetrated in the place alleged to be the location of the offense. This establishes local jurisdiction of the offense, and is called venue. Venue is said to be jurisdictional, but a lack of venue does not deprive a court of jurisdiction to adjudicate the case. Its judgments are merely voidable rather than void.

a. Constitutional Venue Provisions

Article III, § 2 of the United States Constitution provides that criminal trials "shall be held in the State where the said crimes shall have been committed." This safeguard is reinforced by the command of the Sixth Amendment vicinage clause that has been deemed to provide the defendant, at least in federal trials, with a right to venue before an impartial jury of "the State and district wherein the crime shall have been committed." *Johnston v. United States*, 351 U.S. 215 (1956). State constitutions sometimes provide parallel provisions.

b. Multi-Venue Problems

Ordinarily a crime is committed in one place. However, because some offenses may be committed in more than one place, venue may be proper in any location where the crime began, continued, or was completed. Some offenses are said to be continuing in nature because the elements of the offense repeat themselves, and the offense therefore recurs over a period of time in several different places. For example, the offense of kidnapping begins when the defendant takes the victim into custody, and the offense continues in each place where the victim is moved. Embezzlement requires both the conversion of the property and the duty to account for the property, which may occur in different places. Some statutes, such as 18 U.S.C. § 3237, permit venue in any place where the crime was begun or where criminal acts or the forbidden result occurred. Here are two examples from the Supreme Court.

(1) **United States v. Cabrales**

For a money laundering offense, *United States v. Cabrales*, 524 U.S. 1 (1998) held that the essential conduct element was the laundering itself, even though one element of the offense was the associated crime that produced the funds to be laundered.

(2) **United States v. Rodriguez-Moreno**

For a crime prohibiting the use of a firearm "during and in relation to any crime prohibiting the use of a firearm," *United States v. Rodriguez-Moreno*, 526 U.S. 275 (1999) held that ongoing crime of violence is a "critical" conduct element of the offense, along with the element of the use of the weapon. Venue therefore was proper in any district in which that predicate crime occurred, even though it was not a district in which the weapon was also used.

(3) **Comparing *Cabrales* and *Rodriguez-Moreno***

Rodriguez-Moreno distinguished *Cabrales* as a case in which the government attempted to base venue on a "circumstance element," rather than a "critical element" that was an integral part of the offense. The associated crime in *Cabrales* occurred "after the fact" as an offense "begun and completed by others." The predicate crime in *Rodriguez-Moreno*, on the other hand, was ongoing, and one of "two distinct conduct elements" required of the defendant for liability.

c. **Proof of Venue**

Venue is a matter to be proved during trial. The court has the obligation to decide as a matter of law whether the incidents that occurred in the place were sufficient to say that the crime was committed there. The factfinder must then decide whether those events actually did occur within that place. Circumstantial evidence may be relied upon to establish the place in which the offense was committed. If venue is in two or more places, the place in which process is first issued may have exclusive venue during the pendency of the prosecution.

(1) **Raising the Venue Issue**

As a practical matter, venue is seldom contested in a pretrial motion to dismiss unless the lack of venue is evident from the face of the indictment or information. The defendant normally raises lack of venue in a motion for a directed verdict or in a motion for a new trial, where the claim is that the prosecution failed to prove venue. Venue jurisdiction may be waived by the intentional or inadvertent failure to raise the issue.

F. MOTIONS TO DISMISS BASED ON THE UNCONSTITUTIONALITY OF THE CRIME CHARGED

A defendant may move to dismiss an indictment of information on the ground that the statute the defendant is charged with violating is unconstitutional. Motions to dismiss may include the following grounds:

- separation of powers: One branch of government cannot exercise authority in an area over which another branch has inherent authority.
- vagueness: A criminal statute must define the criminal offense with sufficient clarity that ordinary people can understand what conduct is prohibited. *See, e.g., Kolender v. Lawson*, 461 U.S. 352 (1983).
- *ex post facto* laws: A statute is deemed an *ex post facto* law when it imposes punishment for an act which was not punishable at the time it was committed or adds punishment, or changes the rules of evidence by which less or different testimony is sufficient to convict than was previously required. *See, e.g., Stogner v. California*, 539 U.S. 607 (2003).
- first amendment: Statutes may violate constitutional protections of speech, press, or religion. *See, e.g., Texas v. Johnson*, 491 U.S. 397 (1989).
- equal protection: Any distinction in treatment of persons similarly situated must be rational and reasonable.
- police powers: Legislatures have broad powers to regulate conduct which is related to the public welfare and safety.

G. AMENDED PLEADINGS

In federal courts, Fed.R.Crim.R. 7(e) limits the amendment of formal charges to information, but the charge may be amended only upon a proper motion with permission of the court. The amendment may be made at any time before verdict or findings, or even after proof has been taken.

1. Proper Amendments

The amendment may include elements originally omitted from the charge or may correct facts incorrectly stated in the original charge.

2. Improper Amendments

The amendment may not charge a new or different offense, nor shall an amendment be permitted which would prejudice the substantial rights of the defendant. For example, in *Stirone v. United States*, 361 U.S. 212 (1960), a defective constructive amendment of the charge occurred when the prosecution indicted the defendant for one crime (obstructing sand importation) and the evidence showed another crime (interference with steel exportation). Another way for a charge to be impermissibly amended is for the jury instructions to broaden the scope of the indictment by permitting conviction for an uncharged offense. In cases not curable by amendment, if jeopardy has not attached to the prosecution, the defendant may be reprosecuted. See Chapter 29.

3. Variances between Proof and the Charge

Unlike a constructive amendment, a variance occurs when the proof offered at trial differs from the allegations of the indictment or information. A variance is less likely to produce a conviction for a different crime than charged in the indictment. Thus, courts regard a variance as a less serious encroachment, than an amendment, on the right to be tried only upon the charging instrument. Variances may relate to differences in the time a crime occurred, the number of alleged conspiracies, or the number of individuals participating in a conspiracy. The defense may object to the variance either:

- when the prosecutor introduces evidence which the defense claims is irrelevant to the charged offense; or
- when the prosecutor requests a jury instruction grounded on a theory sustained only by evidence which diverges from the charging document. See *Berger v. United States*, 295 U.S. 78 (1935).

CHAPTER 21

JOINDER AND SEVERANCE

A. INTRODUCTION

Joint trials promote efficiency, serve the interests of justice, save public funds, reduce inconvenience to witnesses and law enforcement authorities, and often reduce delays in bringing defendants to trial.

1. Rules Permit Multiple Charges of Defendants in Same Indictment

Most procedural rules allow a prosecutor to combine offenses or defendants simply by charging multiple offenses or defendants in the same indictment or information. In addition, if offenses or parties are charged separately but initially could have been joined in a single indictment or information, criminal rules permit a trial judge the discretion to consolidate the charges for trial in a single charging document.

2. Rules Also Permit Severance of Joined Charges or Defendants

Once multiple offenses or defendants are joined, either by charging document or by court order, the defense or prosecution may ask the court to sever them from one another. In federal courts, even if joinder is proper under the rules, a pretrial motion to sever under Fed.R.Crim.P. 14 leaves the determination of prejudice and any remedy that may be necessary to the discretion of the trial court. If prejudice develops at trial after a motion to sever has been overruled, the defendant should renew the motion and move for a mistrial.

3. Constitutional Consequences from (Not) Joining Charges or Defendants

In addition to joinder and severance issues arising from the application of the criminal rules, the exercise of prosecutorial discretion to join or not to join offenses or defendants may have constitutional consequences relating to Fifth Amendment Double Jeopardy and collateral estoppel issues, as well as Sixth Amendment Confrontation Clause problems.

B. JOINDER AND SEVERANCE OF OFFENSES

1. Joinder of Offenses Under the Federal Rules

Fed.R.Crim.P. 8(a) is typical of joinder rules; it allows but does not require joinder of offenses. Two or more offenses may be charged together against a defendant if they are based upon:

- the same act or transaction (e.g., a rape and an assault), or
- a series of acts or transactions constituting a common scheme (e.g., armed robbery, auto theft, possession of weapon), or
- the offenses being of similar character (e.g., bank robberies in the same neighborhood two months apart).

a. Joinder Based on the Same Transaction or Common Scheme

The first two types of joinder promote judicial efficiency by avoiding repetitious efforts in proving facts. For example, prosecuting a defendant for a rape and an assault arising from the same act or transaction is an efficient use of resources. Likewise, prosecuting a defendant for armed robbery, auto theft during the getaway from the robbery, and possession of a weapon during and after the robbery promotes judicial convenience by combining charges that stem from a series of acts that constitute a common scheme.

b. Joinder Based on Similar Character of Offenses

The third type of permitted joinder is problematic, because it allows a single trial of separate, unrelated offenses only because the offenses are of the same type. However, the judicial convenience is minimal, because the evidence adduced on the several counts will likely involve different proof by different witnesses.

c. Motion to Dismiss for Misjoinder of Charges

A defendant may seek dismissal of joined charges because of the failure to satisfy the procedural rules for joinder. A violation of Rule 8 "requires reversal only if the misjoinder results in actual prejudice because it had a substantial and injurious effect or influence in determining the jury's verdict." *United States v. Lane*, 474 U.S. 438 (1986).

d. Motion to Consolidate Multiple Charges

Because the joinder-of-offenses rule is permissive rather than mandatory, a defendant has no right to have all alleged offenses tried together. However, a defendant's motion to consolidate charges under Fed.R.Crim.P. 13 may succeed if the charges could have been brought together.

e. Motion to Sever Joined Charges

If joinder satisfies Fed.R.Crim.P. 8(a), the defendant may still seek a severance of the offenses from what is described as prejudicial joinder, per Fed.R.Crim.P. 14.

f. Typical Arguments Supporting a Motion to Sever

The joined offenses:

- lead to an inference of criminal propensity,
- involve evidence that is admissible on one charge but inadmissible on another,
- result in the defendant wanting to testify on some but not all of the charges, and
- may involve both substantive charges and a perjury charge resulting from the defendant's prior testimony.

C. DOUBLE JEOPARDY IMPLICATIONS FOR JOINDER OF OFFENSES

When the prosecution charges a defendant with multiple offenses, either in simultaneous or successive prosecutions, a constitutional issue may arise. The Double Jeopardy Clause of the Fifth Amendment shields a defendant from even the risk of being punished twice for the same offense.

1. Double Jeopardy in Simultaneous Prosecutions

In a simultaneous prosecution, suppose a defendant is charged with killing a victim in one count and for assaulting the same victim at the same time. If the defendant is charged with those two offenses constituting the same offense, there are two options for how the court is able to address the double jeopardy issue:

- because local laws may require the judge to instruct the jury on any offense for which there is sufficient proof, the instructions may further direct the jury that it can convict the defendant of the homicide or the assault but not both offenses, or
- local laws instead may require the prosecutor to elect which of the two charges should be submitted to the jury so that the jury

is not confused by jury instructions that it must make the election.

2. Double Jeopardy in Successive Prosecutions

In successive prosecutions, following an acquittal or a conviction for one offense prior to the second trial for the "same" offense, the defendant will seek dismissal of that charge because it is the same offense as the offense for which he has already been tried.

3. The "Same Offense" and the *Blockburger* Test

Double jeopardy protections depend on whether two offenses are considered to be the "same offense." That decision is important not only in the traditional double jeopardy scenario involving successive prosecutions for related acts, but also in a single prosecution involving multiple offenses and punishments.

a. Missouri v. Hunter

A constitutional violation does not occur if the legislature intended to impose cumulative punishments for a single act that constitutes more than one crime. In *Missouri v. Hunter*, 459 U.S. 359 (1983), the Supreme Court held that "[w]here . . . a legislature specifically authorizes cumulative punishment under two statutes, . . . the prosecutor may seek and the trial court or jury may impose cumulative punishment under such statutes in a single trial."

(1) Legislative Intent

To show legislative intent, the statutes defining the two offenses must require:

- a "clearly expressed legislative intent" that supports the imposition of cumulative punishments, or
- proof of different elements.

  Either the legislative history of the statute or the language or organization of a statute may reveal the legislative intent. If the offenses are set forth in different statutes or in distinct sections of a statute, and each provision or section unambiguously sets forth punishment for its violation, courts generally infer a legislative intent to authorize multiple punishments.

b. Blockburger v. United States

In most cases, the issue of legislative intent to impose multiple charges or punishments is ambiguous. Then, the Supreme Court test from *Blockburger v. United States*, 284 U.S. 299 (1932) governs whether multiple offenses and punishments in a single or successive prosecutions are constitutionally permissible. *Blockburger* held that:

- two offenses do *not* constitute the same offense when each offense requires proof of elements that the other offense does not. The test may be satisfied despite substantial overlap in the evidence used to prove the offenses.

(1) United States v. Felix

In *United States v. Felix*, 503 U.S. 378 (1992) the Supreme Court held that an attempt to commit a substantive offense and a conspiracy to commit that offense are not the same offense for double jeopardy purposes even if they are based upon the same underlying facts.

(2) Multiple Victims

When a single act affects multiple victims, different offenses are committed. If one person is killed and another is wounded by the same bullet, multiple criminal offenses have been committed.

(3) Different Time Periods

In *Brown v. Ohio*, 432 U.S. 161 (1977), the Court suggested that the legislature may divide a continuous course of conduct into separate offenses, even for conduct which occurs within a very short period of time. For example, when the defendant fires six gunshots at police during a chase, the result is six different counts of reckless endangerment.

c. Defining the Same Offense

Two offenses *do* constitute the same offense when only one of the offenses requires proof that the other offense does not. A lesser included offense is the same as the greater offense because by definition the greater offense includes all the elements of the lesser. Thus, multiple punishments following a single prosecution for both offenses are barred, in the absence of a clearly expressed legislative intent to the contrary.

(1) Whalen v. United States

In *Whalen v. United States*, 445 U.S. 684 (1980), the Supreme Court held that because rape is a lesser included offense of felony-murder committed in the course of that rape, double jeopardy prohibited convictions in the same trial for both offenses. Only the felony-murder required evidence that proof of the rape did not: killing the same victim in the perpetration of the crime of rape. By contrast, proving that the defendant raped the victim did not require the prosecutor to show anything different than what was necessary to prove the rape as to the felony-murder charge. Because rape and the felony-murder were the "same offense," cumulative punishments could not be imposed absent clear legislative intent. The same principle applies in successive trials of rape and felony-murder.

(2) Harris v. Oklahoma

Unlike *Whalen*, which involved simultaneous charges, *Harris v. Oklahoma*, 433 U.S. 682 (1977) was convicted of felony-murder in the first trial and later charged with robbery (the predicate felony to prove the intent necessary in the first trial, and thus the same offense as the homicide). The Double Jeopardy Clause barred the second trial, because the conviction of the greater crime, murder, could not have been had without conviction of the lesser crime.

(3) United States v. Dixon

In *United States v. Dixon*, 509 U.S. 688 (1993) the Court applied *Blockburger* in an unusual factual context. Defendants were prosecuted for criminal offenses after they had been convicted of criminal contempt based upon the same conduct. Dixon was released on bond, and he could not commit any crime during his pretrial release. He was then arrested for a drug offense, which the court that had released him determined that he had committed and held him in criminal contempt of its release order. The Court found that Dixon's drug offense was a prohibited lesser included offense of criminal contempt.

(4) Exception for Subsequent Events

When all the events needed for the greater crime have not occurred when the trial for the lesser crime began, a defendant convicted of assaulting a victim can still be convicted for that person's death if he died after the assault trial began. See *Diaz v. United States*, 223 U.S. 442 (1912).

d. *Blockburger*'s Lesson for Prosecutors

The lesson for prosecutors from the *Blockburger* line of cases is to be careful not to trigger double jeopardy by not charging multiple offenses permitted by the joinder rules. For example, if a lesser offense is tried separately from a greater included offense, double jeopardy will probably prevent the prosecutor from being able to try the defendant on the greater offense. In the context of *Dixon*, a prosecutor must choose whether to pursue a contempt conviction and jeopardize not being able to charge the defendant with the substantive offense that had led to the contempt charge.

4. A Criminal Charge and a Civil Case May Implicate Double Jeopardy

Recently, the Supreme Court has begun to consider another effect of charging a defendant with related offenses. As noted, double jeopardy may preclude multiple punishments for essentially the same conduct. Double jeopardy regarding punishments assumes that there is a dual "punishment." Most double jeopardy cases involve the prohibition of two criminal prosecutions. Double jeopardy also may apply to a criminal charge and another type of proceeding.

a. Hudson v. United States

In *Hudson v. United States*, 522 U.S. 93 (1997), the Court examined whether a civil penalty can be characterized as criminal and therefore subject to the double jeopardy concern. Bank officers were indicted for misapplication of bank funds, following imposition of monetary penalties by the Office of Comptroller of Currency (OCC). "A court must first ask whether the legislature, 'in establishing the penalizing mechanism, indicated either expressly or impliedly a preference for" a criminal or civil penalty. Even if the legislature has labeled the penalty a civil, it still may be so punitive in its purpose or effect that it is regarded as a criminal penalty.

b. *Kennedy v. Mendoza-Martinez* Factors as a Guide

In making the determination of whether a civil remedy is equivalent to a criminal penalty, the factors in *Kennedy v. Mendoza-Martinez*, 372 U.S. 144 (1963), provide useful guideposts, including:

- "[w]hether the sanction involves an affirmative disability or restraint",
- "whether it has historically been regarded as a punishment",
- "whether it comes into play only on a finding of scienter",
- "whether its operation will promote the traditional aims of punishment-retribution and deterrence",

- "whether the behavior to which it applies is already a crime",
- "whether an alternative purpose to which it may rationally be connected is assignable for it", and
- "whether it appears excessive in relation to the alternative purpose assigned."

It is important to note, however, that "these factors must be considered in relation to the statute on its face," and "only the clearest proof" will suffice to override legislative intent and transform what has been denominated a civil remedy into a criminal penalty.

c. Applying the *Kennedy* Factors to *Hudson*

When the Court applied the *Kennedy* factors to *Hudson*, it concluded that the OCC penalties had been civil rather than criminal In cases considering the question whether confinement is criminal or civil, the Supreme Court has looked to the actual conditions of confinement. For example, because involuntary confinement pursuant to a civil commitment statute is not punitive, that statute's operation does not raise double jeopardy concerns when it follows completion of a sentence for a criminal conviction.

D. COLLATERAL ESTOPPEL AND JOINDER OF OFFENSES

As previously discussed, a single criminal transaction or activity may be divided into multiple statutory crimes. If the prosecution chooses to divide the offenses into separate prosecutions or decides to bring the charges successively rather than simultaneously, an acquittal on one offense may preclude a trial on the other offense under the doctrine of collateral estoppel.

1. Defining Collateral Estoppel

Collateral estoppel provides that determination of a factual issue in a defendant's favor at one proceeding may estop the prosecution from disputing the fact in another proceeding against the same defendant. Thus, when different offenses are charged, double jeopardy would normally not bar a second prosecution. Collateral estoppel may, in effect, bar the second trial when a fact previously found in the defendant's favor is necessary to the second conviction. For collateral estoppel to apply, the defendant must be contesting relitigation of an issue of ultimate fact previously determined in his favor by a valid and final judgment.

a. Same Parties as First Trial

The second prosecution must involve the same parties as the first trial. A defendant cannot estop the prosecution from relitigating a fact found against the prosecution in a proceeding against a different defendant. In *Standefer v. United States*, 447 U.S. 10 (1980), a unanimous Court held that one defendant's acquittal on a bribery charge did not preclude a later prosecution of another defendant for aiding and abetting the same bribery.

b. First Factfinder Decided the Factual Issue

The factfinder must have "actually and certainly" determined the issue of fact in the earlier proceeding. For example, in *Schiro v. Farley*, 510 U.S. 222 (1994), in a homicide case, the jury was given ten possible verdicts and returned a verdict on only one of the verdict sheets, convicting the defendant for rape felony murder. Defendant claimed that the state was collaterally estopped from showing intentional killing (one of the other verdict sheet possibilities) as an aggravated factor supporting a death sentence. The Court held that "failure to return a verdict does not have collateral estoppel effect . . . unless the record establishes that the issue was actually and necessarily decided in the defendant's favor."

2. Determining What Facts Were Decided in the First Case

The most difficult problem in applying collateral estoppel is ascertaining what facts were established in the earlier case. Because juries render general rather than special verdicts in most criminal cases, a determination of which facts support the verdict requires careful analysis of the trial record. Only those fact determinations essential to the first decision are conclusive in later proceedings. Not only must a court be able to determine that the fact issue was litigated in defendant's first trial, but also the nature of the reason for acquitting defendant in the earlier trial determines whether collateral estoppel applies in the current case.

a. Ashe v. Swenson

In the Supreme Court's leading case of *Ashe v. Swenson*, 397 U.S. 436 (1970), the defendant allegedly robbed six participants in a poker game. At the first trial, however, the charge related to only one of the alleged robberies. Because there was no doubt that a robbery had occurred and that Knight had been a victim, the only issue at the first trial was whether the defendant had robbed Knight. After the defendant's acquittal for robbing Knight, the prosecution charged defendant was robbing Roberts, another participant in the poker game. In reversing a conviction on the second robbery charge, the Court believed that it was possible to identify why the first robbery trial had resulted in an acquittal. The resolution of the first trial's only issue established that the defendant had not been present to rob either Knight or anyone else at the poker game.

b. Applying Collateral Estoppel

Assume that Defendant is charged with assaults against two victims at the same time and place, but the offenses are not joined. If she is acquitted at the first trial for assaulting Victim #1 because there is doubt as to whether she was present at the time of the assaults, her acquittal acts as a collateral estoppel defense to the second assault charge. On the other hand, if the acquittal at the first trial resulted from doubt about whether Defendant actually assaulted Victim #1, the prosecutor can still try to prove that she assaulted Victim #2.

c. Special Verdicts to Figure What Was Decided in First Trial

In limited circumstances, it may be easier to identify the basis for a criminal trial verdict under statutes effectively requiring the use of special verdicts to clarify the reason for an acquittal in a first trial. For example, in cases where the defendant has tried to prove a mental defect or mental retardation, the jury may be ordered to make a specific finding that the defendant was mentally defective or retarded. And in cases where the prosecution seeks the death penalty, the jury may need to designate in writing which aggravating circumstance it found to be applicable before the court can sentence the defendant to capital punishment.

d. Using Evidence from Prior Acquittal at Later Trial

Evidence of a crime for which the defendant was acquitted may be introduced at a later trial involving the same circumstances. In *Dowling v. United States*, 493 U.S. 342 (1990), while prosecuting a defendant for bank robbery, the Court held that the prosecution may introduce evidence of a burglary for which the defendant had been acquitted. The Court reasoned that the evidence was admissible at the robbery trial because the acquittal did not prove that the defendant was innocent but only that there was a reasonable doubt about the defendant's guilt. The difference in burdens of proof was the key distinction for the Court: in the first trial, the government failed to show beyond a reasonable doubt that Dowling had committed the act; to introduce evidence of the same act in another trial, the government need show only that a jury could reasonably conclude that the defendant committed the first act.

E. JOINDER AND SEVERANCE OF DEFENDANTS

1. Joinder of Defendants Under the Federal Rules

The rules of criminal procedure also address joinder and severance procedures where multiple defendants are jointly alleged to have committed one or more crimes. The policy behind this type of rule is improved judicial economy and efficiency, since one trial is faster and less expensive than two. The joinder of defendants is permissive and severance is discretionary with the trial court. When multiple defendants are jointly charged, a severance may be available based upon specific allegations of prejudice.

a. Standard for Joinder of Defendants

In most jurisdictions, joinder of defendants is permitted where the defendants allegedly participated either in the same act or transaction or in the same series of acts or transactions. Unlike the rules on joinder of offenses, in order to be joined defendants must have committed offenses that are part of the same series of acts rather than being of a similar character.

b. Applying the Standard

Joinder of defendants looks to the factual connecting link. Where the link is part of some larger plan, or there is some commonality of proof, joinder is permitted. For example, suppose that Defendants A and B are charged with two robberies committed at different times against different victims. To join the two robbery charges, they must be part of the same series of acts or transactions. If that link is lacking, the prosecutor has two options. Under Fed.R.Crim.P. 8(a), the prosecutor may charge defendant A with both robberies in one indictment and charge defendant B with both crimes in another indictment. The alternative for the prosecutor would be to charge both A and B with one robbery in one indictment and to charge A and B with the other robbery in a second indictment.

c. Complete Overlap of Charging is Not Required

Most rules like Fed.R.Crim.P. 8(b) provide that defendants may be charged in one or more counts together or separately, but each defendant does not have to be charged in each count.

d. Motion to Dismiss for Misjoinder of Charges

A defendant may seek dismissal of joined charges because of the failure to satisfy the procedural rules for joinder. Misjoinder is subject to a harmless error analysis.

e. Motion to Consolidate Multiple Defendants

Because the joinder-of-defendants rule is permissive rather than mandatory, a defendant has no right to have a trial of all alleged offenses tried together with another defendant. However, a motion to consolidate charges under Fed.R.Crim.P. 13 may succeed if the defendants' charges could have been brought together.

f. Motion to Sever Joined Charges

If the joinder satisfies Rule 8(b), one or more of the joined defendants may still seek a severance from what is described as prejudicial joinder, per Fed.R.Crim.P. 14, based upon specific allegations of prejudice in a joint trial.

(1) "Spill Over" Effect

One prejudicial aspect of a joint defendant trial is commonly considered as the "spill over" effect of one defendant's heinous conduct affecting the jury's view of the others charged with that defendant.

(2) Multiple Attorneys

While the prosecution is unified, the defense is fragmented. Each defendant has an attorney and each attorney's view of the case may differ.

(3) Weight or Type of Proof as to One Defendant

Factual prejudice may depend on the weight or type of proof as to the respective defendants. For example, the evidence of guilt or the number of counts against each defendant may be disproportionate.

(4) Calling the Codefendant as a Witness

One defendant may want to call the codefendant as a witness.

(5) Antagonistic Defenses

The Court in *Zafiro v. United States*, 506 U.S. 534 (1993) defined the issue of whether two defendants have antagonistic defenses as whether it was necessary for the jury to disbelieve one defendant's defense in order to believe the other defendant's defense.

(6) Pretrial Confession of a Codefendant

The allegation of prejudicial joinder when one or more codefendants have given a pretrial confession is discussed in the next section.

F. SIXTH AMENDMENT ISSUES FOR THE JOINDER OF DEFENDANTS

Chapter 27, *infra*, includes discussion of *Crawford v. Washington*, which describes an out-of-court confession as one example of a hearsay testimonial statement. In a joint trial, a *Bruton* claim relates to the admissibility at trial of a non-testifying *codefendant's* out-of-court statement in order to prove the culpability of the other defendant. A *Bruton* claim involves a narrower set of circumstances than a *Crawford* claim.

1. Bruton v. United States

Bruton v. United States, 391 U.S. 123 (1968) held that in a joint trial the admission of a codefendant's pretrial confession *directly* incriminating the defendant violates the defendant's Sixth Amendment right to confrontation when the confessing codefendant does not testify at trial.

a. When the Confessing Co-Defendant Testifies

Incriminating out-of-court statements are likely to be introduced during the prosecution's case-in-chief before the confessing codefendant decides whether to testify. Where the confessing codefendant does testify, there is no confrontation issue because the codefendant is subject to cross-examination (regardless of whether the codefendant admits or denies making the confession).

2. Richardson v. Marsh

In *Richardson v. Marsh*, 481 U.S. 200 (1987), a codefendant's pretrial confession did not directly but merely inferentially (e.g., "me and some other guys committed the crime") implicated the other defendant. The Court held that a trial court must admonish the jury that the confession does not implicate the non-confessing defendant.

3. Cruz v. New York

When *both* defendants give pretrial confessions incriminating each other, a nontestifying codefendant's confession facially incriminating the defendant is not directly admissible against the defendant. The Confrontation Clause bars its admission at their joint trial, even if the jury is instructed not to consider it against the defendant, and even if the defendant's own confession is admitted against him. *Cruz v. New York*, 481 U.S. 186 (1987).

4. Redaction of References to the Nonconfessing Defendant

Regardless of whether a pretrial confession directly or inferentially implicates a codefendant, courts have held that all references to the nonconfessing defendant must be deleted from the confession that is presented to the jury.

a. Gray v. Maryland

All references to the person's existence must be removed, even if that falsely suggests sole culpability by the confessor. In *Gray v. Maryland*, 523 U.S. 185 (1998), the prosecution erroneously redacted the codefendant's confession by substituting for the defendant's name in the confession a blank space or the word "deleted." The Court held that when the confession directly *or* inferentially incriminates the nonconfessing defendant, no redaction that merely substitutes a blank space, "delete," a neutral pronoun, or symbol is permitted. Such substitutions do not make a significant legal difference and "*Bruton*'s protective rule applies."

b. Timing for Redaction

The prosecutor must delete all references to the nonconfessor *prior* to introducing the abridged codefendant's statement during its case-in-chief. If the codefendant later testifies, the prosecutor may then introduce the full, unabridged version of the codefendant's pretrial statement.

5. Strategic Alternatives for the Prosecutor

When a codefendant already has confessed but may not testify at a joint trial, the prosecution has several strategic options.

a. Sever the Case of the Nonconfessing Defendant

The first alternative is to grant a severance to the nonconfessing defendant. In this way, the codefendant's confession will not be used against the defendant. In ruling on a motion for separate trials, the trial judge may order the prosecutor to deliver to the court for *in camera* inspection any pretrial statements or confessions made by defendants that the prosecutor intends to introduce in evidence at a joint trial. The prosecution may also desire a severance where the other evidence against the codefendant is weak and an unredacted confession is necessary to convict the codefendant.

b. Do Not Present the Pretrial Confession at Trial

A second alternative is that the prosecution not use the codefendant's confession in its case-in-chief in a joint trial. If the confessing codefendant testifies, the prosecution could then impeach the codefendant with the statements made in the confession. This would not constitute a denial of confrontation even if the codefendant denied making the statement. However, it is risky to hope the codefendant testifies in initially denying a severance and allowing introduction of the statement into evidence during the prosecution's case-in-chief.

c. Present the Confession, But Redact References to the Defendant

A third alternative is to redact all references to the moving, nonconfessing defendant. Redaction is accomplished by (1) removing parts of or retyping the confession, or (2) requiring the witness to paraphrase the confession in such a manner as to avoid any references that might directly implicate other defendants. To be effective, the deletion must not call attention to the fact that the statement implicates other persons who are obviously at trial.

CHAPTER 22

SPEEDY TRIAL

A. PRE-CHARGE DELAY IN CHARGING THE DEFENDANT

Many jurisdictions do not apply a statute of limitations to felony prosecutions, but most still use them for misdemeanor charges. *See* Section B.4. Constitutional due process rights may protect a defendant from delay between commission of the crime and the earlier of the arrest, indictment or information. However, proving a constitutional violation is difficult.

1. United States v. Lovasco

In *United States v. Lovasco*, 431 U.S. 783 (1977), the defendant tried to invoke the Fifth Amendment due process right when the indictment was filed seventeen months after the investigator's report. The Court held that there was no due process violation even if the defendant is somewhat prejudiced, if the delay in obtaining the indictment ensures that the correct charges are brought against the appropriate defendants.

2. Proving a Due Process Violation

To establish a federal constitutional due process violation based on pre-charge delay, a defendant must show that:

- a long delay occurred between the crime and the earlier of the defendant's arrest or his formal charge,
- the delay resulted in actual prejudice to the ability of the defense to present its case; and
- the reason for the delay was motivated by the prosecutor's intent to gain a tactical advantage over the defendant.

There is no requirement that the defendant demand a speedy arrest or charge. In each case, the reasons for the delay and the prospective impact on a trial are relevant.

a. Difficulty of Proving Prejudice

The burden of establishing actual prejudice is a heavy one, with the defendant having to provide proof that the delay substantially prejudiced the defense. The defendant must show how any evidence or witnesses now unavailable would have assisted the defense or what exculpatory evidence would have been offered. Prejudice is not established merely by a claim of faded memory, inability to locate a witness, or a witness's refusal to testify. In addition, even if the defendant is able to show actual prejudice, there must be evidence that the delay was used deliberately by the prosecution to gain a tactical advantage over the defendant. The requirement of purposeful delay reflects a judicial reluctance to interfere with the daily exercise of prosecutorial discretion.

b. Example of Sufficient Prejudice

Suppose the defendant alleges that he was prejudiced by a delay that resulted in the loss of a witness's testimony. A sufficient showing of prejudice would require that the defendant show that the witness would have been available at an earlier time, he would have testified for the defendant, and the testimony would have aided the defense without being merely cumulative.

B. POST-CHARGE DELAY IN BRINGING THE DEFENDANT TO TRIAL

The right to a speedy trial attaches from the earlier of the date of the indictment or information, or the date of the arrest, i.e., when the person becomes "accused." Similarly, the right to a speedy trial attaches when a detainer is lodged against an accused who is serving a sentence on other charges. Once the right to a speedy trial attaches, it continues until the charges are dismissed.

1. How Speedy Trial Rights Differ from Other Rights

First, society has an interest in a speedy trial to prevent the accused from endangering public safety by committing other crimes. Second, violating the right may work to the accused's advantage, because the passage of time results in witness unavailability and fading witness memories. Third, because the speedy trial right is a more concept, courts do not apply it as a bright-line test. *See* Section C., discussing statutory speedy trial rights.

2. Barker v. Wingo

In *Barker v. Wingo*, 407 U.S. 514 (1972), the Court held that any inquiry into a constitutional speedy trial claim requires a balancing of at least four factors:

- the length of the delay,
- the reasons for the delay,
- whether and how the defendant asserted the speedy trial right, and
- the amount of prejudice from the delay suffered by the defendant.

a. Rejected Approaches

The Court rejected two alternate approaches: that a defendant must be tried within a specific time period, and a defendant's demand for a speedy trial right is a necessary precondition to judicial consideration of a constitutional violation. The first approach was rejected because there is no *constitutional* basis for quantifying the right as a function of a specific number of days or months. The latter approach was disapproved as inconsistent with the Court's pronouncements about the waiver of constitutional rights as an "intentional relinquishment or abandonment of a known right or privilege."

b. Length of the Delay

Barker held that the length of the delay serves as a threshold requirement or "triggering mechanism" for finding a violation of the speedy trial right. Although the length of the delay alone does not establish a constitutional violation, a court need not inquire into the other factors unless it finds the delay to be presumptively prejudicial. Later decisions have suggested that a delay of at least twelve months triggers further analysis under *Barker* because that delay was presumptively prejudicial. Further, in *United States v. Loud Hawk*, 474 U.S. 302 (1986), the Court held that the time between dismissal of an indictment and a defendant's reindictment is excluded from the length of delay.

c. Reason for the Delay

Courts weigh delays intended to gain a trial advantage more heavily against the prosecution than unintentional delays resulting from institutional dysfunction. In the absence of a showing of bad faith or dilatory motive, the prosecution is not responsible for delays attributable to its own acts. Neutral reasons such as negligence and overcrowded calendars weigh less heavily, but are still considered because responsibility for such conditions rests with the prosecution. A period of delay attributable to tactics by the defendant is deemed a waiver of the right to a speedy trial for that period of delay.

d. Demand for Speedy Trial

Despite the view that a defendant does not have the duty to bring himself to trial, the defendant's failure to demand a speedy trial undercuts the defendant's constitutional argument. By contrast, a vigorous and timely assertion of the right provides strong evidence that the defendant is interested in a speedy disposition. A court will not treat a claim seriously that a trial started too late unless the defendant has sought a speedy trial.

e. Prejudice to the Defendant

Barker stated that a court must weigh any prejudice to the defendant in light of the interests protected by the speedy trial guarantee: preventing oppressive pretrial incarceration, minimizing anxiety of the accused, and limiting impairment to the defense. Courts typically do not take the first two types of allegations very seriously. The third allegation is serious, and if demonstrated usually will result in a finding of prejudice.

(1) Reed v. Farley

Reed v. Farley, 512 U.S. 339 (1994) suggests a modification of the balancing test announced in *Barker*. The Court asserted that a "showing of prejudice is required to establish a violation of the Sixth Amendment Speedy Trial Clause, and that necessary ingredient is entirely missing here."

(2) Doggett v. United States

Doggett v. United States, 505 U.S. 647 (1992), signaled a change in the *Barker* test by suggesting a relationship between the reason for the delay and the allocation of the burden of proof on the prejudice issue. On the one hand, when the reason for the delay is attributable to reasonable diligence by the prosecution, the defendant must show specific prejudice. At the other extreme, when the reason for the delay is intentional misconduct by the prosecution, a presumption of prejudice is "virtually automatic," with the burden of proof on the government to overcome the presumption. It is uncertain which party has the burden of proof when the reason for the delay is governmental negligence.

f. Remedy for Sixth Amendment Violation

Barker expressly stated that dismissal with prejudice is the only possible remedy for a violation of the Sixth Amendment speedy trial right. Trial courts therefore cannot devise less extreme remedies such as a sentence reduction. The reprosecution prohibition probably results in fewer decisions finding constitutional violations. An alternative disposition is to find a violation of the relevant speedy trial statute (e.g., 18 U.S.C. § 3161 et seq.) or the relevant docket control rule, e.g., Fed.R.Crim.P. 48(b), both of which may prescribe dismissal without prejudice as an available method of enforcement. Still another remedy is to provide a writ of mandamus to compel a trial court to set a trial date for the defendant's case.

g. Speedy Trial Rights for Incarcerated Defendants

An inmate in one jurisdiction has a Sixth Amendment right to a speedy trial on charges pending in another jurisdiction. *Smith v. Hooey*, 393 U.S. 374 (1969). A prosecutor must make a good faith and diligent effort to prosecute inmates confined in other jurisdictions. Congress and most state legislatures are signatories to the Interstate Agreement on Detainers, which enables an inmate in one state to force the expeditious disposition of outstanding charges in other states. Prosecutors also can obtain prisoners for trial under the compact. When there is a pending charge in another county of the same state, separate *intra*state statutes may permit the inmate to request a speedy disposition of the untried charge. *See, e.g.*, the Uniform Mandatory Disposition of Detainers Act.

C. STATUTORY RIGHTS TO A SPEEDY TRIAL

In addition to the constitutional speedy trial standard and interstate compacts, many state legislatures and the Congress have enacted speedy trial legislation that establishes specific time limits for completing stages of a criminal prosecution. For example, the federal Speedy Trial Act (18 U.S.C. § 3161 et seq.) provides that an arrested defendant be formally charged within thirty days after the arrest and that the defendant's trial must begin within seventy days after the formal charge is filed. To compute whether there has been a statutory violation, the court calculates the gross elapsed days and subtracts the number of days attributable to excludable time, leaving the net elapsed days for determination about a violation.

1. Excludable Periods of Time

Certain types of pretrial delays are automatically excluded from the computation of time limits, e.g., periods of delay like the absence or unavailability of the defendant or an essential witness, delays resulting from the joinder of a codefendant, and delays resulting from other proceedings involving the defendant. The "other proceedings" provision requires exclusion of all delays attributable to pendency of pretrial motions regardless of whether the delays are reasonably necessary. For example, 18 U.S.C. § 3161(h)(1)(D) covers the delay from the filing of any pretrial motion through the hearing or other disposition of the motion. The running of the 70-day period from indictment to trial stops upon the filing of the pretrial motion regardless of whether it actually causes or is expected to cause a delay in starting the trial. *United States v. Tinklenberg*, 131 S.Ct. 2007 (2011). In *Bloate v. United States*, 559 U.S. 196 (2010), the Court held that 3161(h)(7) permits a court to exclude a "delay resulting from a continuance" it grants, provided it makes required findings.

2. Remedies for Violation of Speedy Trial Act

The Speedy Trial Act is not self-executing. To avoid a waiver of her rights, a defendant who seeks dismissal because of a federal statutory violation must file an appropriate motion. *Zedner v. United States*, 547 U.S. 489 (2006). If the Speedy Trial Act's time limits are not met, the charges against a defendant must be dismissed. The key determination for the trial judge is whether the dismissal must be with or without prejudice. The judge considers three factors in exercising discretion to dismiss charges with or without prejudice:

- the seriousness of the offense,
- the circumstances leading to dismissal, and
- the effect of reprosecution on the administration of justice and the legislation.

18 U.S.C. § 3162(a)(1)–(2). It is an abuse of discretion if the trial judge fails to consider each statutory factor and explain other factors relied upon in deciding whether to dismiss charges. For example, the Court in *United States v. Taylor*, 487 U.S. 326 (1988) reversed a dismissal with prejudice because the trial judge failed to consider all statutory factors.

3. No Prospective Waiver of Statutory Rights

A defendant cannot prospectively execute a written waiver of statutory speedy trial rights. In *Zedner v. United States*, 547 U.S. 489 (2006), the Supreme Court stated that, while under § 3162(a)(2) a waiver of the right to dismissal for a past statutory violation occurs when a defendant fails to file a motion for dismissal before trial or entering a guilty plea, that provision does not indicate that

Congress intended to permit prospective waivers, i.e., a defendant cannot opt out of the Act's requirements *prior* to a violation.

4. Statutes of Limitation

Federal statutory crimes and almost all states have statutes that precisely define limits for bringing a criminal prosecution. *See. e.g.*, 18 U.S.C. § 3282, imposing a five year limitations period after commission for prosecuting felonies. While the length of the period often increases with the seriousness of the crime, may states have no time limitation for charging felonies or capital crimes.

SUMMARY OF PROMPT DISPOSITION THEORIES

Speedy Disposition Element	**Due Process-Assessing Pre-Charge Delay**	**Sixth Amendment-Assessing Post-Charge Delay**	**Federal Speedy Trial Act— 18 U.S.C. § 3161 et seq.**
When Does the Right Apply?	Delay between commission of the crime, and the earlier of arrest or indictment.	Delay between the earlier of arrest or indictment and when the motion to dismiss is filed.	Arrest → charge 30 net days; Charge → trial 70 net days
Is Time Lapse Dispositive or a Trigger?	Time operates as a trigger, but no definitive time lapse has been identified.	Trigger-time lapse in excess of twelve months presumptively triggers the remaining analysis.	Dispositive
What Is the Reason for the Delay?	Prosecutor's intent is to gain a tactical advantage over the defendant.	If attributable to the defendant, court may find waiver.	§ 3161(h)–excludable time is subtracted from gross days to calculate net days.

Speedy Disposition Element	Due Process-Assessing Pre-Charge Delay	Sixth Amendment-Assessing Post-Charge Delay	Federal Speedy Trial Act—18 U.S.C. § 3161 et seq.
Must Defendant Demand Speedy Disposition?	N/A (defendant would not ask to be indicted or arrested)	Probably, if a defendant is aware that an indictment has been returned or has been arrested.	No, the statute is self-executing.
Must Actual Prejudice Be Shown?	Yes, defendant must prove actual prejudice to the ability to present testimony or documents.	Yes, defendant must show impairment to the defense. Cases suggest a relationship between the reasons attributable to government and allocation of the burden of proof on the prejudice issue, e.g., when the reason for delay is due to reasonable prosecution diligence, defendant must show specific prejudice, but when the reason is intentional misconduct by the prosecution, the burden of proof is on the government to overcome a presumption of prejudice. When the government is negligent, the length of delay determines the burden of proof.	No, the statute is about the running of time.

Speedy Disposition Element	**Due Process-Assessing Pre-Charge Delay**	**Sixth Amendment-Assessing Post-Charge Delay**	**Federal Speedy Trial Act—18 U.S.C. § 3161 et seq.**
Sanction	Dismissal *with* prejudice	Dismissal *with* prejudice	Dismissal *with* or *without* prejudice, per factors in § 3162

CHAPTER 23

DISCOVERY AND DISCLOSURE

A. INTRODUCTION

Discovery is the process of exchanging information between the prosecution and the defense. Prior to using the discovery rules, the defense may use informal methods for obtaining information from the prosecution. Prosecutors primarily look to police departments and grand jury investigations to uncover relevant facts.

B. DISCOVERY OUTSIDE THE PROCEDURAL RULES

1. Grand Jury Process

a. Discovery for the Prosecutor

The grand jury offers prosecutors many of the advantages that civil litigants obtain through discovery depositions. Prior to the return of an indictment, the grand jury has the power to compel testimony and documents from many sources. Unlike a civil deposition, the grand jury process occurs *ex parte* and in secret. The prosecutor proceeds unhampered by objections. The witness testifies without the presence of counsel. See Chapter 19.

b. Discovery for the Defendant

Defendants, on the other hand, have no control over the grand jury process and in many cases are unaware of the grand jury's investigation until it results in an indictment. Once the investigation is complete, as a general rule defendants are not entitled to the transcribed record of grand jury proceedings unless and until a grand jury witness later testifies for the government at trial.

2. Bill of Particulars

A defendant's motion for a bill of particulars requests more specific information about the charge described in the indictment or information upon which the accused will stand trial. The charging instrument often sets forth the "bare bones" of the crime in conclusory language such as "the defendant did murder the victim at such a time and place."

a. Example of What a Bill of Particulars Seeks

In order to prepare a meaningful trial defense, a bill of particulars might ask for a description of the particular form of murder (e.g., premeditated murder or felony murder) and the specific method by which the alleged murder was committed (e.g., with a gun, knife, or chain saw). The granting of a bill of particulars is largely discretionary with the judge; the important issue in each case is whether the information claimed to be omitted from the indictment has deprived the defendant of a substantial right and subjects him to being tried for a charge for which he has not been indicted.

3. Preliminary Hearing

Although discovery is not an avowed purpose of preliminary hearings, discovery is an inherent byproduct of the requirement that the prosecution present at least a *prima facie* case to a judicial officer. Prosecutors, however, often limit the defense opportunity for discovery at the preliminary hearing by presenting the minimum evidence required to certify the case for trial, and some jurisdictions have been particularly hostile to defense counsel's efforts to expand the preliminary hearing into a discovery vehicle. See Chapter 18.

4. Plea Bargaining

Outside the confines of judicial proceedings, discovery may occur as part of the give-and-take of plea bargaining between defense counsel and the prosecutor. Some prosecutors subscribe to an "open office" philosophy where the prosecutor voluntarily discusses the nature of the government's case and makes documentary and real evidence available for inspection by the defense.

C. GOVERNMENT'S DUTY TO DISCLOSE EXCULPATORY EVIDENCE

Although most discovery occurs under the authority of local statutes and court rules, the United States Constitution requires disclosure of certain information possessed by the government. Beginning with *Brady v. Maryland*, 373 U.S. 83 (1963), the Court has held that intentional *or* inadvertent suppression by the prosecution of evidence favorable to an accused violates due process where the evidence is material either to guilt or punishment. *Cone v. Bell*, 556 U.S. 449 (2009). Whether the prosecution was acting in good faith at the time of nondisclosure is not relevant to constitutional analysis; a showing of materiality, which is interchangeable with prejudice to the defendant, is critical.

1. United States v. Bagley

United States v. Bagley, 473 U.S. 667 (1985) held that a prosecutor's constitutional duty to disclose includes both impeachment evidence and exculpatory evidence. A reversal for failure to disclose is determined by one standard regardless of whether there is no request, a general request, or a specific request for information by the defense: whether there was "a reasonable probability that, had the evidence been disclosed to the defense, the result of the proceeding would have been different." A *Brady* violation does not occur unless nondisclosure is so serious that the "reasonable probability" materiality standard applies. *Strickler v. Greene*, 527 U.S. 263 (1999).

a. Requesting *Brady* Information

Despite the comprehensive nature of this standard, it is probably just as important under *Bagley* to make the request for information as specific as possible. *Bagley* noted the greater potential for prejudice in a specific request case, where an incomplete response by the prosecution might cause the defense to abandon lines of investigation, defenses or trial strategies that it otherwise would have pursued.

2. Smith v. Cain

"[E]vidence impeaching an eyewitness may not be material if the State's other evidence is strong enough to sustain confidence in the verdict." In *Smith v. Cain*, 132 S.Ct. 627 (2012), there was no "other evidence" to support the conviction because the police withheld" plainly material" contradictory pretrial statements by the *only* witness linking the defendant to the crime scene.

3. Banks v. Dretke

Banks v. Dretke, 540 U.S. 668 (2004) noted that the prosecution has a duty to correct concealment of *Brady* information. Prosecutors failed to disclose that one of its two essential witnesses was a paid police informant and that a pretrial transcript showed that the other witness's trial testimony had been intensively coached by police and prosecutors. Further, prosecutors allowed the two witnesses to testify untruthfully without attempting to correct their false statements.

4. Giglio v. United States

In *Giglio v. United States*, 405 U.S. 150 (1972), a key prosecution witness falsely testified that he had not been promised leniency by another prosecutor in exchange for his testimony. Reversing the conviction, the Court held that nondisclosure of such important impeachment proof was material.

5. Kyles v. Whitley

Kyles v. Whitley, 514 U.S. 419 (1995) held that the constitutional determination of materiality for suppressed evidence is made collectively, not item-by-item. The cumulative standard of materiality requires the prosecutor to inquire in every case what, if any, evidence is undisclosed and to disclose when she believes that the materiality standard is satisfied.

6. Evidence: Is It Favorable or Merely Helpful?

If evidence qualifies as favorable, the prosecutor must decide if it is material. Helpful evidence is not necessarily favorable. For example, negative test results are favorable, but inconclusive test results are not. The prosecutor's initial responsibility is to ascertain whether any evidence in the government's possession qualifies as favorable.

7. Admissibility of the Undisclosed Information

Lower courts have differed as to whether *Brady* applies to information that may be favorable to the defense, but which is inadmissible at trial, e.g., inadmissible hearsay that the crime was committed by another person. Some courts limit *Brady* to information that would be admissible at trial, while others apply *Brady* to any information that might be useful in preparing a defense strategy.

8. Knowing Failure to Disclose Perjured Testimony: A Different Standard

Besides failure to disclose exculpatory evidence, the Supreme Court has addressed the prosecution's knowing failure to disclose perjured testimony. *Mooney v. Holohan*, 294 U.S. 103 (1935). The defendant must prove that the witness committed perjury and that the prosecutor knew or should have known about it. The standard of materiality in these cases is whether "there is any reasonable likelihood that the false testimony could have affected the judgment of the jury." *United States v. Agurs*, 427 U.S. 97 (1976).

a. Defense Counsel's Questioning May Negate Proof of Materiality

Even if a prosecutor fails to correct perjured testimony, reversal of the defendant's conviction may not be necessary if the jury was aware of other evidence contradicting the perjured testimony. Thus, if defense counsel notes the inconsistency of statements for the jury, the materiality standard is not satisfied.

b. Prior Inconsistent Statements v. False Evidence

A prosecutor's use of a witness's prior inconsistent statement doesn't by itself constitute the knowing use of false evidence. However, the line between impeaching evidence and evidence that proves perjury may be thin.

9. No Right to Search Government's Files for Exculpatory Evidence

The defendant is entitled to inspect documents or other objects only upon a "plausible" showing that it might have exculpatory relevance. Even if discovery is ordered, the defendant has no constitutional right to search through the government's files free of court supervision. In *Pennsylvania v. Ritchie*, 480 U.S. 39 (1987), the Court held that the defendant's right to discovery could be fully protected by requiring that the requested files be submitted to the trial court for *in camera* review. The trial court could then determine whether the files contain information that probably would change the outcome of the trial, and thus must be disclosed to the defendant.

10. No Right to Exculpatory Impeachment Evidence Prior to Guilty Plea

Suppose a defendant is considering a guilty plea. In *United States v. Ruiz*, 536 U.S. 622 (2002), the Court held that the defendant has no constitutional right to disclosure of impeachment information prior to a guilty plea. Impeachment evidence's value to a defendant depends on how much he already knows about the case against him, and there is a small risk that innocent defendants would plead guilty without impeachment information. The Court left open whether pre-guilty plea disclosure of exculpatory *Brady* material is required.

11. How a Request for DNA Testing Differs from *Brady*

In *Skinner v. Switzer*, 131 S.Ct. 1289 (2011), the Court held that a convicted state prisoner seeking DNA testing of crime-scene evidence may assert a civil rights claim under 42 U.S.C. § 1983. The

Court distinguished claims for DNA testing from *Brady* claims, by noting:

> Unlike DNA testing, which may yield exculpatory, incriminating, or inconclusive results, a *Brady* claim, when successful postconviction, necessarily yields evidence undermining a conviction: *Brady* evidence is, by definition, always favorable to the defendant and material to his guilt or punishment. And parties asserting *Brady* violations postconviction generally do seek a judgment qualifying them for "immediate or speedier release" from imprisonment. Accordingly, *Brady* claims have ranked within the traditional core of *habeas corpus* and outside the province of 42 U.S.C. § 1983.

12. Duty to Preserve Potentially Exculpatory Evidence

The constitutional right to discovery of exculpatory evidence does not require the government to preserve all potentially exculpatory evidence for possible discovery by defendants. A defendant may challenge the government's failure to preserve evidence or its loss or destruction of evidence as a due process violation.

a. Proving a Due Process Violation

Evidence must be preserved when its exculpatory value was apparent before the evidence was destroyed and when the evidence was of such a nature that the defendant would be unable to obtain comparable evidence by other reasonably available means. In addition, the defendant must prove bad faith on the part of the police. *California v. Trombetta*, 467 U.S. 479 (1984).

b. Remedy for Due Process Violation

When lost or destroyed evidence no longer exists, the remedy of a new trial is not effective. Instead, the remedy is for the court to suppress test results from the destroyed or lost evidence, or to instruct the jury to draw adverse inferences from the loss or destruction of the evidence. For example, the instruction could tell the jury to assume that the evidence, if available, would have been favorable.

D. DISCOVERY STANDARDS FOR EITHER PARTY

1. Reciprocity

In *Wardius v. Oregon*, 412 U.S. 470 (1973), the state required the defendant to disclose his intent to present an alibi defense, but the defendant had no right of discovery against the prosecution. The Supreme Court held that ordinarily discovery must be a two-way street. It is fundamentally unfair to require a defendant to divulge the details of his own case while at the same time subjecting him to the hazard of surprise covering refutation of the very pieces of evidence that he disclosed to the State. Fed.R.Crim.P. 12.1, 12.2, and 16 provides reciprocal discovery, as shown in the next section.

2. Continuing Duty to Disclose

If the court orders discovery, the parties have a continuing duty to disclose, as it becomes available, any additional evidence or material covered by the discovery court order.

3. Pretrial Statements of Trial Witnesses

Generally, the federal rules do not authorize pretrial discovery of the identities of prosecution or defense witnesses. However, Fed.R.Crim.P. 26.2 permits both the defense and prosecution on motion to obtain any pretrial statement of any prosecution or defense witness in the possession of the opposition, *after* the witness testifies at trial on direct examination.

a. Defining a "Statement"

The key to understanding Fed.R.Crim.P. 26.2 is the definition of a "statement" in Fed.R.Crim.P. 26.2(f), which can be a written statement made and signed or adopted or approved by the witness, *or* a substantially *verbatim* recital of an oral statement that is recorded contemporaneously and contained in a recording or transcription of a recording.

4. Work Product

Discovery provisions commonly include an exemption from discovery that will exempt some form of prosecution work product. Except as provided in Fed.R.Crim.P. 16(a)(2) and (b)(2) authorizing discovery of the defendant's own statements, prior records, and reports of examinations and scientific tests, the federal rule does not authorize the discovery or inspection of reports, memoranda, or other internal government documents made by an attorney for the defense or the government or other defense or government agent investigating, defending or prosecuting the case. The federal rule provision encompasses non-opinion as well as opinion work product. Unlike civil discovery, the criminal discovery rule does not provide for disclosure of the non-opinion portions upon a showing of substantial need and undue hardship.

5. Protective Orders

The criminal defendant's right to pretrial discovery may conflict with the privacy rights of victims or other third parties, even though the party seeking discovery is entitled to a reasonable opportunity to examine the discovery material and prepare for its use at trial. Fed.R.Crim.P. 16(d)(1) enables a trial court to issue protective orders to protect either party from improper discovery. Upon a sufficient showing of good cause, the court may at any time order that discovery or inspection be denied, restricted, or deferred, or make such other order that is appropriate.

6. Discovery Sanctions

If either party fails to comply with the court's protective or modified discovery orders, the court generally has a number of options for dealing with the violation. If counsel fails to provide adequate discovery, the court may order counsel to make further disclosure, grant a continuance of the trial to allow for additional discovery, prohibit counsel from introducing at trial any undisclosed evidence, or enter any other order that is just under the circumstances. The scope of permissible remedies depends on the degree of the alleged violation as well as the prejudice that the offended party can establish.

a. Taylor v. Illinois

In appropriate cases, *Taylor v. Illinois*, 484 U.S. 400 (1988) recognized that more drastic remedies are constitutionally permissible. In that case, the Court held that no violation of the Sixth Amendment Compulsory Process Clause occurred when the trial judge refused to allow a defense witness to testify because defense counsel engaged in willful misconduct by ignoring the discovery rules to gain a tactical advantage.

(1) Deciding the Appropriate Sanction

In deciding what sanction to apply, *Taylor* noted that the judge balances the defendant's right to offer testimony against:

- the integrity of the adversary process,
- the interest in the fair and efficient administration of justice,
- the potential prejudice to the truth-determining function of the trial process,
- the nature of the explanation given for the party's failure seasonably to comply with discovery requests,
- the willfulness of the violation, the simplicity of compliance, and
- whether an unfair tactical advantage was being sought.

b. Sample Sanctions Under State Rules

Possible sanctions authorized in various state rules include: an instruction to the jury to assume the accuracy of certain facts that might have been established through the nondisclosed material, holding the offending party in contempt of court, declaration of a mistrial, or in the case of a violation by the government, dismissal of the prosecution. The least drastic and preferred remedy for violations of discovery orders is to order immediate disclosure and offer a continuance for the party to examine the material.

E. DEFENSE DISCOVERY UNDER THE FEDERAL RULES

Brady's due process obligation to disclose exculpatory evidence overrides any limitations on discovery provided by a jurisdiction's discovery statutes or rules. In addition to that constitutional standard, each state is free to set discovery requirements as broadly or narrowly as it pleases. The only constitutional limitation on the state's choice is that the state must be even handed in its treatment of the prosecution and the defense.

1. Discovery Methods

In the absence of voluntary disclosure, the parties either must:

- ask the court to order pretrial discovery, or
- conduct discovery outside the purview of the court by making informal requests of each other.

A motion for discovery or an informal request should specify the time, place, and manner of making the discovery. If a court must approve the discovery, it may prescribe such additional terms and conditions as are required to prevent confusion or misunderstandings between defense counsel and the prosecutor. The federal rules operate primarily by informal requests.

2. Typical Subjects of Rule-based Discovery

Although the specific rules of each jurisdiction vary, most jurisdictions' rules require the government to disclose:

- prior statements of the defendant that are in the possession of the prosecution or other government agencies such as the police department,
- a copy of the defendant's prior criminal record,
- documents and tangible objects the prosecution intends to use at trial, and

- scientific reports and tests such as autopsy reports and fingerprint analysis.

In return, many jurisdictions enable the prosecution to learn about the defendant's intent to raise certain defenses such as alibi, insanity, self-defense or entrapment.

3. Discovery of Items Within the Government's Possession, Custody or Control

Discovery provisions commonly extend only to those discoverable items within the prosecutor's possession, custody or control. This concept reflects an extension of discovery beyond information that the prosecution intends to use at trial. It clearly encompasses the files of the police department working with the prosecutor in a particular case, but there may be a question about whether "control" extends to any prosecutorial or law enforcement officer to which the prosecution might have access. Fed.R.Crim.P. 16 states that discovery may be had of information:

- within the possession, custody or control of the government, and
- which the prosecutor knows or by the exercise of due diligence could know of its existence.

4. Discoverable Items Under Fed.R.Crim.P. 16(a)

a. Defendant's Written or Recorded Statements

When a defendant submits a request, Fed.R.Crim.P. 16(a) requires the prosecution to disclose all relevant written or recorded statements of the defendant within the prosecution's possession or control. (While the defendant can obtain his own grand jury testimony, pretrial discovery under the federal rules prohibits access to other grand jury testimony.)

(1) Purposes for Discovery of the Defendant's Statements

The precise wording of the defendant's statement is especially important to defense counsel in preparing for trial or in determining whether a guilty plea is advisable. Disclosure does not pose a substantial threat of successful perjury since the defendant may be impeached effectively by reference to his own statement. The disclosure of the defendant's statement does not create a reciprocity problem, because the government gained discovery from the defendant in obtaining the statement from him. If disclosure were not granted directly by the rule, the defendant would simply use a motion to suppress as an indirect discovery device.

b. Defendant's Oral Statements

In addition to defense discovery of written or recorded statements, Fed.R.Crim.P. 16(a)(1)(A) permits discovery of the substance of any relevant oral statement made by the defendant whether before or after arrest in response to any interrogation by any person then known to the defendant to be a government agent. The rule's language requires *no* discovery of the defendant's blurted statements or of statements made by the defendant to someone he did not know was an agent for the government.

c. Expert Witnesses

If the prosecution intends to present testimony from an expert at trial, it must respond to a defendant's request by giving the defendant a written summary of that testimony during its case-in-chief. Fed.R.Crim.P. 16(a)(1)(G). The nature of the government's disclosure must describe the expert's qualifications, opinions, and its bases and reasons.

d. Reports of Examinations and Tests

In addition to statements from the defendant, defense discovery rules like Fed.R.Crim.P. 16(a)(1)(F) commonly require pretrial disclosure of reports on physical and mental examinations and about scientific tests or experiments that are within the prosecution's possession or control. Pretrial disclosure is justified because once a report is prepared a scientific expert's position is not readily influenced and disclosure presents little danger of encouraging perjury or witness intimidation.

e. Documents and Objects

As with examinations results and scientific reports, Fed.R.Crim.P. 16(a)(1)(E) allows a defendant to inspect and copy books, papers, documents, photographs, tangible objects, buildings or places which are within the possession, custody or control of the government under certain circumstances. Such objects must be either material to the preparation of the defendant's defense, intended for use at trial by the government as evidence during its case-in-chief, or obtained from or belong to the defendant. However, the discovery rules are not intended to enable a defendant to examine documents that are material to the preparation of a constitutional defense such as selective prosecution. *United States v. Armstrong*, 517 U.S. 456 (1996).

f. Defendant's Prior Criminal Record

If the defendant requests a copy of his criminal record, the prosecution must disclose any such record of which it has knowledge or through due diligence should have knowledge. Fed.R.Crim.P. 16(a)(1)(D).

F. PROSECUTION DISCOVERY UNDER THE FEDERAL RULES

Prosecutorial discovery may occur by operation of the general discovery rules, such as Fed.R.Crim.P. 16(b), or by specific rules like Fed.R.Crim.P. 12.1, 12.2, or 12.3. The prosecution's right to discovery is conditioned upon whether the defense has been granted like discovery under Fed.R.Crim.P. 16(a). Thus if the defendant files no motion or request to discover the prosecution's evidence, the prosecution will have no right to discover defense evidence. If, however, the defendant has been granted discovery, the prosecution may be granted a reciprocal right to discovery.

1. Reciprocal Discovery Under Fed.R.Crim.P. 16(b)

If a defendant obtains from the prosecution discovery of information about documents and objects, examination and test reports, or expert witnesses, the prosecution is entitled to seek discovery of similar information from the defense. For the first two categories of information, the prosecution may discover information that is in the possession of the defendant *and* which the defendant intends to use during her case-in-chief at trial. Fed.R.Crim.P. 16(b)(1)(A)–(B). The prosecution may discover information about defense experts whom the defendant intends to use at trial. Fed.R.Crim.P. 16(b)(1)(C).

2. Notice of Alibi Defense

The Federal Rules mandate the disclosure of defendant's intent to raise the defense of alibi under Fed.R.Crim.P. 12.1. At least with respect to an alibi defense, *Williams v. Florida*, 399 U.S. 78 (1970) held that such disclosure rules do not violate the Fifth Amendment even though the defendant has to disclose information before the trial.

a. Williams v. Florida

In *Williams*, the defendant sought to be excused from Florida's notice-of-alibi rule that required him to give notice in advance of trial if he intended to claim an alibi and to furnish the prosecutor with information about the place he claimed to have been and the names of witnesses he intended to call in support of his alibi. The Court concluded that the privilege against self-incrimination is not violated by a requirement that the defendant give pretrial notice of an alibi defense and disclose his alibi witnesses. The Court found that the rule compelled the defendant merely to accelerate the timing of his disclosure.

b. How Fed.R.Crim.P. 12.1 Operates

The federal notice-of-alibi rule requires a prosecutor to initiate a request to the defendant for written notice about his intent to rely on an alibi defense. The notice by the defendant must state the place at which the defendant claims to have been at the time of the offense, along with the same type of information required by the Florida rule. In the spirit of *Wardius*'s call for reciprocity, the prosecution must supply information establishing the defendant's presence at the crime and rebutting the alibi defense. If the defendant later withdraws the alibi defense, the fact of the withdrawal is not admissible against him.

3. Notice of Insanity Defense or Expert Evidence of a Mental Condition

Fed.R.Crim.P. 12.2 requires a defendant to give advance notice about the intent to rely on a defense of insanity, or the intent to introduce expert testimony that he lacked the mental state for the offense.

a. How Fed.R.Crim.P. 12.2 Operates

The scope of the rule is broader than first appears, because it addresses issues far beyond insanity issues. The defendant must notify the prosecutor in writing of such intent, without waiting for the prosecutor to initiate the process. The trial judge may order the defendant to submit to a mental examination, but any statements to the examiner by the defendant are inadmissible on any issue other than his mental condition. As with the alibi notice rule, a withdrawn defense by the defendant is inadmissible.

4. Notice of Public Authority Defense

Fed.R.Crim.P. 12.3 requires a defendant to disclose his intent to claim a defense of actual or perceived exercise of public authority at the time of the offense. In response to the notice, the defendant first must disclose information about witnesses he will call to support the defense and in turn the government must make like disclosures to the defendant.

CHAPTER 24

GUILTY PLEAS

A. INTRODUCTION

Most criminal cases are *not* resolved by a full trial by jury. "Ninety-seven percent of federal convictions and ninety-four percent of state convictions are the result of guilty pleas." *Lafler v. Cooper*, 132 S.Ct. 1376 (2012). While an attorney must obviously render competent services where the defendant's guilt is contested, it is probably also true that an attorney should explore the possibility that a case may be resolved in some manner other than a jury trial.

B. TYPES OF PLEAS

After an indictment or information has been filed, the defendant is typically arraigned on that charging document and is asked to enter a plea in open court. The criminal rules contemplate that a defendant may plead not guilty, which is a constitutional right. A plea of not guilty generally is regarded as a denial of every material allegation in the indictment. A defendant may plead not guilty and rely on all defenses, even those that are deemed to be affirmative in nature.

1. Guilty Plea

A defendant may plead guilty to the charges, even at the arraignment. A guilty plea is a defendant's admission in open court about committing the charges in the indictment. A plea of guilty differs in purpose and effect from a mere admission or an extrajudicial confession in that it is a conviction that is conclusive. A proper guilty plea dispenses with requirements of evidence of guilt. Once a guilty plea is entered, the court has nothing to do but impose sentence.

a. Rights Waived by a Guilty Plea

A guilty plea constitutes a waiver of numerous constitutional rights, including the privilege against self-incrimination, the right to a trial by jury, and the right to confront one's accusers. While there are exceptions, a guilty plea constitutes an admission of all facts alleged and a waiver of all non-jurisdictional and procedural defects and constitutional infirmities in any prior stage of the proceeding. In addition, a guilty plea is a waiver of the right to appeal the conviction.

2. *Nolo Contendere*

In many jurisdictions—if permitted by the procedural rules or by the court in the interests of justice—the accused may enter a plea of *nolo contendere*, i.e. indicating that she is simply not contesting the charges. *See, e.g.*, Fed.R.Crim.P. 11(a)(3). Generally a "*nolo* plea" (as it is commonly called) is identical to a guilty plea except that, unlike a guilty plea, a *nolo* plea cannot be used as an admission of guilt against the defendant in a subsequent civil or administrative proceeding. However, the law still regards a *nolo* plea as the equivalent of a criminal conviction for sentencing and recidivist charges.

3. Guilty But Mentally Ill

In most jurisdictions, instead of pleading guilty or not guilty (or entering a *nolo* plea), the defendant can invoke a psychological condition by pleading not guilty by reason of mental illness or mental retardation or, in some jurisdictions, guilty but mentally ill.

a. Burdens of Proof

A defendant may enter a plea of guilty but mentally ill if the court finds the defendant was mentally ill at the time of the offense. Or, a defendant may be found guilty but mentally ill at a trial if the prosecution proves guilt beyond a reasonable doubt, and the defendant proves by a preponderance of the evidence that he was mentally ill at the time of the offense.

b. Sentencing Consequences for Guilty but Mentally Ill

The court may appoint at least one psychologist or psychiatrist to examine, treat and report on the defendant's mental condition at the time of sentencing. If the defendant is found guilty but mentally ill at the time of sentencing, treatment is provided for the defendant until the treating professional determines that such treatment is no longer necessary or until expiration of the sentence, whichever occurs first. Such treatment must be a condition of probation, conditional discharge, parole or conditional release as long as the defendant requires treatment for the mental illness in the opinion of the treating professional.

4. *Alford* Plea

A defendant may wish to accept a plea bargain and plead guilty but continue to protest his innocence, in order to avoid the risk of going to trial where a higher sentence may be imposed. Because the trial court usually must find a factual basis for a guilty plea and insure that the plea is otherwise voluntary, the validity of such a plea is suspect.

a. North Carolina v. Alford

In *North Carolina v. Alford*, 400 U.S. 25 (1970), the Court allowed the use of a "best interest" guilty plea. Where a defendant is represented by competent counsel and there is a record that strongly evinces guilt, an accused may voluntarily, knowingly, and understandingly consent to the imposition of a prison sentence even though the defendant is unwilling to admit participation in the crime, or even if the guilty plea contains a protestation of innocence.

5. Conditional Guilty Plea

A number of jurisdictions have rules such as Fed.R.Crim.P. 11(a)(2), by which a defendant may, with the approval of the court, enter a conditional plea of guilty. In so doing, the defendant reserves in writing the right to appellate review of the adverse determination of any specified pretrial or trial motion.

a. Purpose of a Conditional Guilty Plea

The conditional guilty plea avoids the necessity of a full trial for a defendant who wants appellate review of a claim (but who previously had to go to trial to preserve the issue for appeal). Conditional pleas require that both the court and the prosecutor approve the conditional guilty plea, and any defendant who prevails on appeal may later withdraw the conditional plea.

C. PLEA NEGOTIATION

The prosecutor frequently attempts to resolve a case by negotiations with the defense attorney. While the prosecutor may decide to negotiate with the defense attorney, the prosecutor is not compelled to do so. A defendant has no constitutional right to plea bargain. When the prosecutor does decide to negotiate, the system "presuppose[s] fairness." While a prosecutor cannot engage in vindictive conduct and must usually honor plea agreements, there are few legal sanctions that may be imposed on the prosecutor. Under the guise of allowing leniency in plea situations, the courts permit the prosecutor to engage in not so subtle threats.

CHAPTER 24

1. Importance of Plea Bargains

The reason defense lawyers continue to negotiate plea agreements is because of the fear that their clients may face uncertain punishment at trial. For example, in *Corbitt v. New Jersey*, 439 U.S. 212 (1978), the Court upheld a statute that allowed for a possibly lesser sentence for those who plead guilty but which was not available for those who went to trial. The practice of plea negotiations similarly encourages defendants to plead guilty rather than go to trial.

2. Bordenkircher v. Hayes

In *Bordenkircher v. Hayes*, 434 U.S. 357 (1978), the Court found that a prosecutor may carry out threats of increased charges made during plea negotiations if the defendant refuses to plead guilty to the original charge. After *Bordenkircher*, a plea is likely to be found voluntary as part of the "give-and-take" of negotiations as long as the prosecutor has probable cause for any charges brought or threatened. (Previously, in *Brady v. United States*, 397 U.S. 742 (1970), the Court took a different view of voluntariness: for a guilty plea to be valid the defense must be aware of "the actual value of any commitments made.") Most courts have no problem with the voluntariness of a plea by a husband to avoid like charges being brought against his spouse, as long as there was probable cause for those threatened charges.

3. Effective Assistance of Counsel

Although there is no constitutional right to plea bargain, the practical reality of the criminal justice system requires oversight of defense counsel in plea negotiations. Defense counsel is ineffective if she fails to properly inform the defendant of a beneficial plea agreement offered by the prosecution, or if she incorrectly advises defendant on the state of the law or the consequences of a guilty plea. *Missouri v. Frye*, 132 S.Ct. 1399 (2012); *Lafler v. Cooper*; *Padilla v. Kentucky*, 559 U.S. 356 (2010). See Chapter 16C.

4. Package Deals

In addition, the prosecutor may offer a "package deal" whereby all defendants in a single case must accept the terms or else the deal applies to none. Prosecutors nevertheless cannot base the decision to plea bargain upon unjustifiable standards such as race, religion or other arbitrary classification.

5. Judicial Participation in Plea Negotiations

A federal judge's participation in plea negotiations, in violation of Fed.R.Crim.P. 11(c)(1), is harmless error and does not require vacating a guilty plea, unless the record shows that the defendant would not have pleaded guilty in the absence of the error. *United States v. Davila*, 133 S.Ct. 2139 (2013).

D. PLEA AGREEMENTS UNDER THE FEDERAL RULES

Fed.R.Crim.P. 11(b)–(g) describes types of "plea agreements" which may be reached between a defendant and the government, and the procedure used to implement and safeguard such agreements.

1. "A" Agreement

Not every criminal charge against a defendant ends in either a conviction or an acquittal. Sometimes, the charges are "dismissed" or other actions are taken. One type of plea agreement (sometimes referred to as an "A" agreement, described in Fed.R.Crim.P. 11(c)(1)(A)) recognizes that, in return for a guilty plea, the prosecutor will not bring, or will move to dismiss, other charges against the defendant.

a. Dismissal of Charges

As part of a plea bargain agreement, the prosecutor may seek dismissal of charges or defendants with the court's permission. A *nolle prosequi*, or *nolle*, is a formal declaration of record by the prosecution that it will not prosecute further, either as to some of the counts of the indictment or as to some of the defendants.

b. Reduction or Amendment of Charges

As part of any plea agreement, the prosecution may reduce or amend a criminal charge on motion with the court's permission. The reduction or amendment of charges is one of the most common elements in bargained pleas. The charge to which the plea is ultimately entered in such cases tends to reflect the severity of the defendant's conduct and the strength or weakness of the prosecutor's case, but it may bear little relationship to the charge initially brought in the case.

2. "C" Agreement

A second plea agreement recognized by the Federal Rules (sometimes referred to as a "C" agreement, per Fed.R.Crim.P. 11(c)(1)(C)) is that the parties agree that a specific sentence or sentence range is the appropriate disposition of the case.

3. Judicial Role with A and C Agreements

The primary distinction between an A or C agreement and a B agreement is that the court must accept or reject an A or C agreement, or may defer its decision until it has considered the presentence report. The necessity of an acceptance or rejection ensures that the defendant will either receive from the court the bargained for concessions or instead be given the opportunity to withdraw the plea. See Fed.R.Crim.P. 11(c)(4)–(5).

4. "B" Agreement

The third type of plea agreement recognized by the federal rules (and sometimes referred to as a "B" agreement, per Fed.R.Crim.P. 11(c)(1)(B)) is that the prosecutor will recommend, or agree not to oppose the defendant's request, that a specific sentence or sentence range is appropriate. Like an A agreement, under a B agreement the prosecutor is supposed to live up to the promise about the recommendation.

a. Judicial Role with B Agreements

The court is not bound in any way by the recommendation under a B agreement. In a B agreement, the court must advise the defendant that the opportunity to withdraw the plea does not exist if it decides not to follow the recommendation or request, because the recommendation or request by the prosecutor was all that the defendant was entitled to under the agreement. The court's advice to the defendant thus precludes the application of the acceptance provisions of Fed.R.Crim.P. 11(c)(4) or a need for rejection of the agreement with the opportunity to withdraw under Fed.R.Crim.P. 11(c)(5).

5. Agreements Are Not Mutually Exclusive

The three types of agreements specified in the federal rules are not mutually exclusive. Thus, for example, if a defendant faces several charges, a B agreement may be reached to recommend a particular sentence on one count, and the prosecutor may move for dismissal of another count under an A agreement.

E. ENFORCEMENT OF PLEA AGREEMENTS

Fed.R.Crim.P. 11 contains an elaborate structure of procedures for judicial consideration of plea agreements reached by parties. In *United States v. Hyde*, 520 U.S. 670 (1997), the Court observed that the Federal Rules:

> explicitly envision a situation in which the defendant performs his side of the bargain (the guilty plea) before the Government is required to perform its side (here, the motion to dismiss four counts). If the court accepts the agreement and thus the Government's promised performance, then the contemplated agreement is complete and the defendant gets the benefit of his bargain. But if the court rejects the Government's promised

performance, then the agreement is terminated and the defendant has the right to back out of his promised performance (the guilty plea), just as a binding contractual duty may be extinguished by the nonoccurrence of a condition subsequent.

"[W]hen a plea rests in any significant degree on a promise or agreement of the prosecutor, so that it can be said to be part of the inducement or consideration, such promise must be fulfilled." *Santobello v. New York*, 404 U.S. 257 (1971).

1. Was There an Agreement Between the Parties?

The threshold question relates to whether there was an agreement between the prosecutor and defendant. The agreement requires an offer and acceptance by both parties.

2. Was the Agreement Broken?

A plea bargain standing alone has no constitutional significance since it is a mere executory agreement that, until embodied in the judgment of a court, does not deprive an accused of any constitutionally protected interest.

a. When the Defendant Received What Was Bargained For

An agreement is not broken where the defendant receives what he or she bargained for. Alleged violations of plea agreements often focus on whether the prosecutor kept an agreement to recommend a particular sentence or at least not to oppose a desired disposition like probation. A prosecutor who keeps a promise to recommend a particular disposition need not do so enthusiastically or state the reasons for the recommendation. *United States v. Benchimol*, 471 U.S. 453 (1985).

3. Who is Bound by the Agreement?

Assuming that a plea agreement exists between a defendant and the prosecution, who is bound by that agreement? In *Santobello*, the successor of the prosecutor who made a promise about sentencing to the defendant was bound by that promise. Generally, a plea agreement in a state prosecution is not binding on prosecutors in other jurisdictions or on officials in other parts of the same jurisdiction if they are not parties to the agreement.

4. Who Decides Whether the Agreement is Broken?

Although the prosecutor may make a pretrial agreement, the agreement is subject to the approval of the court. Some decisions indicate that the prosecution may unilaterally decide whether the defendant has broken the agreement. In *Ricketts v. Adamson*, 483 U.S. 1 (1987), the Court found that if a defendant refuses to provide the testimony he promised against a codefendant in exchange for a reduction of charges, the guilty plea can be vacated because the defendant has breached his agreement. To avoid unilateral rescission of a plea agreement by the prosecution, a plea agreement should explicitly state that questions about the construction of the terms of the plea agreement must be decided by the court and not by the parties.

5. Remedies for a Broken Agreement

In *Santobello*, the Supreme Court left to the discretion of the trial court whether a guilty plea should be set aside or specific performance of the prosecutor's promise should be granted.

F. TENDERING A GUILTY PLEA TO THE COURT

A judge who considers a plea of guilty or *nolo contendere* from a defendant must address the defendant personally in open court and determine that the plea is voluntary. Fed.R.Crim.P. 11(b)(1).

1. Defendant's Competence to Plead

While a defendant's guilty plea will be set aside if it is taken without the physical presence of the defendant, a defendant also must be competent to plead guilty. There is no higher mental standard required to enter a guilty plea than there is to stand trial. *Godinez v. Moran*, 509 U.S. 389 (1993). Prior drug use or addiction will not always make a plea involuntary unless the defendant is under the influence of drugs at the time he or she enters the plea. Where drugs are present at the time of the plea, the intoxication must be such as to render the defendant incompetent so as to lack an understanding of the plea.

2. The Plea Must Be Voluntary, Knowing and Intelligent

The issue of voluntariness includes whether the defendant is capable of pleading guilty as well as whether the plea is the result of force, threats or promises that are not part of a plea agreement. In addition, the federal rules and many decisions suggest that a plea must be intelligently made, i.e., the defendant must have a sufficient amount of information about the charge to which he is pleading as well as the consequences of the plea.

a. *Henderson v. Morgan*: What Is a Voluntary Plea?

In *Henderson v. Morgan*, 426 U.S. 637 (1976), the Court held that a plea was involuntary when neither defense counsel nor the trial court explained that intent was an element of second-degree murder. A guilty plea is involuntary if the defendant is unaware of the essential elements of the offense to which he is pleading.

b. Sufficient for Counsel to Inform Defendant About the Charge

The Court later retreated from its suggestion that the record should reflect the defendant's understanding of the essential elements of the criminal charge. "Where a defendant is represented by competent counsel, the court usually may rely on that counsel's assurance that the defendant has been properly informed of the nature and elements of the charge to which he is pleading guilty." *Bradshaw v. Stumpf*, 545 U.S. 175 (2005).

c. What the Rules Require the Defendant to Know

The Federal Rules address the *Henderson* issue by requiring that the court ensure the defendant's understanding about "the nature of each charge to which the defendant is pleading." Fed.R.Crim.P. 11(b)(1)(G). The Rules establish further procedures that federal courts must follow to ensure that a plea is voluntary.

3. Factual Basis for the Plea

The court may decide not to accept a guilty plea unless there is a factual basis for the plea. Fed.R.Crim.P. 11(b)(3). The purpose of a factual basis is to ensure that the defendant does not mistakenly plead guilty when his actual conduct does not meet all the elements of the crime. A factual basis for the plea may be accomplished by having the prosecutor recite the facts or by having the defendant describe the conduct that gave rise to the charge, or a combination. Most courts recognize that the evidence for the factual basis, whether from the prosecutor or from the defendant, need only be enough from which a court can reasonably find that the defendant is guilty of the particular offense.

4. What the Court Record Must Show

The record of the trial court must affirmatively show that the defendant both voluntarily waived those rights and understood the rights that he was waiving. *Boykin v. Alabama*, 395 U.S. 238 (1969). Per other portions of the federal rule, the court must inform the defendant of and determine that he understands the rights that he is waiving by pleading guilty and the range of penalties of the offenses to which he is pleading. Fed.R.Crim.P. 11(b)(1)(A)–(F), (H)–(N).

a. Effect of Insufficient Explanation of Rights

If a defendant testifies that the judge accepted a plea without explaining the rights or that the defendant did not understand the rights, the prosecution has the burden of proof that the judgment was entered in a way which fully protected the defendant's constitutional rights. A silent record does not suffice. In a recidivist proceeding, however, a presumption of regularity of the prior judgment of conviction exists. *Parke v. Raley*, 506 U.S. 20 (1992).

G. WITHDRAWING A GUILTY PLEA

1. Broken Plea Agreements

It is not uncommon for a defendant who has previously tendered a guilty plea to subsequently seek to withdraw that plea, whether it is days, months, or even years later. In "broken" plea agreement cases, i.e. situations where the defendant believes that he or she has not received the "deal" he or she bargained for, courts generally permit such withdrawal if they agree that the deal was in fact broken.

a. "Recommendations" Do Not Justify Plea Withdrawal

However, where the bargained-for deal is simply to be a "recommendation" or where the prosecutor has agreed simply not to oppose a defense recommendation, and where the prosecutor has not reneged on this particular deal, a defendant cannot count on being able to withdraw a guilty plea if he or she is displeased with the ultimate sentencing outcome. For example, under a B agreement the court must advise the defendant that if the court does not follow the recommendation or request, the defendant has no right to withdraw the plea.

2. Other Reasons for Wanting to Withdraw a Plea

Besides the broken plea agreement cases, there are reasons why a defendant might later seek to withdraw his or her guilty plea. Such reasons range from mere second thoughts about the strategic thinking (defendant's and/or defense counsel's) that resulted in a guilty plea, to dissatisfaction with or surprise at the severity of the sentence received, to the emergence of new evidence or new witnesses (or the disappearance of evidence or witnesses).

a. Plea Withdrawal Prior to Plea Acceptance

Prior to acceptance of a plea, the federal rules permit withdrawal for any reason or no reason. Fed.R.Crim.P. 11(d)(1).

b. Withdrawal After Plea Acceptance But Before Sentencing

After acceptance of a plea agreement, but before imposition of sentence, the court may permit the defendant to withdraw the plea if the defendant presents "any fair and just reason" to do so, or if the court rejects the plea agreement. Fed.R.Crim.P. 11(d)(2).

c. Withdrawal After Sentencing

After the imposition of sentence, the federal rules do not provide for plea withdrawal and withdrawal is rarely permitted absent a finding of manifest injustice or a miscarriage of justice.

d. Constitutional Basis to Withdrawal Plea: Ineffective Assistance

If the reason a defendant pleaded guilty was that he relied on the incompetent legal or tactical advice of defense counsel, when he can demonstrate that "there is a reasonable probability that, but for counsel's errors, [defendant] would not have pleaded guilty and would have insisted on going to trial," a trial court may permit the guilty plea to be withdrawn as a result of ineffective assistance of counsel. *Hill v. Lockhart*, 474 U.S. 52 (1985). *See* Chapter 16.

CHAPTER 25

JURY TRIALS

A. CONSTITUTIONAL RIGHT TO JURY TRIAL

The Sixth Amendment provides in part that in all criminal prosecutions an "accused shall enjoy the right to a public trial, by an impartial jury of the State and district wherein the crime shall have been committed. . . ." Further, Article III of the Constitution states that "[t]he trial of all crimes . . . shall be by jury; and such trial shall be held in the state where the said crimes shall have been committed. . . ." Notwithstanding the breadth of those constitutional standards, the case law differs about the scope of the right.

1. Jury Trial as a Fundamental Right: *Duncan v. Louisiana*

The Sixth Amendment jury trial right is applicable to the states through the Fourteenth Amendment Due Process Clause. In *Duncan v. Louisiana*, 391 U.S. 145 (1968), the defendant was convicted of simple battery, a misdemeanor under Louisiana law, and punishable by a maximum of two years' imprisonment and a $300 fine. He sought a trial by jury, but the trial judge denied the request because the state constitution granted jury trials only when capital punishment or imprisonment at hard labor could be imposed. Duncan was convicted and sentenced to serve 60 days in the parish prison and pay a fine of $150. The Court upheld Duncan's right to a jury trial, and described the rationale and the scope of the jury trial right, as follows.

a. Jury Trial Right Combats Government Oppression

"A right to jury trial is granted to criminal defendants in order to prevent oppression by the Government. Those who wrote our constitutions knew from history and experience that it was necessary to protect against unfounded criminal charges brought to eliminate enemies and against judges too responsive to the voice of higher authority. . . . Beyond this, the jury trial provisions in the Federal and State Constitutions reflect a fundamental decision about the exercise of official power—a reluctance to entrust plenary powers over the life and liberty of the citizen to one judge or to a group of judges."

b. **The Scope of the Jury Trial Right**

"[In] determining whether the length of the authorized prison term or the seriousness of other punishment is enough in itself to require a jury trial, [we] refer to objective criteria, chiefly the existing laws and practices in the Nation. In the federal system, petty offenses are defined as those punishable by no more than six months in prison and a $500 fine. In 49 of the 50 States crimes subject to trial without a jury, which occasionally include simple battery, are punishable by no more than one year in jail. We need not, however, settle in this case the exact location of the line between petty offenses and serious crimes. It is sufficient for our purposes to hold that a crime punishable by two years in prison is, based on past and contemporary standards in this country, a serious crime and not a petty offense. Consequently, appellant was entitled to a jury trial and it was error to deny it."

c. **No Right to Jury Trial in Juvenile Delinquency Cases**

The right to a jury trial does not apply to juveniles convicted in juvenile court, because 1) a juvenile delinquency proceeding is neither civil nor criminal, and 2) accurate fact-finding is possible without a jury trial. *McKeiver v. Pennsylvania*, 403 U.S. 528 (1971).

d. **No Right to Jury Trial in *De Novo* Cases**

A jurisdiction may use a two-tier trial system in which no jury is provided for the first trial, but the defendant has a right to a second jury trial *de novo*. *Ludwig v. Massachusetts*, 427 U.S. 618 (1976). The possibility of a second trial before a jury satisfies the need to protect the defendant from government oppression.

e. **What Juries Decide**

A jury decides: 1) questions of fact, and 2) how to apply the legal elements of the offense to those facts, drawing the ultimate conclusion of guilt or innocence. The jury's constitutional responsibility includes deciding mixed questions of law and fact. *United States v. Gaudin*, 515 U.S. 506 (1995).

2. **The Test for the Constitutional Right: Authorized Sentence**

A jury trial is constitutionally mandated for any offense that carries an *authorized* sentence of more than six months, regardless of whether the *actual* sentence imposed. For offenses with authorized sentences of six months or less, there is a presumption against a jury trial, to be rebutted by a defendant who can show that additional statutory penalties are so severe that the penalties together indicate that the legislature considers the offense to be "serious." *Blanton v. City of North Las Vegas*, 489 U.S. 538 (1989).

a. Rebutting the Petty Offense Presumption Is Difficult

Later decisions applying *Blanton* have not generously construed its holding in favor of a jury trial. In *United States v. Nachtigal*, 507 U.S. 1 (1993), the Court held that a DUI charge with a maximum penalty of six months' imprisonment, a $5,000 fine, a five-year term of probation, and other penalties was not constitutionally serious enough for a jury trial. The Court reiterated *Blanton*'s presumption that offenses are presumptively "petty" when the maximum authorized period of incarceration is six months or less.

b. Jury Trial Right Is Determined Offense-by-Offense

The right to a jury trial based on violations of criminal statutes is determined on an offense-by-offense basis, rather than in the aggregate. *Lewis v. United States*, 518 U.S. 322 (1996). The scope of the federal jury trial right "does not change where a defendant faces a potential aggregate prison term in excess of six months for petty offenses charged. . . . [B]y setting the maximum authorized prison term at six months, the Legislature categorized the offense . . . as petty. . . . [For example,] the fact that the defendant was charged with two counts of a petty offense does not revise the legislative judgment as to the gravity of the particular offense, nor does it transform the petty offense into a serious one. . . ."

3. Apprendi v. New Jersey

Whenever any fact besides a prior conviction increases the maximum penalty for a crime with regard to federal law, Fifth Amendment Due Process and the Sixth Amendment jury trial right require that the fact must be charged in the charging instrument, submitted to a jury, and proved beyond a reasonable doubt. That standard applies as well to the states through the Fourteenth Amendment. *Apprendi v. New Jersey*, 530 U.S. 466 (2000). Thus, a judge alone cannot increase a penalty beyond a statutory maximum by making a factual determination under a preponderance of evidence standard.

a. Ring v. Arizona

In *Ring v. Arizona*, 536 U.S. 584 (2002), the Court addressed the situation in states where juries determine defendants' guilt or innocence and judges alone decide their punishment. The Court held that a sentence imposed by a judge in those circumstances violates a defendant's constitutional right to a trial by jury. Comparing the *Apprendi* result with *Ring*, Justice Ginsburg noted: "The right to trial by jury guaranteed by the Sixth Amendment would be senselessly diminished if it encompassed the fact-finding necessary to increase a defendant's sentence by two years, but not the fact-finding necessary to put him to death. We hold that the Sixth Amendment applies to both." *Ring*'s immediate effect was to overturn death sentences in at least 150 cases in which judges had been allowed to make life-or-death decisions.

b. Alleyne v. United States

The Sixth Amendment right to a jury trial applies to facts that trigger or increase mandatory minimum sentences. *Alleyne v. United States*, 133 S.Ct. 2151 (2013). In *Alleyne*, when an essential fact issue was whether the defendant brandished a weapon, a jury must decide that fact in order to increase the mandatory minimum sentence for the crime.

c. Blakely v. Washington

Blakely v. Washington, 542 U.S. 296 (2004) held that "the relevant statutory maximum for *Apprendi* purposes is the maximum a judge may impose based solely on the facts reflected in the jury verdict or admitted by the defendant." Blakely pleaded guilty to kidnapping, a crime which supported a maximum sentence of 53 months. However, after the trial judge found that the defendant had acted with "deliberate cruelty," the sentence increased to 90 months. Likewise, the Court invalidated California's determinate sentencing law, which gave the judge the authority to elevate a sentence by finding the existence of "circumstances in aggravation." *Cunningham v. California*, 549 U.S. 270 (2007).

d. United States v. Booker

The Court subsequently applied the *Apprendi* and *Blakely* holdings to invalidate the mandatory nature of the Federal Sentencing Guidelines. *United States v. Booker*, 543 U.S. 220 (2005). The remedy from a majority of the *Booker* Court was to consider the mandatory federal standards as "effectively advisory."

e. Southern Union Co. v. United States

Apprendi also applies to sentences of criminal fines. *Southern Union Co. v. United States*, 132 S.Ct. 2344 (2012). Juries must determine the facts that set a fine's maximum amount.

4. Contempt Proceedings

In situations such as contempt proceedings that have no legislatively authorized sentence, a jury must be afforded before an *actual* (as opposed to authorized) sentence of confinement for more than six months may be imposed for a post-verdict finding of contempt. In *Codispoti v. Pennsylvania*, 418 U.S. 506 (1974), the Court held that a contemnor has a right to a jury trial if multiple contempt sentences aggregate to more than six months. Direct contempts in the presence of the court *during* trial are subject to immediate summary adjudication without jury trial.

5. Fines

A jury trial is also required when a court imposes *serious* fines for criminal contempt. In *International Union, United Mine Workers of Am. v. Bagwell*, 512 U.S. 821 (1994), the court held that contempt fines of $52 million for violation of a labor injunction were criminal and were subject to the jury trial right.

6. Waiver of Jury Trial Right

A defendant may waive the constitutional right to a jury trial in favor of a bench trial, but a defendant does not have a right to a bench trial. Because a jury trial is the preferable mode of disposing of factual issues in criminal cases and society also has an interest in the disposition of those cases, *both* the prosecution and the court must concur in a waiver which is unaccompanied by a guilty plea. *See, e.g.*, Fed.R.Crim.P. 23(a). In *Singer v. United States*, 380 U.S. 24 (1965), the Court left open the possibility that the right to waive could belong to the defendant alone. A determination that the defendant's waiver is made voluntarily and with a full understanding of its consequences must precede the acceptance by the court of a waiver.

B. CHARACTERISTICS OF THE JURY TRIAL RIGHT

1. Jury Size

While the federal rules states that a federal jury should consist of twelve jurors, the Supreme Court has upheld state rules requiring fewer than twelve jurors. For example, in *Williams v. Florida*, 399 U.S. 78 (1970), the Court held that a jury consisting of six jurors was constitutionally permissible. Despite the *Williams* holding, many state constitutions require a twelve-person jury for all felony prosecutions and a six-person jury for misdemeanor prosecutions.

a. Six-person Jury

The Court later used empirical data to establish a constitutional minimum of six-person juries and to reject a jury of only five persons as violative of the Sixth and Fourteenth Amendments. *Ballew v. Georgia*, 435 U.S. 223 (1978). Smaller juries are less likely to deliberate effectively, and "they are less likely to have members who remember each of the important pieces of evidence or argument. Furthermore, the smaller the group, the less likely it is to overcome the biases of its members to obtain an accurate result."

2. Jury Unanimity

While federal courts and most state courts require a twelve-person jury verdict to be unanimous, there is no federal constitutional requirement of unanimity. *Apodaca v. Oregon*, 406 U.S. 404 (1972). *Burch v. Louisiana*, 441 U.S. 130 (1979) later held that a unanimous verdict is required of a jury consisting of six members. The Federal Rules require unanimous jury verdicts unless the parties stipulate otherwise. Fed.R.Crim.P. 31(a).

a. State Exceptions to Unanimity

Only Louisiana and Oregon allow juries to convict on less than unanimous votes such as 11–1 or 10–2 in felony cases. The Court has upheld a conviction based upon a 9–3 vote. *Johnson v. Louisiana*, 406 U.S. 356 (1972).

b. Schad v. Arizona

Issues addressed by the courts since *Apodaca* have been more complex. For example, in *Schad v. Arizona*, 501 U.S. 624 (1991), the defendant was convicted of first-degree murder which included both premeditated and felony-murder theories. The prosecution offered proof on both. With a general verdict, it was uncertain whether the jury had been unanimous about premeditated murder. A plurality of the Court characterized the issue as whether alternative actions and mental states could constitute the basis for one crime. The Court held that Schad's due process rights had not been violated when the trial court grouped felony murder and premeditated murder as alternative ways of committing the single crime of first-degree murder.

c. Richardson v. United States

In *Richardson v. United States*, 526 U.S. 813 (1999), a federal statute prohibited engaging in a continuing criminal enterprise (CCE), which is defined as a violation of the drug statutes where the "violation is part of a continuing series of violations." The Court had to decide whether the phrase "series of violations" refers to one element—a "series"—or whether it creates several elements, or violations, each of which requires unanimity. The Court held that a jury must agree unanimously not only that a defendant committed a "continuing series of violations" but also which specific violations made up that "continuing series of violations."

d. Jury Instructions to Enable Jury Unanimity

In some instances the jury will report that it is unable to reach a unanimous verdict. Where the jury reports that it is unable to reach a verdict and the trial court determines that further deliberations may be useful, the court may deliver a limited number of instructions to the jury before considering whether to declare a mistrial. The court may instruct the jury that, in order to return a verdict, each juror must agree to that verdict; jurors must consult with each other and deliberate to achieve an agreement, without harming individual judgment; each juror must decide the case after impartial appraisal of the evidence with other jurors; during deliberations, a juror may reexamine her views and change his or her opinion if persuaded that it is erroneous; and no juror should relinquish his or her honest beliefs about the evidence solely due to the opinion of the other jurors, or merely to return a verdict. When a jury has been kept together until it appears that there is no probability of agreement upon a verdict, the court then may discharge the jury without a verdict.

3. Inconsistent Verdicts

In criminal trials on multiple charges, the jury may convict on one count and acquit on another. On occasion such an action may seem wholly inconsistent. In some states, inconsistent verdicts as between separate counts are permissible unless there is a logical inconsistency resulting in more severe punishment. For example, it is inconsistent for the jury to return verdicts on two wanton crimes and one reckless crime when all three crimes occurred simultaneously. On the other hand, verdicts on three assault charges are not inconsistent when the injuries occurred as a result of three independent acts that produced the charges. Convictions of different degrees of a crime like burglary for different defendants are not regarded as inconsistent.

C. SELECTING PROSPECTIVE JURORS

In most states, the master list for prospective jurors is drawn from such sources as voter registration lists and/or a list of persons over the age of eighteen holding valid drivers' licenses. A computer periodically may generate a randomized jury list of prospective jurors. The jury panel in a court consists of as many names as are necessary for impaneling of the number of jurors required.

1. Juror Qualification Form

Each person drawn for jury service may be served with a summons directing him to report at a specified time and place and to be available for jury service for a period of time. A jury qualification form to be completed and returned often accompanies the summons. The form may seek information about the person's address, date of birth, level of education, employer, and immediate family members. The form also may seek prior litigation information, as well as information which could disqualify the person under statutes from serving as jurors, e.g., United States citizenship, ability to speak and understand English, physical or mental disabilities which may prevent effective jury service, a current indictment or a past felony conviction against the prospective juror, or recent jury service. Unless the court determines in a particular case that the information contained on the form must be kept confidential or its use restricted in the interest of justice, the form is made available to the parties or their attorneys.

2. The Fair Cross-Section Requirement

The Sixth Amendment grants to criminal defendants the right to a "jury of the state and district wherein the crime shall have been committed." From this language has evolved the concept that the trial jury in a criminal case must be selected from a fair cross-section of the community where the crime occurred. A jury panel from which a cognizable class of citizens has been systematically excluded is not a representative jury. The requirement applies only to the jury panel (also known as the jury array or jury venire) from which the petit jury is selected. A grand jury and the jury that *actually* decides the case do not have to reflect a cross-section of the community. The Equal Protection Clause of the Fourteenth Amendment also dictates restrictions on the composition of the petit jury.

a. Purpose of the Requirement

The purposes of the cross-section requirement are:

- avoiding "the possibility that the composition of juries would be arbitrarily skewed in such a way as to deny criminal defendants the benefit of the common-sense judgment of the community,"

- avoiding an "appearance of unfairness," and
- ensuring against deprivation of "often historically disadvantaged groups of their right as citizens to serve on juries in criminal cases." *Lockhart v. McCree*, 476 U.S. 162 (1986).

b. Proving a Violation of the Requirement

In *Duren v. Missouri*, 439 U.S. 357 (1979), the Court held that a defendant must establish three things to demonstrate a *prima facie* violation of the Sixth Amendment fair cross-section requirement, although the defendant does not have to be the same race, ethnicity, or gender as the excluded group. *Taylor v. Louisiana*, 419 U.S. 522 (1975):

- the excluded group is a "distinctive" group playing a major role in the community,
- the group is not fairly and reasonably represented in the jury pool, and
- the underrepresentation is the result of "systematic exclusion" of the group from the jury selection process.

(1) What Is a Distinctive Group?

Case law has held that young adults and college students are not a distinctive group; jurors excluded from jury duty for cause as a result of their beliefs on capital sentencing are not a distinctive group. Likewise, the exclusion of young people due to periodic recompiling of the jury lists has been justified in the interest of judicial economy.

(2) People with Shared Attitudes Not a Distinctive Group

"[G]roups defined solely in terms of shared attitudes that would prevent or substantially impair members of the group from performing one of their duties as jurors" are not part of a distinctive group for purposes of the fair cross-section requirement. *Lockhart v. McCree*, 476 U.S. 162 (1986) (anti-death penalty views).

c. Proving an Equal Protection Violation Relating to Jury Selection

Castaneda v. Partida, 430 U.S. 482 (1977) defined a *prima facie* case of Equal Protection for discriminatory underrepresentation in jury selection. The primary difference between *Partida* and the fair cross-section test relates to the standing requirement. For an equal protection violation, the defendant must be from the same racial, ethnic, or gender group that is alleged to be underrepresented.

D. SELECTING THE ACTUAL JURORS

A jury may be selected with the clerk drawing the number of jurors required for a jury trial from a container holding the names of all members of the jury panel remaining after preliminary proceedings affecting jury qualifications and exemptions. As their names are called, the jurors are tentatively seated in the jury box to be examined under oath concerning their qualifications. If jurors are excused from service following their examination, the clerk draws additional names until they are replaced.

1. *Voir Dire* Examination Purposes

Because of its central role in the selection of a fair and impartial jury, the *voir dire* examination is one of the most important parts of the trial. The purpose of *voir dire* examination is to determine any possible basis for challenging jurors for cause and to develop background information to be considered in the intelligent exercise of peremptory challenges. A second function of the *voir dire* examination is to learn about prejudices and attitudes in order to minimize their effect on the outcome of the case. It is the first opportunity afforded to counsel to address the jury in connection with the case. *Mu'Min v. Virginia*, 500 U.S. 415 (1991).

a. Who Asks Questions During *Voir Dire*?

Except for capital cases that may require individual *voir dire*, examination of individual jurors may be restricted by the court. In most jurisdictions, the court initiates the examination and then permits counsel for the parties to conduct further examination. Even if the court conducts the examination, the parties are often entitled to submit supplemental inquiries. *See, e.g.*, Fed.R.Crim.P. 23(a)(2).

b. What Types of Questions Are Asked?

During *voir dire* examination, the examiner may properly explore all matters which may relate to the case to be tried—the prospective jurors' knowledge and opinions, their relationships and associations, and their attitudes and prejudices. The potential of anything disclosed on *voir dire* examination to affect the outcome of the case may also be explored.

c. Challenges for Cause

If a juror's responses indicate explicit or implicit grounds for a reasonable belief that a juror cannot render a fair and impartial verdict, one of the attorneys or the judge may raise the issue of whether the juror must be excused for cause.

(1) Types of Challenges for Cause

The two general bases for a challenge for cause: an inability to perform the necessary functions, and a bias that could compromise that juror's ability to decide the case impartially. An inability to perform may result from a lack of physical or mental capacity or an inability to understand legal principles. Bias may be actual or implicit, with the former requiring proof that the juror would be biased in the particular case and the latter shown by an assumption that the juror is so likely to be biased that the challenge is appropriate, e.g., membership in a particular interest group.

(2) Example of Removal of Juror for Cause

A challenge for cause must be granted if during *voir dire* a prospective juror hears about a prior conviction of the same defendant in a similar case. *Leonard v. United States*, 378 U.S. 544 (1964).

(3) Challenges for Cause in Capital Cases

In capital cases, the issue is that the court granted the challenges too easily. A juror may be challenged for cause because their opposition to the death penalty is so strong that it would prevent or substantially impair the performance of their duties as jurors. *Wainwright v. Witt*, 469 U.S. 412 (1985). Even a single misapplication of that standard invalidates a death sentence. *Gray v. Mississippi*, 481 U.S. 648 (1987).

(4) Need to Use All Peremptory Challenges?

In some states, a defendant may appeal the presence of an objectionable juror only if she already has used all available peremptory challenges and was thus unable to exclude that objectionable juror. *Ross v. Oklahoma*, 487 U.S. 81 (1988). However, the Court does not require using all peremptory challenges to claim that the defendant was denied a fair trial. *United States v. Martinez-Salazar*, 528 U.S. 304 (2000).

d. Peremptory Challenges

By rule in most jurisdictions, both parties can challenge a number of jurors without giving any reason whatsoever. *See, e.g.*, Fed.R.Crim.P. 24(b). Peremptory challenges, though, are not of constitutional dimension. If multiple defendants are being tried, each defendant usually is entitled to additional peremptory challenges to be exercised jointly with or independently of any other defendant. Typically, the attorneys for each side exercise peremptory challenges and jury selection moves forward. However, if opposing counsel believes that the other attorney has exercised the challenges based on race or gender discrimination, the issue must be raised immediately.

(1) Batson v. Kentucky

Under *Batson v. Kentucky*, 476 U.S. 79 (1986), "a defendant may establish a *prima facie* case of purposeful discrimination in selection of the petit jury solely on evidence concerning the prosecutor's exercise of peremptory challenges at the defendant's trial." The Equal Protection Clause prohibits intentional discrimination in jury selection on the basis of race and gender. *J.E.B. v. Alabama ex rel. T.B.*, 511 U.S. 127 (1994).

(2) Any Defendant Can Object to Peremptory Challenges

In *Powers v. Ohio*, 499 U.S. 400 (1991), a white defendant alleged that the prosecutor used peremptory challenges to exclude African-American jurors based on their race. Using third-party standing principles, the Court held that the white defendant had standing to assert an Equal Protection claim on behalf of the excluded African-American jurors: a defendant suffers injury in fact from exclusion of a different race because "racial discrimination in the selection of jurors casts doubt on the integrity of the judicial process . . . and places the fairness of a criminal proceeding in doubt."

(3) Any Party May Commit a *Batson* Violation

A criminal defendant is prohibited from engaging in purposeful discrimination in the exercise of peremptory challenges. *Georgia v. McCollum*, 505 U.S. 42 (1992). Relying on *Powers* to find that the prosecution had third-party standing to assert the equal protection rights of excluded jurors, the Court observed: "As the representative of all its citizens, the State is the logical and proper party to assert the invasion of the constitutional rights of the excluded jurors in a criminal trial."

(4) The *Batson* Test: Proving a *Prima Facie* Case

Under *Batson*, the complaining party "must show that these facts and other relevant circumstances raise an inference that the [other party] used that practice to exclude veniremen from the petit jury" on account of their race or gender, which is an "inference of purposeful discrimination." It is then for the trial court, considering "all relevant circumstances," such as a pattern of exercising strikes from the venire on the basis of race or gender and the nature of the prosecutor's questions and statements on *voir dire*, to decide if the showing creates a *prima facie* case of discrimination.

(5) The *Batson* Test: Neutral Explanation for Peremptory Usage

If a *prima facie* case of discrimination is shown, "the burden shifts to the [alleged offending party] to come forward with a neutral explanation for challenging jurors," which requires more than a denial of a discriminatory motive. *Batson* does not require the neutral explanation for peremptorily striking a potential juror to be derived from *voir dire*. Nor does the neutral explanation have to rise to a level sufficient to satisfy a challenge for cause.

(6) Comparing Struck and Retained Jurors

In *Miller-El v. Dretke*, 545 U.S. 231 (2005), the Court found reversible error when the trial court accepted offered "neutral" explanations that were pretextual. Peremptory challenges were used to strike ten of eleven qualified black venire panel members. White jurors retained on the jury shared the same characteristic offered as the neutral explanation for striking the black jurors.

(7) The *Batson* Test: Was There an Equal Protection Violation?

After the trial court listens to the neutral explanation, it then decides whether the alleged offending party has acted with a prohibited intent. If a prosecutor's "neutral explanation" is pretextual, there is an "inference of discriminatory intent." *Snyder v. Louisiana*, 552 U.S. 472 (2008).

(8) Timing of *Batson* Objection

It is a "sensible rule" to require counsel to make *Batson* objections after the jury is selected and before they are sworn so that the trial judge can ensure that the jury is properly selected. *Ford v. Georgia*, 498 U.S. 411 (1991).

CHAPTER 26

FREEDOM OF THE PRESS AND FAIR TRIALS

A. WHY FREEDOM OF THE PRESS MATTERS

In the context of the criminal justice process, freedom of the press may promote or undermine significant societal interests. Unfettered expression promotes self-government by exposing judicial or prosecutorial corruption or incompetence. In addition, it serves as a catalyst for reform by heightening the public's political awareness and understanding of the criminal process. While the press can serve these and other useful functions, its presence can be disruptive and can undermine the fairness of the trial process.

1. Benefits of Freedom of the Press

Even before an arrest, reporting may expose the commission of certain crimes and provoke law enforcement authorities to investigate and prosecute, as well as to aid in apprehending suspects. After an arrest, reporting assures the public that the police are doing their job, but also may reveal the suspect's mistreatment. During trial, reporting educates the public about how the criminal process works. Even post-trial reporting produces analysis of how the case was handled and sometimes may indicate that an innocent person was convicted.

2. Adverse Effects of a Free Press

Reporting may expose persons like undercover agents to danger. Reporting also may produce repeated false accusations or invade the privacy of victims or suspects. The case law is most concerned with the impact of reporting on the fairness of a criminal trial, especially as it relates to a public outcry for conviction, the bias of the jury even before it hears any sworn evidence, and the concern that the jury's verdict rests solely on the evidence presented at trial.

B. FAILURE OF COURTS TO CONTROL THE PRESS

A trial judge can impose restraints upon the conduct of newsmen who are in or near the courtroom. The failure of the judge to take steps to restrict such behavior may deprive the defendant of the due process right to a fair trial. *Sheppard v. Maxwell*, 384 U.S. 333 (1966) involved a murder trial in which there was massive media coverage. The Court found a denial of the defendant's fair trial rights based on totality of circumstances and the following facts. During the nine weeks of trial, the courtroom was crowded with representatives of the news media whose movements in and out of the courtroom "often caused so much confusion that, despite the loud speaker system installed in the courtroom, it was difficult for the witnesses and counsel to be heard." Reporters were seated inside the bar, making "confidential talk among Sheppard and his counsel almost impossible during the proceedings." During recesses, television and photographic pictures were taken of the parties, witnesses and jurors, and newsmen even handled and photographed trial exhibits on the counsel table. The trial judge failed to take many steps that could have ensured courtroom decorum.

C. PRETRIAL PUBLICITY AND THE RIGHT TO A FAIR TRIAL

In *Sheppard*, the Court noted that "where there is a reasonable likelihood that prejudicial news prior to trial will prevent a fair trial, the judge should continue the case until the threat abates, or transfer it to another county not so permeated with publicity." During trial, a judge also has broad discretion to sequester the jury and caution the jurors to avoid media accounts of the proceedings. To prove juror partiality, a defendant must show that the publicity *either* actually prejudiced a juror *or* so pervaded the proceedings that it raised a presumption of inherent prejudice. *Skilling v. United States*, 561 U.S. 358 (2010).

1. Change of Venue

The right to request a change of venue belongs to either the defendant or the prosecution, and is largely a creature of statute or rule. When publicity has already occurred, a trial court will consider available procedures for ensuring a fair trial for the defendant. One possibility is a change of venue, i.e., removal of the case to another judicial district within the same system, and beyond the reach of the publicity. A change of venue is of limited value in smaller states, and other states as well, as a result of cable television and internet access. The opportunity to show that a change of venue is required must be available to a criminal defendant. *Groppi v. Wisconsin*, 400 U.S. 505 (1971).

a. Changing Venue for Guilty Plea

While a change of venue is frequently thought of as a contested matter because there is a concern about obtaining a fair trial, the parties may agree to a change where the defendant desires to plead guilty. Fed.R.Crim.P. 20, for example, permits a speedy disposition if a defendant wants to plead guilty without any hardship from transporting him back to the district where he is charged.

b. *Rideau v. Louisiana*: Presumption of Prejudice

In *Rideau v. Louisiana*, 373 U.S. 723 (1963), two months prior to trial a local television station broadcast a twenty-minute film of the defendant personally admitting in detail commission of the charged offenses. The estimated audiences for the three broadcasts were 24,000, 53,000 and 29,000. The Supreme Court held that it was a denial of due process for the trial court to refuse the defendant's request for a change of venue. Prejudicial publicity may be so inflammatory and pervasive that the *voir dire* cannot be trusted to reveal the likely prejudice among prospective jurors. Thus, a change of venue is constitutionally required even though the *voir dire* does not establish an "inference of prejudice." When publicity is pervasive, community pressures can lead jurors to answer with less than full candor about their familiarity with the case.

c. Skilling v. United States

Skilling v. United States, 561 U.D. 358 (2010) identified several factors which may lead to application of a presumption of prejudice:

- the nature of the pretrial publicity,
- the size and character of the community,
- the length of time between the dissemination of the publicity and the trial,
- whether the defendant was acquitted on any of the charges, and
- actions by the trial court which reduced the risk that the defendant would not receive a fair trial.

2. Jury Selection

Frequently, a trial judge will postpone ruling on a motion for a change of venue until after it tries to seat an unbiased jury through *voir dire*. When potential jurors have read or heard prejudicial publicity, a trial judge inquires into the nature and extent of the exposure, i.e., which jurors have actually been exposed to the pretrial publicity and what effect that exposure has had upon them.

a. Irvin v. Dowd

The media in *Irvin v. Dowd*, 366 U.S. 717 (1961) published a "barrage of newspaper headlines, articles, cartoons and pictures" containing prejudicial and inflammatory information, including defendant's confessions to six homicides, his past criminal record, and the alleged willingness to enter a guilty plea in return for a life sentence. The press reports produced a "pattern of deep and bitter prejudice" in the community. Over half of the 430 venire members were excused on challenges for cause, admitting to an opinion about the defendant's guilt. Almost 90% of those examined entertained some opinion as to defendant's guilt and eight of the twelve seated jurors had said they thought that the defendant was guilty. Although those jurors also said that they could put aside that opinion and judge the case impartially, "where so many, so many times, admitted prejudice, such a statement of impartiality [could] be given little weight."

b. Actual Prejudice from Seating a Particular Jury

Irvin established the constitutional framework for determining whether the jury selection process was adequate to address the prejudicial effect of pretrial publicity and thereby deprived the defendant of the constitutional right to an impartial tribunal. In *Irvin*, the Court overrode the trial court's finding of jury impartiality. Despite concerns about pretrial publicity and juror impartiality, jurors need not be completely ignorant of the facts and issues. It is sufficient if the juror can lay aside his impression or opinion and render a verdict based on the evidence presented in court.

c. Actual Prejudice from the Totality of Circumstances

While the Court in *Skilling* stated that there is no "hard and fast formula" to satisfy the actual prejudice test, an inference of actual prejudice is shown in a particular case from examining the totality of circumstances:

- the nature of the pretrial publicity,
- the community atmosphere as reflected in the media at the time of trial, and
- whether the *voir dire* testimony revealed pervasive hostility within the community.

(1) Character of the Publicity

Unlike the *Irvin* "barrage" of inflammatory and prejudicial articles, the Court in *Skilling* and earlier cases has described many of the media reports as "neutral," i.e., merely reporting events without editorial comment.

(2) Community Atmosphere

Whereas in *Irvin* the intense publicity occurred 6–7 months prior to trial, the publicity in *Murphy v. Florida*, 421 U.S. 794 (1975) was more than seven months before trial and the publicity in *Patton v. Yount*, 467 U.S. 1025 (1984) was more than four years before the trial. The *voir dire* resulted in the selection of jurors who had either forgotten what they had heard about the case or would need to be persuaded again of what they had heard. The passage of time between the publicity and trial has assumed paramount importance.

(3) *Voir Dire* Testimony

In both *Murphy* and *Patton*, the *voir dire* statistics were comparable to *Irvin*. In *Murphy*, 20 of the 78 prospective jurors were challenged for cause because of their acquired opinions from the publicity. In *Patton*, 126 of the 163 jurors were challenged for cause, and 8 of the 14 seated believed that the defendant was guilty. On the issue of *voir dire* testimony, the cases since *Irvin* indicate an overwhelming deference to the trial court in assessing such testimony. *Patton v. Yount*, 467 U.S. 1025 (1984).

3. Continuance

Another possible remedy for prejudicial pretrial publicity is for the trial court to grant a continuance of the case. As with change of venue motions, courts are inclined to take a wait-and-see attitude by denying the motion for a continuance while efforts are made to select a jury. As in *Rideau* and other cases, the concern is whether the publicity may be so serious that a continuance should be regarded as a constitutionally necessary solution.

4. Jury Sequestration

A trial judge has broad discretion to sequester the jury and caution the jurors to avoid media accounts of the proceedings during both trial and jury deliberations. Because the prospective jurors have already been exposed to pretrial publicity when the jury is selected, sequestration is not an effective remedy for claims of prejudicial publicity.

D. GAGGING THE PRESS

In *Nebraska Press Association v. Stuart*, 427 U.S. 539 (1976), the Court held that a prohibition on the media's publication of information possibly prejudicial to a defendant will seldom, if ever, be a permissible means for preventing prejudicial publicity from occurring. In *Stuart*, the trial court entered orders prior to trial which barred both the publication of "any testimony given or evidence adduced" in court and the reporting of any confessions or incriminating statements made by the defendant to the police or to anyone else other than the press or of other facts "strongly implicative" of the defendant. The Court concluded that the bar on reporting what happened at the preliminary hearing violated the settled principle that "once a public hearing had been held, what transpired there could not be subject to prior restraint."

1. Prior Restraint

The Court examined the facts of the case to determine whether the danger was great enough to justify such an invasion of free speech, which requires examination of "the evidence before the trial judge when the order was entered to determine (a) the nature and extent of pretrial news coverage; (b) whether other measures would be likely to mitigate the effects of unrestrained pretrial publicity; and (c) how effectively a restraining order would operate to prevent the threatened danger." For the nature and extent of news coverage, the Court found the trial court's conclusion about the effect of the as yet unpublished publicity on prospective jurors to be speculative.

2. Alternatives to Prior Restraint

As to alternative measures, the Court stated that the record did not reflect careful consideration of the "alternatives to prior restraint"—change of venue, continuance, *voir dire*, and jury admonitions. The Court's response was to conclude that in a small community rumors "could well be more damaging than reasonably accurate news accounts." Lower courts following *Nebraska Press*'s standard invariably have found inadequate proof for exercising prior restraint, especially because of the availability of alternatives.

E. PUBLIC ACCESS TO JUDICIAL PROCEEDINGS

A defendant may believe that the right to a fair trial can be compromised by *too much* openness and publicity. However, openness assures that established procedures are being followed and that any deviations become known. It also enhances both the fairness of the trial and the appearance of fairness that is essential to public confidence in the criminal justice system. Questions of access have arisen in the context of both pretrial proceedings and trials.

1. Sixth Amendment Right to Public Trial

The Sixth Amendment right to a public trial is rooted in traditional distrust of secret trials. Its purposes are to safeguard against any attempt to use the courts as instruments of persecution and to inform the public about governmental actions against citizens. Trials themselves historically have been open to the press and public, and the Court has established a presumption in favor of access.

a. Tradition Sometimes Has Cut Both Ways

Tradition, however, has not always cut in favor of open preliminary proceedings. In *Gannett Co., Inc. v. DePasquale*, 443 U.S. 368 (1979), the Court upheld a trial judge's order closing a suppression hearing at the defendant's request. The outcome in *Gannett* reflected an understanding that the Sixth Amendment guarantee of a public trial accrued not to the press or public but to the defendants. The Sixth Amendment established no constitutional right for the press or public to attend a criminal trial. The determination rested on the premise that "that the public interest is fully protected by the participants in the litigation." But five years later, *Waller v. Georgia*, 467 U.S. 39 (1984) held that the Sixth Amendment right to a public trial did not justify the prosecutor's request to close an entire suppression hearing over the defendant's objection. The defendant is not required to prove actual prejudice to obtain relief.

2. First Amendment Right of Access by Press and Public

In *Richmond Newspapers, Inc. v. Virginia*, 448 U.S. 555 (1980), the Court found a qualified First Amendment right of the press and public to attend criminal trials, absent findings sufficient to overcome the presumption of openness. A proceeding may be closed only if the trial judge makes specific findings that:

- there is a substantial probability that the defendant's right to a fair trial will be prejudiced by publicity that closure would prevent, and
- reasonable alternatives to closure cannot adequately protect that right.

In *Presley v. Georgia*, 558 U.S. 209 (2010), the Court held that trial courts must consider alternatives to closing courtrooms during *voir dire*, even if no one identifies the nature of such alternatives, because the "public has a right to be present whether or not any party has asserted the right" and "[t]rial courts are obligated to take every reasonable measure to accommodate public attendance at criminal trials."

a. **Globe Newspaper Company v. Superior Court**

In *Globe Newspaper Company v. Superior Court*, 457 U.S. 596 (1982), the Court invalidated a statute that required the closure of the entire trial involving certain sex crimes. The Court indicated that under limited circumstances a portion of the trial might be closed when there is proof of an overriding interest that is likely to be prejudiced, as where a minor rape victim's testimony related certain sensitive details.

b. **Press-Enterprise Co. v. Superior Court**

In *Press-Enterprise Co. v. Superior Court*, 464 U.S. 501 (1984), the Court held that a trial judge could not close almost six weeks of jury selection. Following *Richmond Newspapers*, the Court noted that limited portions of the selection process may be closed in the case of individual jurors. Another case styled *Press-Enterprise Co. v. Superior Court*, 478 U.S. 1 (1986) emphasized the historical tradition of openness and the functional value of openness for application of the First Amendment right of access to pretrial proceedings.

c. **Tradition and Value of Openness**

As to tradition, because preliminary hearings are open to the public while grand jury proceedings are not, open preliminary hearings are accorded "the favorable judgment of experience." As to the value of openness, a court asks whether public access to the preliminary proceeding is similar to a trial and "plays a particularly significant positive role in the actual functioning of" the criminal justice process. At least when the nature and traditions of a preliminary hearing are congruent with a trial, it is predictable that First Amendment values of openness will be a dominant factor.

d. **Extending Right of Access**

Courts have applied the tests of *Press-Enterprise* for public and press access to court documents, including pre-sentence reports.

3. **What the Cases Teach**

A defendant has a presumptive right to a public and open trial. The right may be overcome by an overriding interest that a public trial will prejudice, and the closure must be nor broader than is necessary to protect the interest. The trial court also must consider reasonable alternatives to any closure, and make specific findings to support the closure.

F. BROADCASTING LEGAL PROCEEDINGS

The right of access to trials and pretrial hearings does not incorporate any freedom for the media to use a particular technology to cover such proceedings. To the contrary, even as cameras and other electronic instrumentalities have become increasingly common in state courts, the judiciary still exercises considerable control over the extent (if any) to which they may be used. Cameras in the courtroom have become a staple in state courts but, except for some experimentation in the civil context, have been disallowed at the federal level.

1. Estes v. Texas

A plurality of the Court in *Estes v. Texas*, 381 U.S. 532 (1965) concluded that televised proceedings entail "such a probability that prejudice will result that it is deemed inherently lacking in due process." In a concurring opinion of significant durability, Justice Harlan stressed the need for adaptability in the event future circumstances warranted it. As technology reinvented the electronic instrumentalities of trial coverage, so that intrusiveness and distraction were diminished, case law veered in the direction of Justice Harlan's concurring opinion.

2. Chandler v. Florida

Responding to provisions for electronic coverage of judicial proceedings, the Court in *Chandler v. Florida*, 449 U.S. 560 (1981) repudiated the notion that cameras in the courtroom *per se* offended due process. *Chandler* upheld a regulated state practice allowing electronic media and still photography coverage of public criminal proceedings over the objection of the accused. The Court emphasized that "no one has been able to present empirical data sufficient to establish that the mere presence of the broadcast media inherently has an adverse impact on that process." It stressed that the televising had occurred pursuant to guidelines designed to assure that the excesses found in *Estes* were avoided.

a. Guidelines for Televised Proceedings

The guidelines included restrictions on the type and manner of equipment used, designed to keep the recording unobtrusive, and a prohibition against the filming of the jury itself. They also required the trial judge to protect the fundamental right of the defendant to a fair trial. A particular defendant could still show that the "coverage of his case . . . compromised the ability of the jury to judge him fairly" or to "show that broadcast coverage of his particular case had an adverse impact on the trial participants sufficient to constitute a denial of due process." However, prejudice is not established by merely showing "juror awareness that the trial is such as to attract the attention of broadcasters."

CHAPTER 27

TRIAL RIGHTS

A. DEFENDANT'S RIGHTS REGARDING THE CHARGE

1. Burden of Proof

Due Process "protects the accused against conviction except upon proof beyond a reasonable doubt of every fact necessary to constitute the crime with which he is charged." *In re Winship*, 397 U.S. 358 (1970). This proof standard is a "prime instrument for reducing the risk of convictions resting on factual error."

a. Proof of Defenses

While the prosecution must prove every element of the crime beyond a reasonable doubt, the defendant may be required to prove defenses such as insanity, self-defense, and duress, by a preponderance of the evidence. *Patterson v. New York*, 432 U.S. 197 (1977). In some jurisdictions, after the defendant offers some proof of a defense, the burden shifts to the prosecution to prove beyond a reasonable doubt or a lesser standard that the defense did not exist.

b. Inferences Allowed, But Not Presumptions

Prosecutors used to try to lighten their burden of proof through jury instructions that make use of presumptions. For example, a common instruction is that a person is presumed to intend the natural and probable consequences of his acts. In *Francis v. Franklin*, 471 U.S. 307 (1985), the Court held that presumptions violate Due Process because they impermissibly shift the burden of proof. Instead of presumptions, a jury instruction may permit the jury to make "permissible inferences." For example, the jury instruction may state that the jury may infer that the defendant intended to kill from the fact that he aimed his weapon at the victim, and fired the shots that caused the victim's death.

2. Order of Proof

After jury selection, the prosecution gives its opening statement, which usually is confined to an overview of the case. The defense may deliver its opening statement, or it may defer until after the prosecution's proof.

a. Prosecution's Proof

After opening statements, the prosecution presents its case "in chief" during which it must satisfy its burden of proving that the defendant engaged in the charged conduct beyond a reasonable doubt. When the prosecution completes its proof, it "rests its case."

b. Defense Motion for Acquittal

Usually, the defense then moves for a judgment of acquittal, claiming that the prosecution has failed to admit sufficient proof of the defendant's guilt beyond a reasonable doubt. The trial judge will deny the motion when she believes that the prosecution has met its burden of proof and that a reasonable jury could therefore find the defendant guilty beyond a reasonable doubt. She will grant the motion if she believes that the prosecution's evidence fails to satisfy the burden of proof. Granting the motion means that the trial is over, and the judge enters a judgment in favor of the defendant.

c. Defendant's Proof

The defense may "rest its case" and present no proof in response to the prosecution's evidence. The Fifth Amendment privilege against self-incrimination permits a defendant to remain silent in the face of the charges. More commonly, the defendant presents evidence which contradicts the prosecution's proof and asserts a defense recognized in that jurisdiction.

d. Rebuttal Proof

After the defendant's case-in-chief, the trial judge has the discretion to allow the prosecution to offer additional proof to respond to the defendant's new evidence or theories. Rebuttal proof may then produce a defense request to present its own rebuttal to meet new prosecution issues raised during rebuttal.

e. Closing Arguments

After the proof concludes, both sides present closing arguments. The Sixth Amendment right to a defense attorney includes the present a closing statement even in a non-jury trial. *Herring v. New York*, 422 U.S. 853 (1975). While prosecutors' closing arguments often produce defense claims of prejudice, appellate courts frequently rely upon the harmless error doctrine to uphold convictions even when the prosecutor's arguments were inflammatory. *Darden v. Wainwright*, 477 U.S. 168 (1986).

3. Defendant's Right (Not) to Testify

The Supreme Court did not explicitly recognize a defendant's constitutional right to testify until *Rock v. Arkansas*, 483 U.S. 44 (1987). The constitutional sources were Due Process, the Sixth Amendment rights of self-representation and compulsory process, and a corollary to the Fifth Amendment privilege against self-incrimination.

a. Order of Testimony

Brooks v. Tennessee, 406 U.S. 605 (1972) recognized that any restrictions on the defendant's choice about when to testify during the defense's case-in-chief violates Due Process. A Tennessee statute required a defendant to testify before any other testimony for the defense is heard. The statute unduly interfered with defense counsel's planning the presentation of her case.

b. Griffin v. California

The trial court cannot instruct the jury and the prosecution cannot comment about the defendant's failure to testify at trial. *Griffin v. California*, 380 U.S. 609 (1965). Such comments are a penalty for exercising a constitutional privilege to remain silent, and suggest evidence of guilt.

(1) Jury Instruction About Silence

Although the trial court cannot refer to the defendant's silence, it can instruct the jury not to make adverse inferences from his decision. *Lakeside v. Oregon*, 435 U.S. 333 (1978). Later, the Court held that trial judges have a constitutional obligation to give such a jury instruction at the defendant's request. *Carter v. Kentucky*, 450 U.S. 288 (1981).

(2) Applies also to Sentencing Hearings

The Court extended the *Griffin* "no adverse inference" rule to defendants who do not testify at a sentencing hearing. *Mitchell v. United States*, 526 U.S. 314 (1999).

(3) Comment on the Content of Defendant's Testimony

The Court refused to extend *Griffin* to a prosecutor's comments on the defendant's opportunity to conform his testimony after he heard the prosecutorial witnesses testify. *Portuondo v. Agard*, 529 U.S. 61 (2000). This comment concerned a defendant's credibility, rather than his silence as evidence of guilt.

4. Right to Jury Instructions

a. Presumption of Innocence

While the law presumes that a defendant is innocent of a crime, the failure to give an instruction about that presumption is not by itself a constitutional violation. *Kentucky v. Whorton*, 441 U.S. 786 (1979). Whether the failure to give such an instruction violates due process depends upon other jury instructions, counsel's arguments, the weight of the evidence, and other relevant factors.

b. Lesser and Greater Included Offenses

The right to a jury instruction on a lesser crime is constitutionally based, because depriving the jury of the option of conviction on a lesser offense increases the risk of conviction on the greater offense. *Beck v. Alabama*, 447 U.S. 625 (1980). However, a trial must give a lesser included offense instruction only if there is evidence supporting a conviction for that offense

B. SCOPE OF SIXTH AMENDMENT CONFRONTATION RIGHTS

In addition to familiar Sixth Amendment rights such as the right to counsel and the right to a jury trial, the Sixth Amendment also provides a defendant with the right to confront adverse witnesses against her, as well as compulsory process to offer the testimony of witnesses in her favor and compel their attendance at trial. Confrontation and compulsory process rights are discussed briefly, with references to longer discussions elsewhere in this book.

1. Identification Procedures

The right to the presence of counsel at pretrial identification procedures established in *United States v. Wade*, 388 U.S. 218 (1967) enables counsel to be more effective in confronting and cross-examining trial witnesses who testify about identifications made at pretrial lineups. See Chapter 14.

2. Preliminary Hearing

Preliminary hearing testimony may be used as substantive testimony at trial without violating the defendant's Confrontation rights, as long as the preliminary hearing witness is unavailable at trial and the defendant had an opportunity to cross-examine the witness at the preliminary hearing. See Chapter 18.

3. Confrontation Rights at Trial

If a prosecution witness testifies against the defendant, but invokes the Fifth Amendment on cross-examination, there is a conflict between the witness's Fifth Amendment privilege against self-incrimination and the defendant's Sixth Amendment right to confrontation and compulsory process. Usually, the witness's right to remain silent overrides the defendant's rights in this context. *Alford v. United States*, 282 U.S. 687 (1931). The trial court may strike all or part of the witness's direct testimony.

a. Confronting and Cross-examining Adverse Witnesses

At trial, the Sixth Amendment Confrontation Clause enables a defendant the right to face adverse witnesses. *Maryland v. Craig*, 497 U.S. 836 (1990). The rationale is that such a "confrontation enhances the accuracy of factfinding by reducing the risk that a witness will wrongfully implicate an innocent person." The right to confront adverse witnesses also includes the right to cross-examine adverse witnesses, and the right to be present at any stage of the trial that would enable the defendant to effectively cross-examine adverse witnesses.

(1) Constitutional Limits on Cross-examination

Statutory or judicial limits on cross-examination are constitutional. *Delaware v. Van Arsdall*, 475 U.S. 673 (1986). "[The Confrontation Clause] guarantees an opportunity for effective cross-examination, not cross-examination that is effective in whatever way, and to whatever extent, the defense might wish."

(2) Joint Trials and the Confrontation Clause

In a joint trial, the admission of a codefendant's extrajudicial confession incriminating the defendant violates the defendant's right to confrontation when the codefendant does not testify at trial. *Bruton v. United States*, 391 U.S. 123 (1968). Where the codefendant later testifies, there is no confrontation issue because the codefendant is subject to cross-examination. See Chapter 21.

b. Right to Confront Witnesses Is Not Absolute

The right to face adverse witnesses, however, is not absolute. Under *Craig*, the defendant's right to face adverse witnesses may give way if "necessary to further an important public policy [if] the reliability of the testimony is otherwise assured."

c. Right to Be Present during Criminal Proceedings

The right of a criminal defendant to be present during criminal proceedings arises from the Confrontation Clause as well as from Due Process. The Confrontation Clause assures a defendant the right to be present at any stage of the proceeding that would strengthen the opportunity for effective cross-examination. *Snyder v. Massachusetts*, 291 U.S. 97 (1934); *Kentucky v. Stincer*, 482 U.S. 730 (1987). Due Process provides a defendant with the "right to be present at any stage of the proceeding that is critical to its outcome if [the defendant's] presence would contribute to the fairness of the procedure."

(1) Waiver of Right to Be Present

A court may deem the defendant to have waived his right to be present either after he voluntarily absents himself from the courtroom, *Taylor v. United States*, 414 U.S. 17 (1973), or after he engages in continuous disruption of the proceedings after warnings from the court. *Illinois v. Allen*, 397 U.S. 337 (1970). The latter decision recognized three "constitutionally permissible ways for a trial judge to handle an obstreperous defendant" within her discretion: bind and gag him, cite him for contempt of court, and remove him from the courtroom until he promises to conduct himself properly.

(2) Being Present in Physical Restraints

How a jury views a defendant may present a constitutional issue as well. Absent a trial court's determination in the exercise of its discretion that there is a state interest specific to the defendant justifying the use of physical restraints, Due Process prohibits the routine use of restraints in a guilt or penalty phase of a criminal trial. *Deck v. Missouri*, 544 U.S. 622 (2005). Compelling a defendant to dress in identifiable prison clothes at his jury trial also violates Due Process. *Estelle v. Williams*, 425 U.S. 501 (1976).

(3) When Defendant Has No Right to Be Present

A criminal defendant has a right to be present at trial, but has no right to be present at a:

- pretrial hearing when the defendant does not indicate how his or her presence could have contributed to a more reliable determination and when there are no questions asked about substantive trial testimony, or
- conference when the defendant could have done nothing by being present and would have gained nothing by attending. *United States v. Gagnon*, 470 U.S. 522 (1985).

d. Crawford v. Washington

The admission of hearsay evidence against a criminal defendant can implicate the Sixth Amendment because the defendant is not afforded the opportunity to confront the person making the out-of-court statement. In *Crawford v. Washington*, 541 U.S. 36 (2004), the interrogation of a domestic violence victim was directed solely at establishing a past crime and was held to be testimonial. *Crawford* noted that the concept of "testimonial" applies "at a minimum to prior testimony at a preliminary hearing, before a grand jury, or at a former trial; and to police interrogations."

(1) Testimonial v. Non-testimonial Statements

Crawford distinguished between "testimonial" and "non-testimonial" evidence. Statements are non-testimonial when made in the course of police interrogation under circumstances objectively indicating that the primary purpose of the interrogation is to enable police assistance to meet an ongoing emergency. They are testimonial when the circumstances objectively indicate that there is no such ongoing emergency, and that the primary purpose of the interrogation is to establish or prove past events potentially relevant to a later criminal prosecution. *Davis v. Washington*, 547 U.S. 813 (2006).

(2) Defining an "Ongoing Emergency"

Assessment of whether an emergency threatening the police and the public is ongoing must focus on whether the threat to the first victim has been neutralized, the type of weapon employed, and the medical condition of the victim; the degree of informality of an encounter between a victim and police also bears on the primary purpose of the interrogation. *Michigan v. Bryant*, 131 S.Ct. 1143 (2011).

In *Bryant*, the Court held that, because the shooting victim's out-of-court statements to police were made to assist them to meet an ongoing emergency, the statements were not testimonial hearsay and were admissible at trial. "[T]he existence and duration of an emergency depend on the type and scope of danger posed to the victim, the police, and the public."

(3) Ongoing Emergency Statement Not Subject to Confrontation Right

Statements made to assist police in addressing an ongoing emergency objectively lack the testimonial purpose that subjects them to the requirement of confrontation. In *Davis*, the Court held that a victim's statements responding to a 911 operator's interrogation were not testimonial.

(4) When Testimonial Hearsay Violates Confrontation Clause and Is Inadmissible

Admission of a "testimonial" hearsay statement violates the Confrontation Clause, unless the person making the out-of-court statement is unavailable. A witness is considered unavailable if the prosecution cannot obtain that witness's attendance at trial, and the defendant had a prior opportunity to cross-examine that person. In *Bullcoming v. New Mexico*, 131 S.Ct. 2705 (2011), a lab report was deemed to be testimonial. Nothing on the record indicated that the forensic analyst was actually unavailable. The defendant did not have an opportunity to cross-examine him, and the analyst who did testify was not an "adequate substitute." *Williams v. Illinois*, 132 S.Ct. 2221 (2012) further develops the *Crawford* line of cases.

(5) When Testimonial Statement Is Admissible

A testimonial out-of-court statement is admissible at trial even if the person making the statement does not appear at trial but there was a prior opportunity for cross-examining her. A non-testimonial out-of-court statement is admissible at trial *regardless* of either the declarant's availability to testify at trial or any prior opportunity to cross-examine her.

f. Compulsory Process

A Sixth Amendment right related to the Confrontation Clause is the Compulsory Process Clause, which grants a defendant the right to offer the testimony of favorable witnesses and to compel their attendance at trial. The Sixth Amendment provides that "[i]n all criminal prosecutions, the accused shall enjoy the right . . . to have compulsory process for obtaining witnesses in his favor." To exercise this right, a defendant must show that the testimony she seeks would be material, favorable to her, and not merely cumulative. *United States v. Valenzuela-Bernal*, 458 U.S. 858 (1982).

(1) Statutory Violation of Compulsory Process

Washington v. Texas, 388 U.S. 14 (1967) invalidated a statute preventing accomplices from testifying for one another but allowing them to testify for the prosecution. The statute violated the Compulsory Process Clause by arbitrarily denying the defendant the right to present a materially favorable witness.

CHAPTER 28

SENTENCING

A. INTRODUCTION

There are certain statutory and constitutional limitations on sentencing that may have the effect of reducing a particular penalty. In general, these include limitations on resentencing, alterations in the punishment, and certain notice rules. While it is seldom successful, counsel may attack a sentence that constitutes cruel and unusual punishment, violates double jeopardy prohibitions, or violates concepts of equal protection. *See, e.g., Hodgson v. Vermont*, 168 U.S. 262 (1897).

B. NONCAPITAL SENTENCING ALTERNATIVES

1. Imprisonment

There are two types of prison sentences. An indeterminate sentence is set within statutory limits, with the parole board having responsibility for deciding precisely when the defendant is eligible for early release. About two-thirds of the states use indeterminate sentences. A determinate sentence (also known as "flat time") is for a fixed period without the possibility of early release, but supervision often accompanies that release.

2. Fines and Costs

The punishment for a violation of the law may include a fine in addition to or, in some cases, instead of imprisonment. Due to certain constitutional limitations, a person may not usually be confined for failure to pay the fine or costs. Fines cannot be imposed upon any person determined by the court to be statutorily indigent. While incarceration is still a possibility for an intentional refusal to pay, the court must explore alternative means of satisfaction of the fine. *Bearden v. Georgia*, 461 U.S. 660 (1983).

a. Reimbursing the State for Incarceration Costs

Recently, states have begun to provide that the sentencing court may order a person incarcerated to reimburse the state or local government for the costs of incarceration. The sentencing court determines the amount to be paid based on the actual per *diem*, per person, cost of incarceration, the cost of medical services provided to a prisoner less any copayment paid by the prisoner, and the prisoner's ability to pay all or part of the incarceration costs.

3. Restitution

By statute, a person convicted of certain types of crimes such as a crime involving the taking of, injury to, or destruction of property can be ordered to restore the property or its value to the victim. *See, e.g.*, 18 U.S.C. § 3663. An order of restitution may defer payment until the person is released from custody. However, the decision by a trial judge not to use this remedy does not deprive the victim of a civil action for the injury sustained.

4. Forfeiture or Confiscation of Property

A person convicted of certain types of crimes such as controlled substances, intoxicating liquors, eavesdropping devices, deadly weapons, gambling devices, and obscene matter can be ordered to forfeit property used in connection with commission of the offense. Forfeitures, as payments in kind, are "fines" if they constitute punishment for an offense. *Austin v. United States*, 509 U.S. 602 (1993). Thus, forfeiture of vehicles and realty used to facilitate commission of drug trafficking is allowed.

a. Due Process Rights in Forfeiture Cases

Generally, under the Due Process Clause, the Government must provide notice and a meaningful opportunity to be heard before seizing real property subject to civil forfeiture. *United States v. James Daniel Good Real Property*, 510 U.S. 43 (1993). However, due process does not preclude forfeiture of property used for unlawful purposes by a defendant but which belongs to another person. *Bennis v. Michigan*, 516 U.S. 442 (1996).

b. Kaley v. United States

Pretrial seizure of property ensures that a criminal defendant's assets are available to be forfeited if he is convicted. Such seizures are constitutional, as long as there is probable cause to believe both that the defendant has committed an offense that can lead to forfeiture and that the assets result from the allegedly criminal conduct. *United States v. Monsanto*, 491 U.S. 600 (1989). A grand jury's determination of probable cause cannot be reviewed by a judge. *Kaley v. United States*, 134 S.Ct. 1090 (2014).

5. Probation and Conditional Discharge

Probation is granted when the sentencing court suspends the execution of a sentence of imprisonment conditionally and releases the defendant under the supervision of a probation officer. Some jurisdictions grant "conditional discharge" when a defendant is released without supervision. These forms of release are regarded as "legislative clemencies," not constitutional rights, granted as a matter of grace. Some constitutional rights apply differently to probationers than to others. For example, in *Griffin v. Wisconsin*, 483 U.S. 868 (1987), the Court upheld a search of a probationer's home that was conducted without either a warrant or probable cause.

a. Eligibility for Probation or Conditional Discharge

In most jurisdictions, not every defendant is eligible for probation or conditional discharge, with eligibility often based on circumstances such as the

- nature of the conviction, e.g., death penalty,
- circumstances of the conviction, e.g., use of a firearm, or
- nature of the victim, e.g., sexual offense against a minor.

b. Conditions of Release

Conditions of release are usually stated in writing and furnished to the defendant. All defendants are required to refrain from committing another offense, as well as other conditions (such as restitution) that the court deems to be reasonably necessary to enable the defendant to lead a law-abiding life. In addition to reasonable conditions, a court may require a defendant to submit to a period of imprisonment in the local jail at times to be determined by the court. This is known as a "split sentence."

c. Revocation of Probation

Proceedings for the revocation or modification of a sentence to a period of probation or conditional discharge may only be initiated before the discharge of the defendant or the termination of the period. Due process entitles a defendant to a prompt preliminary hearing to determine whether there is reason to detain, pending a final hearing. The defendant must be given written notice of the grounds, as well as a reasonable time to obtain evidence and otherwise prepare a defense.

(1) Hearing Rights

The right to counsel at the revocation hearing is case-by-case. *Gagnon v. Scarpelli*, 411 U.S. 778 (1973). The revocation hearing must be held with reasonable promptness, based primarily on the assumption that the defendant is prejudiced by confinement pending the hearing. In most jurisdictions, the rules of evidence are inapplicable to a revocation hearing. See *Wolff v. McDonnell*, 418 U.S. 539 (1974). The defendant must have the opportunity to present evidence in defense or mitigation of the accusation, including the right to confront and cross-examine adverse witnesses. A court cannot revoke probation for failure to pay restitution or a fine unless the failure is willful or alternatives to imprisonment are not adequate. *Bearden v. Georgia*, 461 U.S. 660 (1983). Due process requires the court to make findings as a prerequisite to any unfavorable action. *Morrissey v. Brewer*, 408 U.S. 471 (1972).

6. Home Incarceration

Many states permit defendants convicted of minor offenses to serve all or part of a definite term of imprisonment under conditions of home incarceration. Some provisions prohibit home incarceration for minor offenders with outstanding charges or a recent violent crime conviction. The sentencing judge may have discretion to order home incarceration as another type of "split sentence" for the defendant to serve part of the sentence at home and part of it in the local jail. As with probation and conditional discharge, a defendant under home incarceration signs an agreement listing all of the conditions for confinement.

C. PROPORTIONALITY OF PUNISHMENT

On several occasions, the Supreme Court has grappled with the issue of whether certain sentences are disproportionately severe. The Eighth Amendment, which forbids cruel and unusual punishments, contains a "narrow proportionality principle" that "applies to noncapital sentences."

1. Rummel v. Estelle

In *Rummel v. Estelle*, 445 U.S. 263 (1980), the Court held that a state did not violate the Eighth Amendment when it sentenced a three-time offender to life in prison with the possibility of parole. Rummel was sentenced to a lengthy prison term under a recidivism statute, when his two prior offenses were a felony for fraudulent use of a credit card to obtain $80 worth of goods or services, and a second conviction for passing a forged check in the amount of

$28.36. His triggering offense was a conviction for felony theft—obtaining $120.75 by false pretenses.

a. Solem v. Helm

In *Rummel*, the defendant was eligible for parole but in *Solem v. Helm*, 463 U.S. 277 (1983), the defendant was ineligible for parole. The Court held that the Eighth Amendment prohibited "a life sentence without possibility of parole for a seventh nonviolent felony." The triggering offense in *Solem* was "uttering a 'no account' check for $100." Three factors were relevant to a determination of whether a sentence is so disproportionate that it violates the Eighth Amendment: "(i) the gravity of the offense and the harshness of the penalty; (ii) the sentences imposed on other criminals in the same jurisdiction; and (iii) the sentences imposed for commission of the same crime in other jurisdictions."

b. Harmelin v. Michigan

The Court addressed the proportionality issue again in *Harmelin v. Michigan*, 501 U.S. 957 (1991), which involved a first-time offender convicted of possessing 672 grams of cocaine and sentenced to life in prison without possibility of parole. A majority of the Court rejected the claim that the sentence was grossly disproportionate but it could not agree on why the argument failed.

(1) Justice Kennedy's *Harmelin* Concurrence

Justice Kennedy concurred and identified four principles of proportionality review—"the primacy of the legislature, the variety of legitimate penological schemes, the nature of our federal system, and the requirement that proportionality review be guided by objective factors—[that] inform the final one: The Eighth Amendment does not require strict proportionality between crime and sentence. Rather, it forbids only extreme sentences that are 'grossly disproportionate' to the crime." Justice Kennedy's concurrence also stated that *Solem* "did not mandate" comparative analysis "within and between jurisdictions."

c. Ewing v. California

The proportionality principles in Justice Kennedy's *Harmelin* concurrence directed the Court's application of the Eighth Amendment in *Ewing v. California*, 538 U.S. 11 (2003). The issue there was "whether the Eighth Amendment prohibits the State of California from sentencing a repeat felon to a prison term of 25 years to life under the State's 'Three Strikes and You're Out' law." Justice O'Connor found that the states had an interest "in dealing in a harsher manner with those who by repeated criminal acts have shown that they are simply incapable of conforming to the norms of society as established by its criminal law." The state's interest in public safety and deterrence supported application of the recidivism principle, in the absence of a grossly disproportionate sentence.

D. CAPITAL CASES

The death penalty is currently in effect in about three fourths of the states and the federal system. Methods of execution include electrocution, firing squad, gas chamber, hanging, and lethal injection. In *Furman v. Georgia*, 408 U.S. 238 (1972), the Court found that Georgia had not applied the death penalty fairly. Statistics on executions showed that black males who committed murder were executed far more frequently than white males, even though black males were not committing most of the crimes. The Court stated that capital punishment cannot be used unless the states can prove that it is being applied fairly.

1. When Death Penalty Is Inapplicable

The Eighth Amendment prohibits the death penalty for any crime that does not result in the death of the victim. The death penalty is inapplicable unless the defendant committed the homicide intentionally or with wanton indifference. *Tison v. Arizona*, 481 U.S. 137 (1987).

a. Mental Incapacity

The same provision also prohibits capital punishment for a prisoner who is either insane or mentally retarded at the time of the crime. *Atkins v. Virginia*, 536 U.S. 304 (2002). When a state is deciding whether a death-eligible person is intellectually incapacitated to be executed, it cannot use a fixed IQ score as the measure of incapacity. The defendant must be allowed to offer clinical evidence of intellectual deficit, including the inability to learn basic skills and adapt how to react to changing circumstances. *Hall v. Florida*, 134 S.Ct. 1986 (2014).

b. Age

Capital punishment also is prohibited for a person who was under the age of 18 at the time of the crime. *Roper v. Simmons*, 543 U.S. 551 (2005).

2. Prerequisites for Death Penalty

In *California v. Brown*, 479 U.S. 538 (1987), the Court stated that there are two prerequisites to a valid death sentence. First, "death penalty statutes [must] be structured so as to prevent the penalty from being administered in an arbitrary and unpredictable fashion." For example, some states have adopted statutory requirements to avoid racial discrimination in seeking the death penalty. Second, "the capital defendant generally must be allowed to introduce any relevant mitigating evidence. . . ."

a. Notice of the Intent to Seek Death Penalty

The government must give defense counsel adequate notice that it will seek the death penalty. *Lankford v. Idaho*, 500 U.S. 110 (1991).

b. Proof of Aggravating Circumstance

Before the death penalty can be imposed, the prosecution must prove at least one aggravating circumstance beyond a reasonable doubt. Aggravating circumstances limit the application of the death penalty to the most serious crimes. In states that retain the death penalty, the jury's recommendation as to punishment of death must include a written designation of the aggravating circumstance. If the jury does not find at least one aggravating circumstance, the judge cannot impose a sentence of death. In this situation, the judge can impose a sentence of life.

(1) Types of Aggravating Circumstances

The legislature of each state decides the number and types of aggravating circumstances. One common aggravating circumstance is that the defendant has been previously convicted of a capital offense. *Romano v. Oklahoma*, 512 U.S. 1 (1994). Aggravating circumstance may include a death while engaged in the commission of a serious felony, or a defendant who either pays for or receives remuneration for a murder.

(2) Variations on Felony-Murder Rule as Aggravator

In *Schiro v. Farley*, 510 U.S. 222 (1994), the Court approved the use of an intentional killing during the commission of rape as an aggravating factor during the sentencing proceeding.

(3) Multiple Victims as Aggravator

In *Lowenfield v. Phelps*, 484 U.S. 231 (1988), the Court held that a death sentence imposed pursuant to a finding of an aggravating circumstance of knowingly creating a risk of death or serious bodily harm to more than one person is not improper because it duplicates one of the elements of the homicide.

c. Mitigating Evidence

A defendant must be allowed to introduce proof of any mitigating circumstances for consideration by the jury. *California v. Brown*, 479 U.S. 538 (1987). In *Skipper v. South Carolina*, 476 U.S. 1 (1986), the Court held that when a statute entitles a defendant to present any mitigating circumstance, the defendant can introduce evidence about his peaceful adjustment to prison life. The purpose of the mitigating factors appears to be avoidance of the death penalty.

(1) Types of Mitigating Evidence

Typical statutory mitigating circumstances include: a lack of a significant history of prior criminal activity, the defendant was under extreme mental or emotional disturbance, the victim participated in the act, the defendant believed he had a moral justification for the conduct, the defendant was only an accomplice, the defendant acted under duress, the defendant suffered from some diminished capacity, or the youth of the defendant.

d. Evidence at Penalty Phase Hearing

All evidence may be introduced in a capital sentencing hearing, even beyond factors in aggravation and mitigation, as long as it is relevant, reliable, and not prejudicial. *Zant v. Stephens*, 462 U.S. 862 (1983).

e. Relationship Between Aggravators and Mitgators

There is no uniformity among the states about how juries assess aggravating and mitigating factors. Before deciding on a death sentence, most states require that the aggravating circumstances outweigh the mitigating evidence.

f. Proportionality Review

Many states require by statute that appellate courts conduct a proportionality review, by which the defendant's death sentence is compared with sentences for those convicted of the same crime but did not receive the death penalty. However, that type of review is not constitutionally required, *Pulley v. Harris*, 465 U.S. 37 (1984), if the state has sufficient procedures to avoid arbitrary application of the death penalty.

E. SENTENCING CONSIDERATIONS

Due process plays an important role in the procedures a judge should use before sentencing a defendant. *Williams v. New York*, 337 U.S. 241 (1949). In *Williams*, for example, the Court permitted the sentencing court's consideration of prior crimes for which the defendant had never been charged or convicted, stating that "the fullest information possible concerning the defendant's life and characteristics" is "highly relevant if not essential" . . . to the selection of the appropriate sentence. The Court rejected the defendant's due process challenge to the state sentencing procedure which permitted the sentencing judge to consider information about the offender's "past life, health, habits, conduct, and mental and moral propensities."

1. Perjury by Defendant

In *United States v. Grayson*, 438 U.S. 41 (1978), the Court held that perjury by the defendant is relevant to the sentence to be imposed and does not infringe upon the defendant's right to testify on his own behalf. The Court found that the Constitution guarantees only the right to testify truthfully; thus, any chilling effect on the decision to testify falsely was permissible.

2. Defendant's Refusal to Cooperate

In addition, the judge may consider the defendant's refusal to cooperate with law enforcement authorities. The judge "must be permitted to consider any and all information that reasonably might bear on the proper sentence for the particular defendant, given the crime committed." *Wasman v. United States*, 468 U.S. 559 (1984).

3. Presentence Report

If the defendant has been convicted, the case should proceed to sentencing without unreasonable delay. However, it is customary to postpone sentencing for a short period of time to enable the court to obtain a presentence report. The report must be prepared by a probation officer, must include an analysis of the defendant's background and may include a victim impact statement under appropriate circumstances. *Payne v. Tennessee*, 501 U.S. 808 (1991).

a. Disclosure of Contents

The presentence report is reviewed by the court before sentencing. Before imposing sentence, the trial court must advise the defendant or counsel of the contents of any presentence report. If the defendant wishes to controvert the contents of any report, the court must afford a fair opportunity and a reasonable period of time to challenge them. However, the court need not disclose the sources of confidential information contained in the report.

CHAPTER 29

DOUBLE JEOPARDY

A. GENERAL PRINCIPLES

A defendant has both federal and state constitutional protections against being placed in jeopardy twice for the same offense. The pertinent part of the Fifth Amendment states: "[N]or shall any person be subject for the same offense to be twice put in jeopardy of life or limb." Despite the "life or limb" language of the Fifth Amendment, double jeopardy protection extends to all crimes, capital and otherwise. Double jeopardy protection applies to the states through the Fourteenth Amendment. *Benton v. Maryland*, 395 U.S. 784 (1969).

1. Essence of Double Jeopardy's Prohibition

The defendant would risk conviction for an offense for which the defendant has already been placed on trial and in jeopardy. A successful claim involving double jeopardy will bar a trial on the indictment or information.

a. Raising a Double Jeopardy Objection

The objection may be raised by a motion to dismiss at any time before trial. Although a failure to raise the objection before the second adjudication may operate as a waiver, it may be raised for the first time in a reviewing court if the double jeopardy issue can be decided as a matter of law on the facts established by the record.

2. When Jeopardy Attaches

Double jeopardy bars a second prosecution only if jeopardy attached in the original proceeding. In a jury trial, jeopardy attaches when the jury is sworn. *Crist v. Bretz*, 437 U.S. 28 (1978). If a case is tried before a judge, after waiver of a jury, jeopardy attaches when the first witness is sworn. *Serfass v. United States*, 420 U.S. 377 (1975). Jeopardy also attaches when the trial court accepts a guilty plea. If a case is dismissed or terminated prior to the attachment of jeopardy, jeopardy has not attached and the defendant may have to respond to the same criminal charges in further proceedings.

3. Dual Sovereign Doctrine

The doctrine of dual sovereign does not prohibit multiple prosecutions for the same offense by courts of different sovereigns. In *Heath v. Alabama*, 474 U.S. 82 (1985), the Court held that successive prosecutions by different states are permissible); earlier, *Bartkus v. Illinois*, 359 U.S. 121 (1959) held that successive state and federal trials for same offense are also permissible.

a. Possible Statutory Exceptions

Despite the dual sovereign approach, some states have adopted statutes barring subsequent prosecutions when conduct constitutes an offense within the concurrent jurisdiction of the state and another state, or the state and the United States. *See, e.g.*, KRS 505.050.

b. When Constitutional Dual Sovereign Is Inapplicable

The dual sovereign theory does not apply to state and municipal prosecutions for the same act, because the state and the municipality are regarded as the same sovereign, regardless of how the state chooses to classify its governmental subunits: the subunits derive their power to exist from the sovereign. In *Waller v. Florida*, 397 U.S. 387 (1970), the Court held that successive prosecutions for the same offense based upon violations of state statute and local ordinance are prohibited by double jeopardy.

B. MISTRIALS AND THE POSSIBILITY OF A RETRIAL

Once jeopardy has attached in a criminal trial, circumstances often will suggest that the proceedings should be terminated prior to a formal verdict. In such a situation, called a mistrial, the judge exercises her discretion to decide that the proceedings must end without a verdict in the case. A mistrial is granted whenever an error has occurred in the trial that cannot be cured by any remedial action of the parties or the court.

1. What a Mistrial Declaration Does and Does Not Decide

Under a mistrial declaration, the judge need not decide whether a subsequent trial on the same charge would be permitted; the only question before the court is whether the first trial should be discontinued.

a. When to Seek a Mistrial

Mistrial motions are made orally as soon as the error complained of occurs or is disclosed. If a motion for mistrial already has been denied, a renewed motion should seek a mistrial for the instant error as well as for the cumulation of prior error.

2. Grounds for Mistrial

In most jurisdictions, there is an extensive amount of case law dealing with the types of error in the admission of evidence and the conduct of counsel, witnesses, the court, and jury that are "curable" by instructions to the jury or continuances, and which errors require a mistrial.

a. Assessing the Propriety of a Mistrial

Several factors seem to be significant in assessing the propriety of a mistrial:

- the source of the problem, e.g., prosecutorial error, act of God,
- the motivation for the error, e.g., harassment, good faith,
- prejudice to the defendant associated with a retrial, e.g., loss of tactical advantage gained in the first trial, apart from the fact of the retrial itself, and
- available alternatives to declaring a mistrial, e.g., jury admonition, continuance.

b. Illinois v. Somerville

In *Illinois v. Somerville*, 410 U.S. 458 (1973), soon after the jury was sworn the prosecutor noticed a negligent omission of a vital allegation from the indictment that would require reversal of any conviction on appeal, because state law did not permit amendment of an indictment. The trial court declared a mistrial. Although the prosecution was responsible for the poorly drafted indictment, the Supreme Court upheld the mistake because it was not subject to prosecutorial manipulation, there was no prejudice to the defendant, and under Illinois law there was no alternative such as amending the indictment. The Supreme Court found that there was manifest necessity for the trial court's mistrial declaration.

c. Clashing Interests in Considering Reprosecution After a Mistrial

The prosecution argues that it has a strong interest in obtaining one reasonable opportunity to establish the defendant's guilt. Defense counsel argue that reprosecution is undesirable because it subjects the defendant to serious burdens even if the defendant is acquitted at a retrial. Invariably, the defense arguments return to the defendant's interest in completing the trial before a jury that was favorably disposed to the defendant's case. In *Arizona v. Washington*, 434 U.S. 497 (1978), the Court stated that when a mistrial is justified by a "high degree" of necessity, the defendant's right to a particular tribunal is outweighed by society's right to have one complete opportunity to prosecute the accused.

d. Judicial Discretion in Deciding Whether to Grant or Deny a Mistrial

When mistrials are declared due to hung juries, trial judges have considerable discretion to gauge firsthand the amount of time a particular jury needs to reach a verdict. Likewise, when defense counsel makes prejudicial comments to the jury, the trial judge can observe the impact of the statements on the jury and select the appropriate remedy. The *Washington* Court observed that trial judges need broad discretion to assess the need for a mistrial; otherwise unscrupulous defense attorneys would take unfair advantage of their clients' double jeopardy rights by intentionally biasing the jury. Therefore, appellate courts defer to a trial judge's decision to grant a mistrial, unless there is an abuse of that discretion.

e. Effects of a Mistrial Declaration

Although a double jeopardy claim will not arise until subsequent charges are brought, that double jeopardy claim constitutes an attack on the propriety of the original mistrial declaration, i.e., a motion to dismiss the charge on double jeopardy grounds is effectively arguing that there is no reason to have a second trial because there was no manifest necessity for the mistrial declaration that ended the first case.

f. Defense Consent Waives Double Jeopardy Objection After Mistrial

Defense consent to mistrial ordinarily constitutes waiver of double jeopardy rights. Mistrials are easiest to deal with for double jeopardy purposes when the defendant requests or agrees to the mistrial. The defendant's consent or agreement for a mistrial ordinarily removes any barrier to reprosecution.

(1) Objecting to Mistrial Preserves Double Jeopardy Issue

In order to reserve the possibility of later raising the lack of manifest necessity, the defendant must object to the mistrial, whether it is sought by the prosecutor or by the court. Before declaring a mistrial, a judge is required under Fed.R.Crim.P. 26.3 to permit all counsel to comment on the propriety of a mistrial order, including their right to consent or object, and to suggest alternatives to a mistrial. A retrial is permissible if the defendant actively sought or consented to premature termination of the earlier proceedings.

(2) Oregon v. Kennedy

Oregon v. Kennedy, 456 U.S. 667 (1982) held that a defendant's mistrial motion does not waive his double jeopardy rights if the prosecution or the trial court intended to subvert those rights by provoking him into seeking a mistrial. The provocation must be the result of prosecutorial or judicial intent, not bad faith or harassment.

C. PROSECUTION APPEALS AFTER DISMISSAL OR ACQUITTAL

The assumption underlying a mistrial is that the reason for terminating the first trial is not a fatal defect to having a second trial. By contrast, the question for prosecutors following a dismissal or acquittal is whether it can be appealed or retried.

1. Before Jeopardy Attaches

Prior to the attachment of jeopardy, the reason for terminating a criminal proceeding has no double jeopardy significance. For example, in *Serfass v. United States*, 420 U.S. 377 (1975), the defendant's pretrial motion to dismiss for insufficient evidence was granted. The Court held that double jeopardy does not bar a government appeal even though it could lead to a new trial because jeopardy had not attached.

2. After Jeopardy Attaches

Once jeopardy has attached, the way in which a trial ends is relevant to double jeopardy principles. Whether the cessation of a trial is a dismissal or acquittal is important to resolving whether the government can appeal the adverse termination of the case and whether the defendant can be retried.

a. Statutory Grounds for Government Appeals

All jurisdictions provide statutory authority for the government to appeal from an adverse termination. In the absence of a double jeopardy prohibition, the government can appeal and, if successful, can retry the defendant. *See, e.g.*, 18 U.S.C. § 3731.

3. Acquittal Defined

An acquittal is a termination of the proceedings in favor of the defendant, on the merits. When an acquittal occurs after jeopardy has attached, it forever bars the retrial of the defendant for the same offense, *Martinez v. Illinois*, 134 S.Ct. 2070 (2014), as well as a prosecutorial appeal of the acquittal. An acquittal may be the result of a judge's ruling or a jury verdict. For example, a defendant is acquitted when the trial court rules "that the prosecution's proof is insufficient to establish criminal liability for an offense." *Evans v. Michigan*, 133 S.Ct. 1069 (2013).

4. Dismissal Defined

A dismissal is not the same as an acquittal. Even though it is a termination of the proceedings, a dismissal is not a termination on the merits of the case. For example, when a court dismisses the charge because the indictment is dismissed as legally defective, double jeopardy does not preclude an appeal by the prosecution and a retrial if the appeal is successful.

5. Key Issues about Appealability of Dismissals and Acquittals

Summarizing, it is important to know the nature of a termination and whether it occurs before or after jeopardy attaches:

- is it important when a termination occurs? Yes, before jeopardy attaches its label does not matter,
- after jeopardy attaches, is the type of disposition important? Yes.

a. United States v. Scott

In *United States v. Scott*, 437 U.S. 82 (1978), after the trial began the trial court dismissed the charge for precharge delay before any factfinder had ruled on the defendant's culpability. Thus, *Scott* was a midtrial dismissal; the prosecution could appeal the dismissal because it was not related to culpability, i.e., it was not on the merits.

b. Sanabria v. United States

Even where the judge makes errors in the admission of evidence, a ruling that ends in a functional acquittal bars retrial. In *Sanabria v. United States*, 437 U.S. 54 (1978), the

Court held that when a defendant is acquitted midtrial, he cannot be retried for the same charge, even if the legal rulings underlying the acquittal were erroneous. The trial court erroneously acquitted the defendant on the basis of insufficient evidence tying him to illegal gambling. Erroneous mid-trial judgments of acquittal bar retrial, regardless of their specific nature or cause. *Evans v. Michigan*, 133 S.Ct. 1069 (2013).

6. (Non)Appealability of Judgments of Acquittal

A trial court's judgment of acquittal because the proof was insufficient bars a retrial after a hung jury. In *United States v. Martin Linen Supply Co.*, 430 U.S. 564 (1977), following a mistrial declaration due to a hung jury, the trial court granted defense counsel's timely motion under Fed.R.Crim.P. 29(c) for a judgment of acquittal. The Court treated the disposition as an acquittal and therefore not appealable. Under *Martin Linen* an acquittal is accorded special weight.

a. Untimely Motion for Judgment of Acquittal Is Appealable

However, if after a hung jury the motion for judgment of acquittal is not made in a timely fashion, the case is characterized as being in a pretrial mode and a dismissal of the charge can be appealed and retried. In *United States v. Sanford*, 429 U.S. 14 (1976), the trial judge declared a mistrial after the jury was unable to agree on a verdict. Four months later, the judge dismissed the charge because the government had consented to the conduct that formed the basis of the allegation. The Court held that the dismissal was appealable and was akin to a pretrial order when jeopardy has not attached.

b. Judgment of Acquittal Granted after Conviction Is Appealable

If the judgment of acquittal is granted after a jury's verdict of conviction, the acquittal is appealable by the government since the original verdict of guilt can be reinstated without another trial. *See United States v. Wilson*, 420 U.S. 332 (1975).

D. RETRIALS AFTER DEFENSE APPEALS AND IMPLIED ACQUITTALS

1. Reversal of Conviction Because of Insufficient Evidence

When a conviction is successfully appealed by the defendant, whether there can be a retrial depends on the reason for the reversal of the conviction. If the appellate court reversed due to the insufficiency of the evidence against the defendant, a retrial is prohibited even though the defendant sought the reversal. *Burks v. United States*, 437 U.S. 1 (1978).

a. New Trial Grant Because of Insufficient Evidence

The rule of insufficient evidence applies as well to motions for a new trial made in the trial court after a conviction. A new trial is allowed, however, if the trial judge believes that there was sufficient evidence but she would have decided the case differently than the jury did, based on the "great weight of the evidence." *Tibbs v. Florida*, 457 U.S. 31 (1982).

2. Reversal of Conviction Because of Trial Error

Where the appellate court reverses because of trial errors or defects in the charging instrument, as opposed to insufficiency of evidence, the defendant can be retried. For example, in *Lockhart v. Nelson*, 488 U.S. 33 (1988), the Court permitted a retrial when the appellate reversal was for trial errors in the admissibility of evidence, even though without such evidence there was insufficient proof to support the conviction.

3. Implicit Acquittals of Greater Included Offense

When a defendant is charged for an offense such as first-degree robbery but is convicted of a lesser included version of that offense such as second-degree robbery, on retrial following a successful appeal the defendant cannot be convicted of the robbery in the first degree, the greater included crime. The first verdict operates as an implied acquittal on the greater included offense, thereby precluding a retrial for that crime. Jury instructions on only the lesser included offense can be given at the second trial. However, in the event that the defendant mistakenly is tried and convicted of a jeopardy-barred offense, the conviction can be reduced by an appellate court to a lesser included offense which is not barred by double jeopardy. *Morris v. Mathews*, 475 U.S. 237 (1986).

E. MORE SEVERE PUNISHMENT THAN AT FIRST TRIAL

Suppose the defendant is convicted of a felony and is sentenced to twenty years, but the defendant is successful in obtaining a new trial. Could the judge or jury then sentence the defendant to thirty years?

1. More Severe Sentence May Be Imposed at Retrial

When a defendant successfully appeals his conviction, due process does not bar the imposition of a more severe sentence if he is convicted on retrial. *North Carolina v. Pearce*, 395 U.S. 711 (1969).

A court must record its reasons for the sentence increase at retrial, based upon any relevant event of which it was unaware at the time of the first trial's sentencing, such as a conviction for an offense committed before the original sentencing, or conduct occurring after the first trial. However, in *Chaffin v. Stynchcombe*, 412 U.S. 17 (1973), the Court held that *Pearce* does not apply when a jury at the second trial is recommending the sentence, because the jury would not know of the earlier sentence.

2. More Severe Sentence Cannot Be Imposed at Retrial of Capital Case

The foregoing principle is not applicable to capital cases. When a defendant is sentenced to life and succeeds in obtaining a new trial, she is no longer subject to the death penalty on any retrial. *Bullington v. Missouri*, 451 U.S. 430 (1981). This proposition, grounded on double jeopardy, applies even if a jury is waived. However, if an appellate court corrects a mistaken legal interpretation of an aggravating factor which does not alter the validity of the punishment, a retrial after a reversal for the trial error can result again in a death sentence. *Poland v. Arizona*, 476 U.S. 147 (1986).

CHAPTER 30

APPEALS

A. INTRODUCTION

There are significant differences between the trial and appellate stages of a criminal proceeding. The purpose of the trial stage from the government's point of view is to convert a criminal defendant from a person presumed innocent to one found guilty beyond a reasonable doubt. By contrast, it is ordinarily the defendant, rather than the government, who initiates the appellate process, seeking to overturn a finding of guilt made by a judge or a jury below.

1. Alternative Methods for Reviewing a Conviction

Following conviction, the state defendant has several avenues of relief available and has access to a number of forums where she can obtain review of her conviction. Motions to set aside the verdict and motions for a new trial are addressed to the trial court. Direct appeal lies with the state appellate courts, while *habeas corpus* petitions can be filed in both state and federal court. See Chapter 31.

a. Scope of This Chapter

This chapter addresses the forms of judicial review in the order in which they normally arise, and highlights substantive differences between the forms of judicial review, as well as distinct procedural requirements relating to time and form. Although post-conviction remedies require close attention to details and are addressed in the next chapter, two general themes run throughout the review process.

B. REVIEW BY A TRIAL COURT

In most appeals, a higher court is asked to scrutinize the trial record for errors that would require reversal of the conviction. Many misdemeanor cases, however, are tried in lower courts, such as police courts or magistrate's courts, from which no record or transcript of the proceedings is available for review by a higher court. These lower courts are sometimes referred to as courts-not-of-record and usually operate without a jury and without all of the procedural safeguards provided in the trial of felony cases. A defendant convicted in such a lower court is often granted an absolute right to a trial *de novo* in a superior court, sometimes called a court-of-record.

1. Trial *De Novo*

Although occasionally referred to as an appeal of a conviction, the granting of a trial *de novo* is normally automatic upon the defendant's request. Thus, no error need be alleged as to the first trial, and a defendant who exercises his right to a trial *de novo* is not entitled to judicial review of the sufficiency of the evidence presented to the lower court. *Justices of Boston Municipal Court v. Lydon*, 466 U.S. 294 (1984). The right to a trial *de novo* generally exists even when the defendant pled guilty in the lower court. Neither the defendant's plea nor the lower court's judgment is admissible evidence at the trial *de novo*, but the defendant's prior testimony is admissible at the trial in the higher court.

C. DIRECT APPEAL IN THE STATE COURTS

Most jurisdictions have created a two-tiered appellate structure in which the convicted defendant has a right of appeal to an intermediate appellate court, but any further appeal to a higher court, usually the State Supreme Court, is often discretionary.

1. Right to Counsel on Appeal

The distinction between a right of appeal and discretionary review by an appellate court is important, because the Supreme Court has held that in felony cases, counsel must be provided to indigent persons exercising their *right* to appeal. *Douglas v. California*, 372 U.S. 353 (1963). However, counsel need not be provided to indigent defendants seeking discretionary review. *Ross v. Moffitt*, 417 U.S. 600 (1974). The right to counsel on appeal stems from the Due Process and Equal Protection Clauses of the Fourteenth Amendment, not from the Sixth Amendment. Although the Sixth Amendment guarantees the defendant's right to self-representation at trial, there is no such right at the appellate stage. *Martinez v. Court of Appeal*, 528 U.S. 152 (2000).

2. Waiver of Right to Appeal

Whatever the nature and scope of a right to appellate review, *Ortega-Rodriguez v. United States*, 507 U.S. 234 (1993) demonstrates that the right to appellate review can be waived or forfeited. An appeals court may dismiss the appeal of a defendant who is a fugitive during the appellate process. However, if the defendant flees and returns to custody before the appellate process begins, denial of the appeal is not automatic. Missed deadlines also may result in a waiver of the right appeal.

D. HARMLESS ERROR AND PLAIN ERROR

"The Constitution entitles a criminal defendant to a fair trial, not a perfect one." *Delaware v. VanArsdall*, 475 U.S. 673 (1986).

1. Whether Non-Constitutional Error May Be Harmless

A trial error that is not of constitutional dimension (for example, the trial judge erred in admitting some minor item of evidence) is harmless when it plainly appears from the facts and circumstances of the case that the error did not affect the verdict. Reversal is required for a non-constitutional error only if it "had substantial and injurious effect or influence in determining the jury's verdict." *United States v. Lane*, 474 U.S. 438 (1986). Consider the following from *Kotteakos v. United States*, 328 U.S. 750 (1946):

> If, when all is said and done, the conviction is sure that the error did not influence the jury, or had but very slight effect, the verdict and the judgment should stand. . . . But if one cannot say, with fair assurance, after pondering all that happened without stripping the erroneous action from the whole, that the judgment was not substantially swayed by the error, it is impossible to conclude that substantial rights were not affected. The inquiry cannot be merely whether there was enough to support the result, apart from the phase affected by the error. It is rather, even so, whether the error itself had substantial influence. If so, or if one is left in grave doubt, the conviction cannot stand.

2. Whether Constitutional Error May Be Harmless

Unlike non-constitutional error, the Supreme Court has held that "before a federal constitutional error can be held harmless, the court must be able to declare a belief that it was harmless beyond a reasonable doubt." *Chapman v. California*, 386 U.S. 18 (1967). Application of the harmless error doctrine to a constitutional error depends upon the nature of the error. Structural defects require automatic reversal and are not subject to harmless error analysis. *California v. Roy*, 519 U.S. 2 (1996).

3. Structural Errors Requiring Automatic Reversal

In *Kyles v. Whitley*, 514 U.S. 419 (1995) and *Arizona v. Fulminante*, 499 U.S. 279 (1991), the Supreme Court has recognized a number of structural errors requiring automatic reversal.

4. Case Law Examples of Structural Errors

Type of Error	Case Relating to the Error
Defective reasonable doubt jury instruction	*Sullivan v. Louisiana*, 508 U.S. 275 (1993)
Discrimination in grand jury selection	*Vasquez v. Hillery*, 474 U.S. 254 (1986)
Denial of public trial	*Waller v. Georgia*, 467 U.S. 39 (1984)
Denial of self-representation at trial	*McKaskle v. Wiggins*, 465 U.S. 168 (1984)
Complete denial of counsel	*Gideon v. Wainwright*, 372 U.S. 335 (1963)
Biased trial judge	*Tumey v. Ohio*, 273 U.S. 510 (1927)
Trial by partial fact finder	*United States v. Gonzalez-Lopez*, 548 U.S. 140 (2006)
Non-disclosure of exculpatory evidence	*Kyles v. Whitley*, 514 U.S. 419 (1995)

a. Example of Non-Structural Error

In *Hedgpeth v. Pulido*, 555 U.S. 57 (2008), a conviction based on a general verdict following jury instructions based on multiple theories of guilt (one of which is invalid) was held not to be a structural error, but instead was subject to harmless error review.

b. Trial Errors Are Subject to Harmless Error Analysis

Trial errors occur during the presentation of the case to the jury. For example, the Court held that *Apprendi* violations are subject to harmless error analysis when the trial court fails to submit a sentencing factor to the jury. *Washington v. Recuenco*, 548 U.S. 212 (2006). Such constitutional errors are treated differently depending on whether they are raised on direct appeal or collateral review.

(1) Trial Errors: Collateral Review v. Direct Review

On collateral review, (e.g. *habeas corpus* petitions) trial errors require reversal of the conviction only if the defendant proves "actual prejudice," i.e., the error had a "substantial and injurious effect or influence in determining the jury's verdict." *Brecht v. Abrahamson*, 507 U.S. 619 (1993). On direct review, however, trial errors require reversal of the conviction unless the reviewing court finds such errors to be harmless "beyond a reasonable doubt."

5. Plain Error

A more stringent standard of review for harmless error is applied when the defendant failed to object to a trial error, but now is calling such "plain error" to the attention of the appellate court. Plain error analysis requires a "reasonable probability that the error affected the outcome of the trial," not just "any possibility no matter how unlikely." *United States v. Marcus*, 560 U.S. 258 (2010). *United States v. Olano*, 507 U.S. 725 (1993) established the plain error test requiring that there was error, the error was plain, the defendant show harm to a substantial right, and no error may be corrected unless it "serious affect[s] the fairness, integrity or public reputation of judicial proceedings. Regardless whether a legal question was settled or unsettled at the time of trial, an error is "plain" within the meaning of Federal Rule of Criminal Procedure 52(b) so long as the error was plain at the time of appellate review. *Henderson v. United States,* 133 S.Ct. 1121 (2013).

E. APPEALS OF LAST RESORT

A defendant who fails to obtain a reversal on direct appeal may make collateral attacks on the conviction, such as a petition for a writ of *habeas corpus* discussed in the next chapter.

1. Appeals to Executive Authority

As a supplement to judicial review, all jurisdictions grant a convicted defendant an opportunity to appeal to executive authority for a pardon or grant of clemency. For example, Article 2, Section 2, Clause 1 of the U. S. Constitution gives the President the power to "forgive the convicted person in part or entirely, to reduce a penalty in terms of a specified number of years, or to alter it with conditions which are in themselves constitutionally unobjectionable." *Schick v. Reed*, 419 U.S. 256 (1974).

CHAPTER 31

COLLATERAL REMEDIES

A. INTRODUCTION

A defendant who fails on direct appeal from a criminal conviction may file a collateral attack on the conviction, the most common form being a petition for a writ of *habeas corpus*. Most states have *habeas corpus*-like proceedings that closely follow federal *habeas corpus*, discussed in the remainder of this chapter. Failure to prevail in state habeas proceedings does not bar a subsequent federal *habeas* action. In fact, the filing of a state petition is often a necessary component of the federal petition.

1. *Habeas Corpus* Defined

Habeas corpus, a Latin term meaning "you have the body," is a collateral attack because it is not a continuation of the criminal process, but instead is a civil suit brought to challenge the legality of the restraint under which a person is held. In this civil suit, the petitioner having lost the presumption of innocence upon conviction, has the burden to prove by a preponderance of evidence that his confinement is illegal. The respondent in a *habeas* action is the prisoner's custodian—the prison warden or other official.

2. Summary Disposition of *Habeas Corpus* Petition

Merely filing a *habeas corpus* petition does not insure that a federal court will review the merits of the petitioner's claim. If the *habeas corpus* petition is patently frivolous, or if the court can determine the merits of the allegations by reference to records of previous state or federal judicial proceedings, the petition may be denied without a full evidentiary hearing.

B. JURISDICTION AND VENUE

A state prisoner may petition for a writ of *habeas corpus* in the federal district in which the prisoner resides or in the district where the state sentencing court is located. 28 U.S.C. § 2241(d). In states with more than one federal district, then, the prisoner has a choice about where to file the petition. By contrast, a federal prisoner may file a petition only in the federal sentencing court. 28 U.S.C. § 2255(a).

1. Comparing *Habeas Corpus* with Civil Rights Actions

Unlike a civil rights complaint by which a prisoner challenges the conditions of confinement, a state prisoner who petitions the federal court is challenging the fact or the duration of the confinement. The petition challenges the prisoner's custody based on an alleged violation of the U.S. Constitution, federal laws or federal treaties. 28 U.S.C. § 2254(a). Federal petitioners for *habeas corpus* relief are challenging the imposed sentence as being in violation of the U.S. Constitution or federal laws. 28 U.S.C. § 2255(a). Trial errors that are fundamentally unfair are cognizable because they allegedly violate the Due Process Clause.

C. TIME CONSIDERATIONS

At common law, any person illegally detained could use the writ of *habeas corpus* to make repeated efforts to gain his freedom. "*Res judicata*did not attach to a court's denial of *habeas* relief . . . [instead a] renewed application could be made to every other judge or court in the realm, and each court or judge was bound to consider the question of the prisoner's right to a discharge independently, and not to be influenced by the previous decisions refusing discharge." *McCleskey v. Zant*, 499 U.S. 467 (1991).

1. No Time Constraints at Common Law

The common law courts heard multiple petitions and petitions filed years after the initial trial because the writ of *habeas corpus* originally performed only the narrow function of testing either the jurisdiction of the sentencing court or the legality of executive detention. The scope of the writ later expanded beyond its original narrow purview to encompass review of constitutional error that had occurred in the proceedings leading to conviction. Prior to enactment of the Antiterrorism and Effective Death Penalty Act of 1996 [AEDPA] there was no time limitation on the filing of a writ of *habeas corpus*, although some courts applied the equitable doctrine of *laches* on a case-by-case basis. The doctrine of *laches* did not operate as an effective statute of limitations, because it required that the government prove actual prejudice from the delay, which cannot be presumed merely from the passage of time.

2. AEPDA One-Year Time Limit on Filing *Habeas Corpus* Petitions

In order to promote speedy punishment and the finality of criminal justice proceedings, the AEPDA created a rigid one-year limitation for filing a petition for habeas corpus relief. The year runs from the latest date of the final judgment on direct review or "the expiration of the time for seeking such review"; removal of any state-imposed impediment that unconstitutionally prevented the filing of such a petition; the Supreme Court's recognition of a new, retroactively applicable constitutional right; or the emergence or recognition of any new facts supporting the petitioner's claim that "could have been discovered through the exercise of due diligence." 28 U.S.C. § 2244(d)(1)(A)–(D).

a. Example of Due Diligence

An example of the last ground occurs when a prisoner collaterally attacks his federal sentence on the ground that a state conviction used to enhance that sentence has since been vacated. In that situation, the limitations period begins to run when the prisoner receives notice of the order vacating the state conviction, provided that he showed due diligence in seeking to vacate the state conviction. See *Johnson v. United States*, 544 U.S. 295 (2005).

b. Tolling the One-year Limitation

Tolling under 28 U.S.C. § 2244(d)(2), is triggered by judicial review of a state prisoner's request that the trial court use its discretion to reduce his sentence. *Wall v. Kholi*, 131 S.Ct. 1278 (2011). The one-year limitation is tolled while an application for state post-conviction or other collateral review is pending, even if it contains procedurally-barred claims. *Artuz v. Bennett*, 531 U.S. 4 (2000).

(1) When There Is No Tolling

An application for federal *habeas corpus* review is not an "application for state post-conviction or other collateral review," and the limitation period therefore will not be tolled. *Duncan v. Walker*, 533 U.S. 167 (2001).

(2) Equitable Tolling

In *Holland v. Florida*, 560 U.S. 631 (2010), the Court held that the concept of equitable tolling could apply to the AEDPA's one year time limit for filing a writ of *habeas corpus*.

"We have previously made clear that a 'petitioner' is 'entitled to equitable tolling' only if he shows '(1) that he has been pursuing his rights diligently, and (2) that some extraordinary circumstance stood in his way' and prevented timely filing. In this case, the 'extraordinary circumstances' at issue involve an attorney's failure to satisfy professional standards of care. . . . T]he facts of this case present far more serious instances of attorney misconduct." Counsel was unaware of the time limit for filing and failed to communicate with his client for a long period.

c. When One-year Limitation Does Not Apply

The filling deadline does not apply if there is compelling evidence of the petitioner's innocence, i.e., no reasonable juror aware of the new evidence would have voted to convict. *McQuiggin v. Perkins*, 133 S.Ct. 1924 (2013).

D. CUSTODY

To apply for a writ of *habeas corpus*, a person must be in "custody," which is liberally construed by the courts and includes significant restraints on personal liberty as well as physical incarceration. *Jones v. Cunningham*, 371 U.S. 236 (1963). Thus, the writ may not be used to attack a sentence that has been fully served, to attack a conviction that merely imposed a fine or collateral civil disability not resulting in incarceration, or to challenge a conviction after the sentence has expired, because there is no longer "custody" under that conviction.

1. Custody for Consecutive Sentences

In *Peyton v. Rowe*, 391 U.S. 54 (1968), the Supreme Court ruled that a petitioner serving consecutive sentences is considered "in custody" under any one of the sentences for purposes of filing a *habeas* petition. A consecutive sentence that has not begun, is currently running, or already has expired may be challenged until all of the sentences have been served.

2. Past Custody

Generally, a person who has completed service of a prison sentence prior to filing a petition is not deemed to be in custody merely because of suffering from economic hardship, loss of civil rights, or other harms flowing from the fact of conviction. On the other hand, if a petitioner is released from custody *after* filing a petition, a court may still hear the petition as long as the petitioner is subject to negative collateral consequences from the challenged conviction, e.g., barred from jury duty, voting, or certain jobs requiring licenses. *Sibron v. New York*, 392 U.S. 40 (1968).

a. Prior Convictions as a Basis for Present Custody

A person can attack a sentence already served if there is a direct relation between the prior conviction and the present confinement, e.g., the petitioner is serving a sentence that was enhanced on the basis of a prior conviction for which the sentence has been fully served. *See, e.g., Maleng v. Cook*, 490 U.S. 488 (1989).

E. SUCCESSIVE PETITIONS

Pre-AEPDA law permitted a petitioner to file the same claim for relief in successive petitions. However, under 28 U.S.C. § 2244(b), the AEPDA establishes procedures for the disposition of second or successive petitions. Any claim that was presented in a prior application for relief must be dismissed.

1. Successive Petition Rules Are Modified *Res Judicata* Rules

In *Felker v. Turpin*, 518 U.S. 651 (1996), the Supreme Court upheld the limits on second or successive petitions as "a modified *res judicata* rule, a restraint on what is called in habeas corpus practice 'abuse of the writ.' " A problem arises when a petitioner returns to federal court with a second *habeas corpus* petition raising previously dismissed claims. The Court does not regard *habeas* petitions filed after a dismissal without prejudice of an earlier petition as a second or successive petition. *Slack v. McDaniel*, 529 U.S. 473 (2000).

a. Civil Rule Motion for Relief from Judgment Is Also Considered a Successive Petition

Because collateral proceedings are governed by civil rather than criminal rules, a Fed.R.Civ.P. 60 motion may also constitute a successive petition (and is therefore subject to the AEPDA's gate-keeping provisions) when it contests the merits of the court's denial of relief or seeks to advance new grounds for relief. On the other hand, Fed.R.Civ.P. 60(b) challenges to the integrity of the trial court proceeding do not implicate the provision on successive petitions. *Gonzalez v. Crosby*, 543 U.S. 1086 (2005).

2. Claim for Relief Defined

A claim usually is construed as transactional, rather than based on a separate legal theory. For example, if a petitioner in a prior application has sought relief from a trial court's refusal to suppress a confession on Fifth Amendment grounds, the "claim" regarding the admissibility of the confession has been heard; another petition challenging its admission, this time based on a Sixth Amendment violation, must be dismissed. 28 U.S.C. § 2244(b)(1).

3. Claim Challenges a New Judgment

In *Magwood v. Patterson*, 561 U.S. 320 (2010), the Court addressed the issue of "whether an application is 'second or successive' if it challenges a new judgment." In *Burton v. Stewart*, 549 U.S. 147 (2007), the Court held that because both of the petitioner's *habeas* petitions had challenged the same judgment, the second petition was statutorily precluded. However, *Burton* acknowledged that the result might have been different if there had been a new judgment intervening between the *habeas* petitions. In *Magwood*, there was such an intervening judgment. Thus, Magwood's second petition was his first application to challenge the intervening judgment where the trial court had conducted a full resentencing.

4. Claim Not Previously Presented May Also Be Summarily Dismissed

A claim that was not presented in a prior application also must be dismissed, per 28 U.S.C. § 2244(b)(2), unless:

- the claim relies on a new rule of constitutional law, made retroactive by the Supreme Court to *habeas corpus* cases, or
- the factual basis for the claim could not have been discovered by due diligence and the facts underlying the claim would show by clear and convincing evidence that but for the constitutional error, no reasonable factfinder would have found the petitioner to be guilty of the underlying offense.

5. Certification From Court of Appeals Is Necessary to Consider Successive Petitions

Prior to filing, a second or successive petition must pass through a "gatekeeping" system requiring a petitioner to move for an authorization order from a three-judge panel in the appropriate court of appeals before a district court may hear the petition. *Burton v. Stewart*. This certification decision is not appealable and is not subject to rehearing. 28 U.S.C. § 2244(b)(3).

F. EXHAUSTION OF STATE REMEDIES

Before a federal court will review a constitutional claim in a *habeas corpus* proceeding that seeks review of a state conviction, the claim first must be fairly presented to the state court system by properly pursuing a claim throughout the entire appellate process of the state. 28 U.S.C. § 2254(b)(1)(A). In order to exhaust the state remedies on a claim, the petitioner must have pursued the claim *either* on direct appeal *or* through the state version of *habeas corpus*. The latter remedy is often used when the claim was not raised at trial or on appeal, or it involves matters not in the trial record.

1. Exhaustion Includes Presentation of Claim for Discretionary Review

Exhaustion of remedies includes the presentations of claims to the state supreme court even though its review is discretionary. *O'Sullivan v. Boerckel*, 526 U.S. 838 (1999). The state court need not actually address the claim in a written opinion to satisfy this requirement. Federalism considerations simply will not permit a state prisoner to bypass the state courts and initiate the first review of his conviction in the federal courts.

2. Petitions with Both Exhausted and Unexhausted Claims

In *Rose v. Lundy*, 455 U.S. 509 (1982), the Court held that a federal district court must dismiss a petition that combines unexhausted and exhausted claims. Following dismissal, the petitioner must either return to state court to present the unexhausted claims or resubmit only the exhausted claims to the federal court. A state prisoner who submits such a "mixed petition" may either return to the state courts to exhaust all claims or amend the petition to present only exhausted claims to the federal district court. A federal district court has discretion to stay a "mixed" petition while unexhausted claims are presented to a state court, and to return to federal court for review of the perfected petition within the statute of limitations. *Rhines v. Weber*, 544 U.S. 269 (2005).

3. Unexhausted Claims May Be Dismissed

If the petitioner fails to exhaust state remedies, the federal court may dismiss the petition until such time as the petitioner has exhausted the available state remedies. The only exceptions to the exhaustion of remedies doctrine are when there is an absence of available state remedies or special circumstances render such remedies ineffective to protect the rights of the petitioner. 28 U.S.C. § 2254(b)(1)(B). Because the exhaustion of state remedies doctrine is based on comity and is not a jurisdictional requirement, the government may waive the requirement. *See Strickland v. Washington*, 466 U.S. 668 (1984).

G. EVIDENTIARY HEARINGS

Following the filing of a petition, the state's answer to the petition and the record of the state court proceedings, the *habeas* court must determine whether an evidentiary hearing is required.

1. Evidentiary Hearing When Facts Were Not Developed in State Court

If the petitioner has failed to develop the factual basis of a claim in state court proceedings, the federal court can hold an evidentiary hearing only when the petitioner has shown that (1) either the claim relies on a new, retroactive rule of constitutional law that was previously unavailable, or the claim relies on a factual basis that could not have been previously discovered by an exercise of due diligence; and (2) the facts underlying the claim show by clear and convincing evidence that, but for the constitutional error, there would have been no conviction.

a. Williams v. Taylor

In *Williams v. Taylor*, 529 U.S. 420 (2000), the Supreme Court held that the failure to develop a factual basis of a claim requires a "lack of diligence or some greater fault, attributable to the prisoner or to the prisoner's counsel." However, a claim pursued with diligence in state court may still be heard by a federal court if it was undeveloped due to government misconduct such as concealment of information.

2. Evidence Presented at Hearing

If a federal district court grants a hearing on the *habeas* petition, both the petitioner and the government must be given the opportunity to present evidence. The federal court must apply a presumption of correctness to state court factual determinations, unless the petitioner shows by clear and convincing evidence that the findings were erroneous.

3. Dispositions After Hearing

Upon denial of the petition, the petitioner is remanded to custody. If the court grants the petition, the petitioner is discharged from custody, but the court may suspend execution of its order to allow the government to appeal or to institute a new trial within a specified period of time.

a. Admitting Petitioner to Bail

The court also has authority to admit the petitioner to bail, pending the government's appeal or initiation of a new trial. Under *Hilton v. Braunskill*, 481 U.S. 770 (1987), when deciding whether to grant release pending appeal to a state prisoner who has won habeas relief, a federal court may consider:

- the risk that the prisoner may flee,
- the danger the prisoner may pose to the public,
- the state's interest in continuing custody and rehabilitation, and
- the prisoner's interest in release pending appeal.

H. VIOLATIONS OF FEDERAL LAW ONLY ARE COGNIZABLE

Only federal issues are cognizable in federal *habeas* proceedings; state constitutional or statutory violations are not. The most common *habeas corpus* claims are ineffective assistance of counsel, incriminating statements obtained by illegal police interrogation, improper judicial or prosecutorial conduct, and insufficient evidence. Although 28 U.S.C. § 2254 speaks of a "violation of the

Constitution or laws or treaties of the United States," almost all federal *habeas* petitions allege a violation of the Constitution.

1. Warren Court's Attitude About Scope of *Habeas* Review

A defining characteristic of the Warren Court in the 1960's was its willingness to increase federal *habeas* review of state court convictions by "constitutionalizing" many aspects of criminal procedure. The Warren Court's approach to federal *habeas corpus* was partially premised on a belief that the state courts could not be trusted to protect the constitutional rights of criminal defendants.

a. Modification of Warren Court's Approach

In *Gideon v. Wainwright*, 372 U.S. 335 (1963), Justice Harlan expressed dissatisfaction with many state courts' discharge of their "front-line responsibility for the enforcement of constitutional rights." Courts, however, recently embraced the concept of a "new federalism" by resurrecting faith in the state courts as protectors of individual freedom. *Stone v. Powell*, 428 U.S. 465 (1976) altered the judicial availability of federal *habeas* relief in Fourth Amendment cases, and was the first step in the Supreme Court's efforts to rein in federal judges reared on the Warren Court's "judicial activism" and distrust of state courts.

2. Stone v. Powell

In *Stone v. Powell*, the Supreme Court limited the scope of federal *habeas corpus* review of Fourth Amendment violations by holding that a state prisoner is not entitled to *habeas corpus* relief on the ground that evidence obtained in an unconstitutional search and seizure was introduced at trial, if the state provided an opportunity for full and fair litigation of the Fourth Amendment claim. This limitation on federal *habeas* claims does not apply to Sixth Amendment claims of ineffective counsel based on deficient representation in litigating a Fourth Amendment issue. See *Kimmelman v. Morrison*, 477 U.S. 365 (1986).

a. No Extension of *Stone v. Powell* to Guilt-Related Issues

Although the Court's opinion in *Stone v. Powell* led to speculation that defendants might be denied *habeas corpus* review of other constitutional claims, the Supreme Court has refused to extend that limiting principle to legal issues that are guilt-related.

b. Jackson v. Virginia

For example, in *Jackson v. Virginia*, 443 U.S. 307 (1979), the Court held that a claim that a prisoner was convicted on insufficient evidence is cognizable on federal *habeas corpus* review as a violation of due process. Unlike the Fourth Amendment exclusionary rule, the reasonable doubt standard of proof was deemed to relate to the accuracy of fact-finding. A federal court can hear an insufficiency of evidence claim, even if it was already heard by the state court.

c. Withrow v. Williams

In *Withrow v. Williams*, 507 U.S. 680 (1993), the Court declined an opportunity to apply *Stone v. Powell* to another favorite target of Court opinions—*Miranda v. Arizona*. *Miranda*'s exclusionary rule is similar to the Fourth Amendment rule—both are designed to deter police violations, and both arguably are unrelated to accurate fact-finding. Nevertheless, the *Withrow* Court found that a federal court can hear a petition concerning a *Miranda* violation even if the prisoner had an opportunity for a full and fair hearing of the issue in state court. *Miranda* safeguards a fundamental trial right that is not "necessarily divorced from the correct ascertainment of guilt."

d. Rose v. Mitchell

In *Rose v. Mitchell*, 443 U.S. 545 (1979), the Court held that a claim of racial discrimination in the selection of a state grand jury is cognizable on federal *habeas corpus*, even though the claimed error did not affect the determination of guilt and had been heard by the state court. The Court distinguished *Stone* on three grounds. First, the Court was unwilling to assume that state judges could fairly consider claims of grand jury discrimination, since those claims required the state courts to review their own procedures rather than those of the police. Second, the right to an indictment by a grand jury free from discrimination in its selection process is a personal constitutional right rather than a judicially created remedy. Third, state courts could be expected to respond to a determination that their grand jury selection procedures failed to meet constitutional requirements, i.e., deterrence is effective.

3. Legal Error: The State Decision Involved an Incorrect or Unreasonable Application of Federal Law

Habeas corpus relief will not be granted for any claim adjudicated on the merits in state courts unless the decision was "contrary to, or involved an unreasonable application of" federal law clearly established by the Supreme Court. 28 U.S.C. § 2254(d)(1). The determination that a state court's judgment was contrary to or involved an unreasonable application of clearly established federal law under 28 U.S.C. § 2254(d) must be based on the record that was before the state court that decided the claim. *Cullen v. Pinholster*, 131 S.Ct. 1388 (2011).

a. Adjudication on the Merits

A state court denial of post-conviction relief without stating its reasons qualifies as a § 2254(d) "adjudication on the merits," deserving deference as a reasonable decision. *Harrington v. Richter*, 131 S.Ct. 770 (2011). Similarly, when a petitioner raises a federal claim in state court that is not expressly addressed, federal courts apply *Richter*'s presumption of deference to state decisions being decided on the merits. *Johnson v. Williams*, 133 S.Ct. 1088 (2013).

b. Williams v. Taylor

In *Williams v. Taylor*, 529 U.S. 362 (2000), the Court defined the distinction between the "contrary to" category and the "unreasonable application" category.

c. "Contrary to" Clearly Established Federal Law Defined

"Contrary to" means that a state court either has arrived at a conclusion on a question of law opposite to that reached by the Supreme Court, or when confronted with materially indistinguishable facts from a Supreme Court precedent, arrived at an opposite result.

d. "Unreasonable Application" Defined

"Unreasonable application" of established federal law means that a state court either identified the correct legal rule but unreasonably applied it to the facts of the case, or unreasonably extended the legal principle to a new context that should not apply. Section 2254(d)(1) provides a remedy for instances in which a state court unreasonably *applies* Supreme Court precedent; it does not require state courts to *extend* that precedent or enable federal courts to treat the failure to do so as error. *White v. Woodall*, 134 S.Ct. 1697 (2014) (trial court refused to instruct the jury not to draw any adverse inference from his decision not to testify during the penalty phase). A state court's decision applying federal law must be *both* erroneous and unreasonable.

(1) Yarborough v. Alvarado

In *Yarborough v. Alvarado*, 541 U.S. 652 (2004), the Court elaborated on whether a state court decision was an unreasonable application of clearly established law under

Williams v. Taylor. Whether a decision is "unreasonable" can depend in part on the specificity of the legal rule. The more general the rule, the longer it may take for its meaning to emerge. The more specific the rule, the narrower is the range of a reasonable judgment. In *Yarborough*, the state court's failure to consider a juvenile suspect's age and inexperience with police interrogation in deciding that he was not "in custody" for *Miranda* purposes did not result in an "unreasonable application" of federal law, § 2254(d)(1).

(2) Examples Where the Standard Was Satisfied

In *Abdul-Kabir v. Quarterman*, 550 U.S. 233 (2007) and *Brewer v. Quarterman*, 550 U.S. 286 (2007), the trial court's jury instructions prevented the jury from giving meaningful consideration and effect to relevant mitigating evidence during a capital trial's penalty phase.

(3) Example Where the Standard Was Not Satisfied

Per § 2254, a state court applied Sixth Amendment precedent in a reasonable manner by deciding that there was no ineffective assistance by counsel who advised the defendant about a plea offer before moving to suppress a confession when defendant had admitted the crime to others. *Premo v. Moore*, 131 S.Ct. 733 (2011).

4. Factual Error: The State Decision Involved an Incorrect or Unreasonable Determination of Facts

When a state prisoner challenges the factual basis for a prior state court decision rejecting a claim, the federal court may overturn the state court's decision only if it was "based on an unreasonable determination of the facts in light of the evidence presented in the State court proceeding." §2254(d)(2). The prisoner bears the burden of rebutting the state court's factual findings "by clear and convincing evidence." §2254(e)(1). The state prisoner must "show that the state court's ruling on the claim being presented in federal court was so lacking in justification that there was an error . . . beyond any possibility for fairminded disagreement." *Harrington v. Richter*, 131 S.Ct. 770 (2011). "A state court factual determination is not unreasonable merely because the federal habeas court would have reached a different conclusion in the first instance." *Wood v. Allen*, 558 U. S. 290 (2010).

I. OVERCOMING PROCEDURAL DEFAULTS

Prior to *Wainwright v. Sykes*, 433 U.S. 72 (1977), a procedural default in state court did not prevent a federal court from providing *habeas corpus* relief, unless the state proved that the defendant had deliberately bypassed the state's procedural rules by failing to object to the evidence. With *Wainwright*, the failure to object bars federal *habeas* review in order to preserve the integrity of state procedures, and to promote federalism and comity.

1. Failure to Object to Admission of Evidence

The most common form of procedural default is the defendant's failure to present a federal constitutional claim to the trial court and thus preserve the issue for appellate review. The consequence of a procedural default is that the petitioner may be barred from judicial review of the forfeited claim in both state and federal courts. Unlike *Stone v. Powell* which bars federal *habeas* relief only when Fourth Amendment issues are given a full and fair hearing in the state courts, if there is a procedural bar, there is no hearing on the constitutional challenge in *any* state or federal court.

a. Wainwright v. Sykes

Sykes had sought relief on the ground that his conviction was based on a confession obtained in violation of *Miranda*. The Florida rules required at least a contemporaneous objection to the admission of illegally obtained evidence, but Sykes had made no objection before or during the trial. The Court found that contemporaneous objection rules serve valid interests such as ensuring the development of a factual record when witness recollections are freshest.

2. What a Petitioner Must Prove for *Habeas* Relief

When a defendant procedurally defaults, i.e., fails to comply with state contemporaneous objection rules, *habeas* corpus relief is available only when a prisoner can show either

- cause for the procedural default and actual prejudice from a violation of federal law, or
- that the federal court's failure to review the claims will result in a fundamental miscarriage of justice, because the petitioner is actually innocent.

3. Cause for the Procedural Default

In *Murray v. Carrier*, 477 U.S. 478 (1986), the Court stated that the "cause" usually depends upon whether the prisoner can prove that some objective factor external to the defense prevented counsel from complying with the state's procedural rule.

a. Ineffective Assistance of Counsel as Cause

Cause may be proved by showing that the failure was due to constitutionally ineffective assistance of counsel at trial or on appeal, or that governmental interference rendered procedural compliance impracticable. A lawyer's error is insufficient cause, unless it amounts to a violation of the Sixth Amendment right to effective counsel. See Chapter 16. An ineffective assistance of counsel claim that is asserted as cause for the procedural default of another claim may *itself* be barred by procedural default. *Edwards v. Carpenter*, 529 U.S. 446 (2000).

b. Governmental Interference as Cause

An example of government interference was shown in *Amadeo v. Zant*, 486 U.S. 214 (1988), when the Court held that governmental concealment of evidence that women and African-Americans were intentionally underrepresented on jury lists constituted cause for the defendant's failure to raise a timely challenge to the jury panel.

c. Ineffective Post-Conviction Counsel as Cause

Inadequate assistance of counsel in state post-conviction proceedings may excuse a procedural default of an ineffective assistance of trial counsel. *Trevino v. Thaler*, 133 S.Ct. 1911 (2013); *Martinez v. Ryan*, 132 S.Ct. 1309 (2012).

d. What Does *Not* Constitute Cause

(1) Futility of Raising the Issue Is Not Cause

If defense counsel says that she did not raise an issue in the state court proceedings because the state court would have been unsympathetic to the claim, the apparent futility of making an objection does not constitute cause. *Engle v. Isaac*, 456 U.S. 107 (1982).

(2) Novelty of the Defaulted Issue Is Not Cause

An allegation that an issue was not raised due to its novelty does not excuse a procedural default if the claim "had been percolating in the lower courts for years" at the time of the default. *Smith v. Murray*, 477 U.S. 527 (1986).

4. Prejudice to the Petitioner's Case

Prejudice requires a showing that had the constitutional claim been raised in accordance with state rules, there is a "reasonable probability that the result of the trial would have been different."

Strickler v. Greene, 527 U.S. 263 (1999). A reasonable probability is sufficient to "undermine confidence in the verdict."

a. Applying the Prejudice Standard

Prejudice is a stricter standard than the "plain error" doctrine applicable on direct review because direct appeal is designed to afford a means for the prompt redress of miscarriages of justice. See Chapter 30. This standard is "out of place when a prisoner launches a collateral attack against a [criminal] conviction after society's legitimate interest in the finality of the judgment has been perfected by the expiration of the time allowed for direct review or by the affirmance of the conviction on appeal." Thus, in *United States v. Frady*, 456 U.S. 152 (1982) prejudice did not follow simply from the fact that a jury instruction was erroneous. The Court held that the petitioner failed to show that the error "worked to his actual and substantial disadvantage, infecting his entire trial with error of constitutional dimensions." In other words, prejudice must be evaluated by the effect of the error in the context of the whole trial.

5. Actual Innocence to Overcome Procedural Default

Despite a procedural default, a federal *habeas* court will consider a claim based on proof that the petitioner is actually and factually innocent.

a. What a Petitioner Must Prove

Before a federal court reviews allegations of actual innocence to excuse the procedural default, it first must address the nondefaulted claims for comparable relief. Dretke v. Haley, 541 U.S. 386 (2004). For actual innocence, the petitioner must then show that it is more likely than not that no reasonable juror would have convicted him. Schlup v. Delo, 513 U.S. 298 (1995).

b. Factual Innocence

Innocence claims, however, must be based on actual innocence rather than mere legal insufficiency. *Herrera v. Collins*, 506 U.S. 390 (1993). When a petitioner seeks relief from a conviction following a guilty plea, actual innocence means "factual innocence" based on "any admissible evidence of petitioner's guilt even if that evidence was not presented during petitioner's plea colloquy." *Bousley v. United States*, 523 U.S. 614 (1998).

(1) Schlup v. Delo

Schlup v. Delo, 513 U.S. 298 (1995) characterized petitioner's claim based on ineffective assistance of counsel and the prosecution's failure to disclose evidence as procedural, in contrast to the substantive claim of innocence based on newly discovered evidence raised in *Herrera*. The Court characterized "actual innocence" cases as "extraordinary."

c. House v. Bell

In *House v. Bell*, 547 U.S. 518 (2006), the Court held that petitioner had satisfied the difficult showing required by the actual innocence exception to defaulted claims, and that his federal habeas proceeding therefore could go forward. DNA testing established that semen on the murder victim's clothing came from her husband rather than from House, the defendant; that evidence was the only forensic evidence linking House to the murder. In addition, House in his post-trial proceedings had presented evidence that the murder victim's husband had confessed to the murder. The Court found this to be the "rare" case where, if the jury had heard all the conflicting evidence, it likely would have viewed the record as a whole as creating reasonable doubt.

TABLE OF CASES

INDEX

References are to Pages